Ask Me Anything

A Sex Therapist Answers the Most Important Questions for the '90s

Marty Klein

A Fireside Book
Published by Simon & Schuster
New York   London   Toronto   Sydney   Tokyo   Singapore

FIRESIDE
Simon & Schuster Building
Rockefeller Center
1230 Avenue of the Americas
New York, New York, 10020

Manufactured in the United States of America

10 9 8 7 6 5 4 3

Library of Congress Cataloging in Publication Data is available

ISBN: 0-671-76114-5

To Donn King, Jack Morin, and David Steinberg—
who love and support me whether I write or not

Acknowledgments

I am grateful for the assistance of Marcia Millman, Ph.D., Henry Ritter, M.D., Carol Wells, R.N., and Beverly Whipple, Ph.D. All four were very generous with their time, knowledge, and experience, helping me arrive at the format and content you have before you. They helped make writing this book an adventure.

Thanks also go to my colleagues around the country in the Society for the Scientific Study of Sex. In these sex-negative times, being a sexologist leads to a certain amount of frustration, sadness, anger, and self-doubt. The bright, articulate, loving professionals in the Society support me emotionally and challenge me intellectually. Both are crucial for me to do my best work.

I appreciate my primary editor, Marilyn Abraham, and my agent, Pam Bernstein, for helping to develop the book's original concept and subsequent shape. I am grateful to Fireside's Sheridan Hay for lavishing time on it. And I appreciate Jon Winokur, Robert Byrne, John Gross, and Abby Adams, whose wonderful collections of quotations helped me express the many amusing sides of human sexuality.

Finally, I thank my wife, Randi, for her graceful, sensitive, powerful presence in my life. If every writer had such an influence, how much better most books would be.

Contents
....

Introduction   1

Part I
Your Body

Part II
Turn-ons and Arousal

Part III
Love and Intimacy

Part IV
Concerns

Part V
Parenting

Introduction
····················

Using This Book

You can use this book in several ways. If you read it cover to cover, I think you'll find it's written in a pretty logical order.

You can also use it as a reference book. It has a detailed index, which you can use to locate specific information. And to make it even easier, some answers refer you to related questions in other parts of the book. Follow the bouncing ball!

If you have a mate, feel free to share this book with him or her. You can read chapters together, or you can leave it on the kitchen table with a note: "Honey, see question # X—it's really interesting!"

About "Advice"

Although this book answers almost six hundred questions, it can't address the details of every single situation. So as you read, try to feel the "music"—the sense of the answers—along with the words. Apply the reasoning and the attitudes to your own circumstances.

There's no substitute, of course, for your own judgment. Sometimes, though, emotions interfere with judgment. If you're having trouble with a situation, ask yourself: What feelings are getting in the way? Throughout the book you'll find creative interpretations of feelings that may be helpful.

Some of the answers suggest confronting your partner with how you feel or what you want. I know this can be difficult, but some problems just can't be fixed any other way. It will be easier, and the results will be better, if you keep your positive intention in mind. If necessary, tell your partner several times: "I'm not saying this to hurt you or to cause conflict. I want to be close to you. I want each of us to be happier. I think talking about this will help."

I often advise people to consider professional counseling. There is no doubt that therapy can be helpful; with certain serious problems, it may be the only thing that can help. Individual counseling can be a wonderful gift to give yourself. Many people enjoy great insight and change after only eight to twelve sessions.

If you feel couples counseling is important, ask your partner to join you, even if he or she will only agree to go once. Explain that wanting to see a counselor reflects both how committed you are to this relationship and how much pain you're in. If your partner refuses, go yourself.

Unfortunately, therapy can be expensive. If you have health insurance, it may cover part of the cost. Use it—regardless of what the insurance clerk in your company may think. You can also check with county mental health services, low-cost family planning clinics, and private therapists who have sliding fee scales.

This is the nineties: You don't have to be "sick" to benefit from therapy.

Doctors and Patients

"Why didn't my doctor tell me?" "Why didn't my doctor ask me?" These are two of the most common questions people ask sex therapists about their physicians.

Many doctors do not discuss sex with their patients. It's not entirely their fault; they're often rushed for time, and they're focused on the symptoms that brought you into the office. Some wonder if you'll get offended by sexual questions.

And like many people, some physicians are not comfortable with sexuality. The real problem, I think, is what they learn about sex in medical school: practically nothing. As a result, most doctors don't learn to "think sex." And whatever immature sexual attitudes they have when they enter training usually go unchallenged.

In general, you have to be the one to raise sexual questions with your physician. Talk about any changes in your sex drive or sexual functioning. Talk about the sexual side effects you've noticed from any drugs you take, and always ask about the sexual side effects of new prescriptions the doctor gives you.

The simple, reassuring image of TV doctors is not reality. Be a smart health-care consumer. Working *with* your doctor will create the best results.

Communication

Throughout the book I encourage people to talk to their partners. I know this can be difficult, but there is simply no substitute for communication. Most of us never learned to talk about sex comfortably, so we rarely approach it enthusiastically. But it's the *only* dependable way to get what you want sexually.

If part of my answer to one of your questions is "communicate," do it *now*. Don't wait until it's easy. If communicating about a particular subject were easy for you and your partner, you probably wouldn't have questions about it.

What Is Normal?

The single most common question about sex is "Am I normal?" There are two reasons for this.

1. Unlike other important activities, we don't observe others having sex, don't hear anyone discussing their sexual feelings or experiences seriously, and don't have access to reliable information about what other people feel and do.
2. This wouldn't be such a problem if not for Normality Anxiety. This is the worry that you may not be sexually normal. We all learn this, as we grow up, from the media and from some religions. Both are eager to sell us something (products or salvation) based on the sexual insecurity created in us by this process.

Normality Anxiety, I'm afraid, is very common. The trick is recognizing the form it takes in you, and finding creative ways to minimize its effect. Ultimately, the solution is not needing to be sexually normal, but wanting to be sexually centered and satisfied.

Most people don't know just how huge the range of common sexual behavior is, either in America or around the world. Anthropologists tell us that virtually every form of sexual expression is or has been considered "normal" in one place or another. Bisexuality is standard in many cultures. Sex with prostitutes was considered more normal than marital sex in Victorian England.

So what is sexually normal? This is a trickier question than you might think, and there are many different ways of answering it. Here are some of the ways various people define what is sexually normal:

- What's common or typical
- What's morally right
- What experts say is right
- What the church says is right
- What's traditionally done, and
- What's normative; that is, society's official version of what people do

Compare, for example, some common ideas about how much masturbation is "normal" for happily married men:

- What's *common:* several times per week
- What *society* claims: rarely
- What the *church* says: not at all, and
- What's *moral:* a man and his wife may differ, depending on how satisfied she is with their lovemaking

So what is normal?

This is why I dislike answering the question "What is normal?" As a scientist, I can tell people how often the average person of a certain age has sexual fantasies about Lassie. Or how many marriages experience extramarital affairs. Or how many middle-aged women fantasize about man B while making love with man A. But my experience, over and over, is that people use such numbers to decide whether or not they are okay—which is the opposite of what I want to achieve. I want people to decide for themselves about their sexuality, regardless of what other people do.

Am I saying "If it feels good, do it?" Not exactly. The criteria for making responsible sexual choices are:

- Is it consenting (and is the other person really in a position to give consent)?
- Is it exploitative?
- Is it self-destructive?

These criteria—and they are not always simple—are far more important than what's "normal." One of society's goals should be for everyone to have the sexuality education and moral principles necessary to evaluate their sexual decision-making in this way.

So during the course of the book, when I hesitate to answer questions about "normal" sex frequency, "normal" ways to climax, or "normal" anything else, I'm not being stingy or stubborn. I'm declining to cooperate with people who want to discount their own good sense and decline responsibility for their sexual choices. I'd much rather give you information, encourage you to interpret situations creatively, and help you communicate.

Part I

Your Body

1

....

Erogenous and Other Zones

A kiss is a lovely trick designed by nature to stop speech when words becomes superfluous.

—Ingrid Bergman

1. What exactly is an "erogenous zone?"

Traditionally, the expression refers to the breasts, genitals, buttocks, anus, and mouth. *Taber's Cyclopedic Medical Dictionary* defines it as an "an area of the body that may produce erotic desires when stimulated." It notes that this can also include "the special senses that cause sexual excitement," such as smell.

Although this definition sounds precise, it is actually pretty vague. This is appropriate, because virtually every square inch of the body can be involved in sexual arousal.

2. Why do some say that the most important erogenous zone is the brain?

Now that even Ann Landers is saying it, you *know* it must be true.

Sexual response is generally based on some stimulus from our five senses, which is processed by the brain. Only when the brain interprets a touch, sound, or other stimulus as erotic does the body respond in a sexual way. Thus, you can say that the brain is the ultimate, or super, erogenous zone.

Actually, the concept of *erogenous zone* is narrow and outdated, part of our culture's ongoing attempt to separate sex from the rest of life. The very idea divides each of us into two different bodies, the sexual one and the "other" one. From there, it is easy to decide that enjoying stimulation outside the sexual zone (for example, having your fingers sucked or kneecaps licked) is "perverse."

Erogenous is a useful word only in very specific instances. Don't use it to limit the way you think about your sexuality.

3. Can you expand your erogenous zones? If so, how?

Definitely. That's because, as noted above, your brain mediates the whole erotic stimulus/arousal process. And there's one thing anthropology, history, and our own experience teaches us: *Any* part of the human body can be a sexual part, either as giver or receiver of pleasure.

How do you figure out how you like to be touched? The answer is similar to that given to the young violinist who stopped a New Yorker and asked how to get to Carnegie Hall: "practice."

In this case, practice includes masturbating, occasionally touching yourself in new ways or in new places. Be adventurous with your partner as well. Ask for new things, try new things, and invite your partner to do the same.

Pay attention to how these new stimuli feel; don't just assume that you know—*feel* them. Breathe deeply, open your senses, and appreciate texture, pressure, sensuality. Look, really *look* at your body being touched or kissed. Listen to what it sounds like, and smell what it smells like.

You can also play with the meaning of these new touches. You "know" that having your hair stroked is intimate, perhaps sexy. You know this because you learned it, not because it's intrinsically sexy. What about having your body's less familiar corners and treasures caressed and licked? Can they "mean" sexy, intimate, playful, daring, sensuous?

To expand your horizons, use babies as role models. They aren't aware of having sexual and nonsexual parts; as a result, their entire bodies, and every touch, are sensual and sexual. Conceptualizing a distinction between sexual and nonsexual body parts is what starts a baby on the dubious road to "civilization."

In all of this, a flexible, nonjudgmental attitude is the key. Watching or criticizing yourself will make experimentation less comfortable. Play with your sexuality. Enjoy what you discover, and discard what doesn't appeal to you.

4. Are men's breasts sensitive? Are they as sensitive as women's?

Like most questions about sexual arousal, the answer is "Sometimes, for some people."

In her 1981 study of 7,000 men, Shere Hite documented the wide range of feelings men have about their breasts' sexual sensitivity. Here's what a few of them said:

"A man doesn't have breasts. I thought this questionnaire was for males."

"I'm very into my tits."

"There is nothing erogenous about my chest."

"Breasts has been the greatest discovery for me sexually. Drives me wild."

Why are some men's breasts sensitive? For the same reason many women's are: the concentration of sensitive, erectile tissue, flooded with nerve endings. That's why breast tissue changes color and shape during sexual arousal and orgasm.

More men would enjoy breast stimulation if they just let themselves.

Although women's breasts are typically more sensitive than men's, there is tremendous variation among women, as there is among men.

5. I'm a healthy young woman who enjoys sex in most respects. So why don't I enjoy having my breasts fondled?

This is not uncommon, and it seems unrelated to breast size. Sometimes the reason is too-early development; when a girl's breasts are a social problem for her, she learns to ignore or even hate them. Sometimes the reason is the too-rough or too-feathery way she is touched. And sometimes the reason is simply constitutional—that's just the way her body is.

Many highly sexual women are uninterested in breast stimulation. As long as you enjoy sex in other ways, I'd suggest you relax and not worry about "performing adequately" in this one.

6. My vaginal lips are long and stretched-looking, sort of hanging down like a chicken's neck. Could I have done this by masturbating too often or too hard as a teenager?

No. Your vaginal lips, or labia, are not like your neck—the shape isn't affected by too much sun, too many cookies, or too much sexual pleasure. You can't change their shape, because it's hereditary. But how many women are able to look at their mothers' vaginal lips to learn about their heritage?

Labia are like noses. They all share the same structures and overall appearance, but each one is unique, exactly like no other. Thus, your concept of what labia "should" look like is arbitrary. You can see drawings of a wide variety of "normal" vaginal lips in Betty Dodson's wonderful book, *Liberating Masturbation.*

Your "chicken neck" lips are not a problem. Not only is there nothing wrong with them; in some cultures such lips would be prized. Rather than thinking of your lips as "long and stretched," can you think of them as having a "come kiss me" look?

7. What is the G spot?

The G spot, named for physician Ernst Grafenberg, is a sensitive area located inside the vagina on the upper wall, an inch or two behind the back of the pubic bone. This area swells when stimulated; in some women, this provides an orgasmic response that feels different from the orgasms they get from clitoral stimulation. A few women report that they "ejaculate" a fluid from their urethra when climaxing from G spot stimulation.

This "ejaculation" is still considered controversial within the medical profession; indeed, the very existence of the G spot is still being debated. The women who enjoy sex this way, however, are not questioning its delight.

To experiment with stimulating your or your partner's G spot, use one or two fingers in a 'come here' motion against the inside roof of the vagina about one-third of the way back. To discover what feels best, vary the location and pressure of the touch.

8. What is the hymen? What is its purpose?

The word *hymen* comes from the Greek *humēn,* or "membrane," which provided the name for the Greek god of marriage. The hymen is a small membrane that partially covers the vaginal opening. Most—although not all—women are born with one.

Traditionally, people have focused on the fact that the hymen breaks during intercourse and is therefore an indicator of virginity or the lack of it. But the hymen can also be torn or separated in other ways, including exercise, work, bicycle riding, and tampon use.

In addition, the hymen can be so small or flexible that it remains intact even after intercourse. Each year, in fact, thousands of women have their hymens surgically removed prior to childbirth.

Some women experience great discomfort and/or bleeding when their hymen breaks during sex or other activities, while others experience little or none. Because of the premium some people place on virginity, the lack of bleeding is sometimes used to create unnecessary problems.

At this time the biological function of the hymen is not known.

9. Help—my penis is crooked. What should I do?

You should probably relax, because it's probably nothing. Like fingers, toes, and the rest of our bodies, penises are never perfectly straight and smooth. When erect, some penises curve to the side, some up or down, and some both. If you have no physical discomfort, just accept your unique shape.

Hard, inflamed tissue in the penis can create a pronounced curvature, making erection and sex painful. This is known as Peyronie's disease and requires medical attention.

10. Why do I get unwanted erections now, as an adult? What should I do about them?

Nature, of course, doesn't know that some erections are unwanted, any more than it knows that freckles or a blush are unwanted. Unwanted erections are more common in adolescence because the teenage threshold of arousal is far lower than the adult threshold—that is, it take less stimulation to arouse a boy than a man.

Adults get these erections for the same reasons that teens do: unintentional physical stimulation, such as from clothing, furniture, or a hand; mental or emotional stimulation, through fantasy, desire, guilt, or embarrassment; urethral stimulation, because of infection or the need to urinate.

What to do about unwanted erections? Repeating "I'm losing my erection" doesn't work. Thinking of disgusting things (like the amount of money Michael Jackson makes) isn't dependable either. You end up with a sour face in addition to an unwanted hard-on.

There are several time-tested ways to get rid of unwanted erections. These include root canal, a speeding ticket, and a tax audit.

If you're positive that your arousal system is completely

out of whack, see a urologist. Otherwise, appreciate the fact that your penis does, apparently, respond in a youthful, enthusiastic way. Don't be embarrassed—that "problem" down there is just an erection. The surest way to get it down is to let it down, by ignoring it.

11. Certain nonsexual smells turn me on. Why?

You're not alone in this regard. The nonsexual smells that arouse various people are almost limitless and include those of foods, cleaning materials, clothing, machines, animals, furniture, and even medicine.

Why does this happen? Because smells trigger memories. Your first kiss may have been in a kitchen filled with fresh-baked pie; mine was under a recently polished mahogany desk. The first place we have sex, the breath of a special person, the hideaway where we met a secret lover, the soap we used when preparing for a date—all get an honored place in our olfactory hall of fame.

Like taste, smell bypasses the cognitive, rational part of the brain. This makes it a perfect way to store memories connected with feeling rather than thought. The smell of mahogany polish—and the taste of the boysenberry jam my six-year-old girlfriend had been eating—will *always* excite me just a bit.

12. What are pheremones?

A pheremone is a body secretion that provides a chemical form of communication between living beings. A crucial part of sex and reproduction in many insect and animal species (including rhesus monkeys), it is typically detected by the sense of smell, which, we're learning, involves a lot more than just the nose.

The data on human pheremones is mixed. They are probably what make women who spend a lot of time together (such as in dormitories) begin menstruating on similar schedules. Some studies indicate that the smell of others' sweat, vaginal secretions, and semen can affect our biological rhythms even without their owners' actual presence.

As other studies on this subject are inconclusive, the issue of the role of human pheremones is still considered controversial. Our body is, however, packed with odor-producing glands. And the highly successful perfume industry is based on the obvious reality that certain smells that have no intrinsic meaning do attract and arouse us.

Pheremones, which we can neither see nor taste, may explain why some people who don't even like each other can't live without touching each other.

13. During oral sex, I sometimes worry that I'll urinate and ejaculate at the same time. What can I do to prevent this?

Good news—evolution has taken care of this for you, to prevent the acid in urine from weakening your sperm. A clever valve system inside your urethra (the tube that carries both semen and urine out of your penis) allows only one of these processes to occur at a time. When you are close to ejaculating, the neck of the bladder is closed off so that urine can't escape.

Women with this concern should see question 29.

14. Why do different people respond differently to being touched in the same way?

No one really knows. "Personal preference" is about as close as we can come to an answer, and that's not much of an answer.

Your observation is, however, accurate: Whatever the kind of touch, there are people who love it, people who hate it, and people who don't understand all the fuss one way or the other. Examples of touch that some people love and others hate include being scratched by long fingernails; being deeply massaged; and having the toes licked, the ears kissed, the breasts bitten, and the hair pulled.

Each person's preferences also vary according to such factors as mental state, degree of arousal, and time of month. For example, as our pain threshold increases during sexual excitement, the kind of touch we enjoy changes.

Since people are not interchangeable in their preferences,

and since even individuals' preferences change, communication is a key factor in sexual satisfaction.

15. How can my husband truly enjoy my body with these breasts? He says they turn him on, but I feel very self-conscious.

I've left out your actual breast size, because it's irrelevant to the question. As a group, women seem to believe that breasts come in only two sizes: too big and too small.

There's no denying that many men have distinct preferences regarding women's breast size. But do you know what your husband's is? And do you know what other things he likes about your breasts? This could include the way they smell, taste, or feel; or their texture, color, shape, etc. Maybe he likes them because they're particularly responsive.

Or maybe he likes them because they're attached to you. That's not such a bad reason, is it?

16. How big should an adult penis be?

While there is no such thing as a bad question, this is one question that I don't like answering. I don't want to support the penis envy that so many men seem to feel. Most women say that penis size matters little or not at all, and men should believe them.

Penis size is generally irrelevant because the clitoris, not the vagina, is the main female sexual organ. And penis size is no predictor of the gentleness, skill, or sense of humor of the owner. If there's any male organ whose size women do care about, it's the heart, not the hard-on.

So how big should a penis be? Small enough to fit through a doorway and big enough to find in the dark.

17. Is it my imagination, or do some people taste different than others?

In a recent album, David Bowie gives a woman the ultimate sexual compliment: "I like the taste of your flesh." Yes, different people taste different. The way each person tastes changes during the course of a typical day and month, too, along with the rest of our body chemistry.

This is particularly true of male ejaculate and female lubrication. Diet and general health seem to affect these the most. The semen of vegetarians, for example, is often sweeter and less salty than that of meat eaters.

Taste, of course, is partly a function of smell. This is especially true of warm, damp body areas like the genitals. Don't be shy about asking your partner to shower or not to shower, whichever you prefer. Keep in mind that a taste (or smell) you dislike isn't *wrong*, it's just not to your liking.

18. I'm confused. Is massage supposed to be sexy or not?

If you're talking about downtown massage parlors with names like The Dew Drop Inn, Kitten's Purrfect Touch, or Candy Barr's Boom Boom Room, the answer is yes, they're supposed to be sexy. For a fee, a friendly person gives you a massage and then an orgasm. This is the public side of massage.

Considering massage seriously, however, confronts us with our definitions of sexuality. Legitimate, private massage is a totally sensuous experience. We put our body in someone else's hands, letting him or her nurture us. We *feel* skin, muscles, and joints normally taken for granted. Our focus becomes, simply, whatever the body wants and needs.

Is this sexual? It's not genital and there's no orgasm. But you do bond with another person on a physical level. You breathe deeply, subordinating your thinking mind to your feeling body. You enjoy your body for its own sake, experiencing it as animals do—without any external "meaning." We can say this isn't sexual, but if so, how exactly do we define sex?

19. I hate tickling. Why does my partner keep doing it when we make love even though I say ''don't?''

Tickling can be a hostile, controlling thing to do to someone, particularly during sex. Most adults dislike the frustrating, powerless feeling of being tickled. The laughter of someone being tickled is easily misunderstood; it doesn't express pleasure, but is merely a reflexive response to a peculiar kind of touching.

You have to be clear that it's *your* body, that you make the rules, and that this one isn't negotiable. Then you have to show you're serious by refusing to continue lovemaking when you've been interrupted in this way.

During a nonsexual moment of closeness, ask your partner, "Why do you insist on disrupting our sexual experience together, when I've clearly asked you not to?" And ask yourself, "Why am I in a relationship with someone who repeatedly violates me? Exactly how seriously am I willing to take my own needs?"

2

Body Image and Self-Consciousness

They made love only during total eclipses of the sun, because they wouldn't take off their clothes unless it was dark in the whole world.

—Robert Byrne

Shame begins as a wordless concept. It stems from the toddler's concept that one part of him is less acceptable than the rest.

—Alayne Yates

20. **I like sex, but I feel inhibited, like someone is watching me. What should I do?**

Many people have the vague discomfort that they're being watched during sex, by their parents, their ex-spouse, even God. It all comes down to the same thing: feeling bad about your sexual feelings or behavior or body.

Recognize this feeling for what it is. Don't dismiss it as "just being stupid" or "the way I am"; acknowledge that this is a personality dynamic you have the power to change. Commit yourself to discovering what it is about sex and your body that you feel distant from, and decide what you need to overcome that distance. Books, massage, meditation, and therapy can all help.

Then, focus on *sex* during sex, and nothing else. Get into your breathing, as well as the sounds and smells of lovemaking moment by moment. That won't leave much of your attention for guilt. And after sex, affirm your sexual experience for yourself: "That was enjoyable. I satisfied myself and my partner. The world has room for my sexual pleasure."

21. I don't like to be looked at during sex. Why can't we make love with the lights out?

Lovemaking doesn't have to be limited to penises and vaginas; we can make love with our hands, ears, noses, and any other body parts that can sense and enjoy. Sex can be a feast for the eye—and your mate apparently likes to feast on you.

The self-consciousness that makes us want to hide during sex starts in youth, when we learn that sex is bad. It continues in adulthood, when we compare ourselves to culturally certified sexy people, like movie stars and athletes.

Your partner is appreciating your body, not judging it. *You're* judging it. When you stop doing that, you'll enjoy sex, and your partner's enjoyment of your body, a lot more.

You don't have to make love with the lights on. But as a compromise, try candlelight. It flatters everyone it touches, and its mystery will help you feel cloaked a bit.

22. Most people say I'm pretty nice-looking, including my husband. But if I gain just three or four pounds, he starts nagging and won't make love until I lose the weight. What should I do?

It depends on what you want. You could try to control your weight to please your husband. A healthier approach is to get off the merry-go-round of failure-punishment-promise-failure. Doing so challenges you and your husband to join together to create a new kind of intimacy.

The issue here is not weight. Although neither of you will admit it, your marriage is a battleground in a struggle for con-

trol. By legitimizing your husband's manipulation, you participate in the game.

This situation will not resolve itself without professional
counseling. Your husband may not go unless you demand it,
and perhaps not even then. If he won't go to counseling with
you, go alone. You'll have to show that you are serious about
ending the sex/weight/control game forever.

23. I gain five pounds and I want to hide in the bathroom. My husband gains five pounds and he still feels sexy. Why?

Being a man is no picnic (as rock singer Patti Smith says,
"Being *any* gender is a drag"), but one blessing men do have is
not learning that our looks are the source of our power. Men
do, of course, exaggerate the importance of their erections, but
that's another story. Besides, most men's erections are dependable many years longer than their looks.

Many women, on the other hand, are sure that their sexual
power comes directly from their looks. This is not some neurotic fantasy that they generate themselves in the middle of the
night; every part of American culture delivers this message con-
tinually. As a result, most women view weight gain as humiliating, a dreadful mistake waiting to be made.

Your husband may not be perfect, but he does understand
that his sexuality is not tied to standards of external beauty.
Try this freeing concept—that your body is there to please you,
not betray you.

24. Do women prefer circumcised or uncircumcised men?

There is no, uh, hard data on this. Many women have had
experience with only one kind or the other; they generally have
no opinion. Most women who can compare also seem to have
no opinion; those who do care seem split about fifty-fifty. Most
women, I think, prefer the kind of penis that they're used to.

25. The truth is, I'm about forty pounds overweight. I just can't relax while my husband strokes and plays with my different areas of flab. What should I do?

Generally, we feel discomfort when having certain body parts looked at or touched because we criticize them and assume the other person does too. Typically, the person swears, "But I'm not criticizing you!"—which we don't believe.

Where you see "flab," your mate sees or feels *you*. He also sees or feels texture, color, shape, and so on. Despite your discomfort and disbelief, his experience is clearly erotic. Somehow, you need to learn to trust that your man is enjoying you rather than judging you. If you can't, you'll never really enjoy his touch, and you'll create sexual frustration for both of you.

You can wish to improve your body *and* enjoy it as it is now. The nerves that transmit sexual pleasure within your body don't know that you think there are too many of them.

26. Although my vagina smells bad, my new boyfriend likes to give me oral sex. What should I do? Should I use one of those female deodorants?

Since your boyfriend isn't complaining, how do you know that your vagina smells bad? I don't like the smell of broccoli, but that doesn't mean *it* smells bad.

The vagina is a self-cleansing organ, like the eye. A healthy one is clean, and it smells like living tissue—not like flowers or "spring," as the deodorant ads imply. Your boyfriend may *love* your healthy smell and taste, even if you don't.

If you believe you smell bad, see a gynecologist, who will either treat whatever vaginal problem you have or tell you you're healthy. Either way, do *not* let *any* female deodorant product within 100 yards of your vagina. Because they alter the vagina's delicate chemical balance, *they can be dangerous.*

27. How does a guy get a penis as big as Long John Holmes's?

The same way you acquire a nose exactly like his—you get born Long John Holmes.

When we see Steffi Graf play tennis or Michael Jordan play basketball, we admire their bodies and their performances—but we don't believe we can duplicate either. When viewing an X-rated video, however, we forget that we're watching professional athletes with extraordinarily unusual bodies. The magic of film editing also enhances X-rated performances quite a bit.

Because the penis has no skeletal muscle, it cannot be enlarged by any means. Erection pumps, growth creams, and exercises are all worthless in this regard. Fortunately, penis size doesn't affect sexual satisfaction. How many women have ever told you they wanted a larger penis?

28. My husband wants me to wear erotic underwear. How can I make him understand that I'm just not pretty enough or sexy enough?

If you don't want to wear Fredericks of Peoria's finest, just say so. End of conversation. But don't disqualify yourself because you don't meet some arbitrary standard of "sexy" (say, twenty-two years old, perfect teeth, and breasts the size of Montana).

Try to keep things in perspective: Lingerie is just a toy for people to play with, like Silly Putty or Hula-Hoops. Apparently, your husband is willing to see past your imperfections to the sexy woman he knows is perfect for him. This is something to celebrate, not talk him out of.

29. I'm a sexually active woman with a terrible secret—I wet the bed when I climax. As a result, I usually hold back during lovemaking. How do I explain this to my partners?

I'd rather discourage you from holding back than help you do it better. Many women lose a few drops of urine during climax, because the muscles that spasm so pleasurably during orgasm are the same muscles that normally hold urine in. Also, many women "ejaculate" a small amount of fluid when they climax from G spot stimulation.

By all means, explain your situation to your partners, and let them reassure you of their acceptance. Put a towel underneath you during lovemaking, and celebrate, rather than hide, your body's sexual expressiveness. There are many times in life to hold back, but lovemaking is not one of them.

30. One of my breasts is bigger than the other, they both have a few

hairs growing out of them, and the nipples are inverted. Still, my partner insists on caressing them during sex. How do I get him to stop?

If you'd said your breasts hurt, or even that you don't enjoy the touching, that would be one thing. But your discomfort seems to be about the *idea* of your breasts as they are. Please reconsider your attitude.

Your breasts sound normal, normal, normal. But, like your nose and knees, they aren't perfect. Your distress about the contrast between your real breasts and society's ideal breasts is understandable but oppressive; it hinders both you and your mate from enjoying sex. Instead, let go of your judgments about what breasts are "supposed" to look like, and enjoy the way they *are*—and the way your mate enjoys them.

Without question, you have the right to sex without unwanted touching. If you wish, tell your partner that you're serious about not wanting your breasts touched and that not respecting your wishes will destroy this sexual relationship.

31. What's with all these self-exams we're being told to do? I notice it's always our sexual parts. Are doctors getting off on telling us to touch ourselves, or what?

A doctor's reputation, said George Bernard Shaw, is made by the number of eminent citizens who die under his care. But as strange as many doctors are, I think your accusation is unfounded.

In fact, the trend toward breast, testicle, and other self-exams is a very good one. It gives people permission to take the health of their sexual organs as seriously (or lightly, for that matter) as they take the rest of their health. It helps educate us about the way our sex organs look and feel when healthy. And it normalizes the idea of touching these parts of the body just as we touch the rest of it.

For information on how and why to do these simple self-exams, contact the American Cancer Society.

32. I really want to have my breasts enlarged. Why are so many people trying to talk me out of the surgery?

Be grateful that you have such good friends.

While some cosmetic breast surgery works out fine, too much of it *doesn't*. Additional, unplanned follow-up surgery is sometimes necessary. Complications include lumps, hardness, reduced sensitivity, scars, and pain, all from surgery that was supposed to be "safe" and "routine."

As University of California sociologist Marcia Millman says: "We learn to dream of having perfect bodies, and we've convinced ourselves that surgery now makes this possible. It doesn't, and many women are paying the price for their fantasy with pain and disfigurement that is very real."

33. Since my hysterectomy, I just don't feel like a real woman, so sex is out. How do I deal with my husband, who still wants to make love?

Because hysterectomy involves the removal of the uterus, many women question their essential femaleness afterwards. But this is so unnecessary—femininity resides in who you are, not in what body parts you have.

The typical hysterectomy does not detract from a woman's sexual capacity in any way. If anything, the freedom from worrying about unwanted pregnancy and the healing of your preoperative symptoms can make you *more* comfortable with sex. And right now, you and your husband surely need the comfort of physical affection.

You should anticipate the need for time to recuperate physically from your operation. Perhaps you are afraid of your husband's weight or thrusting. Do not hesitate to discuss these concerns with him and/or your physician.

A hysterectomy that removes the ovaries is more serious. It can create hormonal difficulties which the woman and her partner need to understand thoroughly. If you are not satisfied with your doctor's explanation, see a nurse practitioner or family-planning specialist.

In fact, a recent study of six thousand hysterectomies by Blue Cross of Illinois found one-third to be unnecessary. That's why some people say, sarcastically, that the diagnostic indicators for hysterectomy are paid-up health insurance and a few days to spend in the hospital. If you're told you need a hysterectomy, get a second opinion.

34. My doctor says I can have a sex life after my colostomy, but who is she kidding?

There is sex after ostomy (a surgically formed opening that links an internal organ, such as the intestine, to the outside of the body), although it requires some creative thinking, working through feelings, and practical planning. The keys are patients' comfort with their bodies and their willingness to discuss their (and their partners') feelings. It's hard to feel aroused, for example, if you're still full of rage about your illness.

A nurse, medical social worker, or sex therapist can enhance your sexual communication and comfort level tremendously. You can also get information and support through the United Ostomy Association or the American Cancer Society.

35. I had a medium-size heart attack about six months ago, and my doctor says I've recovered. But I just can't relax during sex—I keep wondering if too much excitement will kill me.

This is a common fear, which men deal with in many ways. A study in the *American Journal of Cardiology*, for example, showed that emotions caused 10 percent of male patients to develop serious erection problems after a heart attack.

Eventually, most coronary patients can resume their former level of sexual activity. Lovemaking and orgasm are usually safe for patients without complications six to ten weeks after their initial incident.

Cardiac rehabilitation must include an exercise and conditioning program. Like any other exercise, sex must be resumed gradually. In this situation:

Do:

• Experiment with intercourse positions to find less stressful ones
• Know and monitor your own warning signs of overexertion, such as shortness of breath and sleeplessness
• Remember that depression can reduce sex drive
• Consider masturbating with a partner until intercourse is physically and emotionally comfortable

- Know that sex is good for you, both physically and mentally
- Discuss your concerns with a physician

Don't:

- Mix alcohol, large meals, and sex
- Make love in an excessively hot or cold room
- Have sex in situations filled with emotional stress, such as performance anxiety or the fear of discovery

When can a heart-attack patient return to lovemaking? When you can walk around the block without getting tired, you can probably have low-stress sex. When you can walk up a flight of stairs without any problem, you can probably have vigorous sex.

36. I'm recovering from a mastectomy. My husband says he still desires me, but how can he enjoy sex with half a woman?

You're not half a woman. You're a whole woman with one breast. Your husband, apparently, loves you *and* your body.

It is quite common, after a mastectomy, to feel angry, sad, and frightened. Working through these feelings is crucial to re-establishing a normal life; self-disgust is not a good way to do this.

The source of sexuality is inside our bodies, not outside. Surely you know flat-chested or plain-looking women who men find desirable. Women who feel sexy *are* sexy. It's as simple—and as real—as that.

When writer and sexual pioneer Deena Metzger had a breast removed several years ago, she decided to uncover and chronicle her experience for the world. She also had a lovely grapevine tattooed across her bosom. She writes, in part:

> There was a fine red line across my chest where a
>   knife entered, but now a branch winds about the
>   scar and travels from arm to heart.
> I have relinquished some of the scars.
> I have designed my chest with the care given to an
>   illuminated manuscript.

For the moving, exhilarating account of her battle and triumph, see her book, *Tree*. You might also enjoy *No Less a Woman* by Deborah Kahane.

Bear in mind, too, that reconstructive surgery, a far more complex approach, is also an option.

37. A car accident has put me in a wheelchair. Am I supposed to go without sex for the rest of my life?

Not if you don't want to. Most disabilities that limit movement do not limit libido. When desire declines after an accident or illness, the causes are typically anger, fear, guilt, depression, or misinformation.

For most people, disability does not reduce the need or ability to be affectionate, passionate, adventurous, and playful. So feel free to continue expressing those parts of yourself in whatever ways feel comfortable.

On the other hand, an illness, accident, or surgery that damages the nervous system can hamper or even eliminate orgasm and erection. Nevertheless, people with such conditions can still function sexually. A willingness to experiment and explore new definitions of sex and satisfaction is crucial.

Don't let society's belief that the disabled should be asexual control you. Rather, keep in mind the film *Coming Home*. Even though Jon Voight's character was confined to a wheelchair, he was still able to give Jane Fonda's character the best sex she'd ever had.

38. I have only one testicle, so naturally I'm self-conscious. Are there surgical implants of some kind that can make me look more normal when I'm nude?

Yes. For more information, consult a urologist. I would, however, strongly discourage you from pursuing this.

You don't have to *like* having one testicle, but neither do you *have* to feel self-conscious. No one notices, and frankly, no one cares. And as I hope your doctor explained, your masculinity, reproductive life, and sexual functioning are completely unaffected (unless you have an unusually low sperm or hormone count, which the doctor can easily check). This is also true if one of a man's testicles is undescended.

You can use your physical variation to create sexual or psychological problems, or you can accept it as a nonissue, like your shoe size.

39. Sometimes I have to urinate during sex. What should I do?

This situation perplexes us only because we believe that a sexual "mood" is so fragile that we must never, ever interrupt it. Let's end this oppressive belief. Any sexual mood can be recaptured in a moment if both people want to.

So if you have to go to the bathroom during sex, kiss your partner, look him or her straight in the eye, and say, "I'll be right back; don't finish without me!" Then go to the bathroom—and don't hide the flushing sound by running water in the sink.

40. I was getting along great with this new man. But the first time we made love, I farted. How can I possibly face him again?

During sex, most of us like to pretend that our bodies are perfectly clean. Good sex, however, is like gourmet cooking—we don't *have* to make a mess, but we usually seem to.

Real lovemaking involves relinquishing control of our bodies. For better or worse, this can mean crying or farting in addition to moaning or coming. That's part of our vulnerability during sex: We expose our bodies without the social niceties that sustain our illusions of cleanliness and wholesomeness.

Look at your experience in perspective, rather than judging it by the standards of nonsexual behavior. This is how we accept other "impolite" behaviors during sex, like drooling, yelling, and clutching.

Your partner probably appreciates your willingness to let go during sex far more than he resents the gas. So be brave. Tell him you enjoyed making love, hope to do it again, and that you're embarrassed about what happened. If he accepts it, forget it happened. If he doesn't, forget him.

3

....

Menstruation and PMS

Orthodox medicine has not found an answer to your complaint. Luckily for you, however, I happen to be a quack.

—Richter cartoon

41. What exactly is menstruation?

During the course of the monthly cycle, the lining of the uterus (*womb*) thickens, as it prepares to nurture a fertilized egg that might attach to it. If no pregnancy occurs—that is, if no sperm fertilizes an egg that month—this blood-rich lining is unneeded. It is conveniently shed at the climax of the cycle.

That shedding of blood, tissue, and secretions is described as *menstrual discharge*. The flow typically lasts from three to seven days and occurs about every twenty-eight days, although the length of women's cycles varies tremendously.

The onset of a girl's periods (*menarche*) starts between the ages of nine and sixteen, averaging around age twelve. In the

United States this figure has been steadily falling, as the population physically matures earlier and earlier. Although menarche is anticipated and celebrated as a rite of passage in many cultures, in ours it is shrouded in fear and ignorance. To prevent this problem, boys and girls should be educated about menstruation about the time they start school.

42. Why isn't my cycle exactly twenty-eight days long, like it's suppose to be?

Aye, there's the rub. We need to understand that a "normal" period isn't twenty-eight days; it's anywhere between twenty-four and thirty-two days. Each woman's cycle varies around its own average, and different women's averages differ from each other. So menstrual facts are more complex than a simple tally of numbers; as they say, there are lies, damn lies, and statistics.

Periods are regulated by rising and falling levels of several hormones. This hormonal tide changes subtly from month to month, affected by conditions such as stress, medication, and exercise. Women, in fact, tend to have shorter cycles in cold weather and climates.

By the way, the fact that most women's cycles fluctuate from month to month is part of what makes the rhythm method of birth control so dangerously unreliable.

43. Why are my periods so irregular?

Although the length of a woman's cycle tends to be similar from month to month, it does vary. Irregular periods are most frequent during adolescence and the year before menopause, when the production of the ovarian hormone that regulates menstruation fluctuates most.

Stress (including fear of pregnancy), crash diets, dramatic weight change, and cancer can affect hormone flow and create irregular periods. Women with extremely erratic periods should see a gynecologist.

44. Why does my period sometimes skip a month?

Because menstruation is an expression of a woman's entire system, a missed period can reflect a wide variety of physical conditions. These can include stress, tumors, hormone imbalance, genital tract defects, and infertility.

A woman may also begin skipping periods if she develops anorexia, experiences significant weight fluctuations, exercises intensely (many Olympic athletes have chronic menstrual difficulties), or overuses recreational drugs.

45. Why do I sometimes bleed in between periods?

Generally caused by a slightly unbalanced hormone flow, occasional *breakthrough bleeding* (or *spotting*) is nothing to worry about. It is most common among adolescents whose periods haven't stabilized yet, and in menopausal women whose periods are phasing out.

Persistent spotting should be checked with a health-care professional.

46. Why does my period hurt so much?

Dysmenorrhea, or painful menstruation, is one of the most frequent gynecological complaints. It may persist throughout a woman's entire reproductive life or begin spontaneously after many pain-free years. This condition can be caused by pelvic congestion or inflammation, or temporary circulation problems combined with uterine muscle contractions.

Treatments that various women find helpful include applying heat, taking analgesics or antispasmodics, and massage. Drugs such as the anti-inflammatory indocin and oral contraceptives are often helpful, but have potential side effects. Changes in diet are sometimes reported to decrease pain dramatically.

Masturbating or lovemaking to orgasm often relieves menstrual pain, because the uterine contractions can dislodge and help discharge uterine material.

47. Is there such a thing as PMS?

Yes, *premenstrual syndrome* (PMS) is a common, very real problem affecting millions of people. It is caused by changes in a woman's hormone levels (estrogen and progesterone) the week or two before her period. Common symptoms include depression, irritability, anxiety, headache, cramps, sleeplessness, breast tenderness, backache, and craving for sweets.

This reality should not be used to characterize women as hysterical or undependable—a bad rap laid on women by ignorant people of both genders. Virtually all women handle their normal responsibilities and make decisions adequately during this time. According to a *Ms.* article about the Olympic games, "Women have won gold medals and established new world records during all phases of the menstrual cycle."

48. What can I do about my PMS?

In most women, PMS seems affected by dietary intake. To reduce its symptoms, avoid caffeine and alcohol. Instead of one major meal, eat several small meals per day, preferably ones low in salt and high in protein, calcium, and vitamins B and C. Exercise can also help.

The only complete cure for PMS is menopause—eventually experienced by all PMS sufferers. This is yet another demonstration of nature's extraordinary sense of balance.

49. My sister said she got pregnant during her period. Isn't that impossible?

While it is very unusual, it's not impossible.

Normally, a woman will release a single egg when she ovulates each month. It will hang around, waiting to be fertilized by a sperm; when that doesn't happen, the body flushes out the unneeded uterine lining and menstruation occurs.

On rare occasions, however, a woman releases a second egg during a month's ovulation. Since eggs and sperm can live up to seventy-two hours in the body, they can survive menstruation if released late enough in the woman's period. Thus, fertilization can actually occur during or immediately after menstruation.

50. How do I prepare my daughters for their first period? When should I do this? I don't want to scare them.

The beginning of menstruation, called *menarche,* occurs between the ages of nine and sixteen, typically around twelve. This climaxes a series of events that include, in order, the development of breasts, pubic hair, and underarm hair.

For a young girl approaching puberty, there is absolutely no substitute for information. After all, unexpected bleeding can be terrifying, not to mention embarrassing. In the wonderful *Talking with Your Child About Sex,* Drs. Mary Calderone and James Ramey offer brief sample conversations about menarche, which you should start when a girl is around nine.

In addition to explaining the actual mechanism of menstruation, discuss the following points:

• Menstruation means you're becoming a woman and that you'll be able to get pregnant
• When your period starts it may be a brownish discharge; eventually it will look like blood, but it's just tissue your body doesn't need
• Some people make a fuss about menstruation or think it should be kept a secret, but I/we think it's a normal, natural thing you can ask me/us about whenever you want to

51. Is it okay to have sex during a woman's period?

It's okay to have sex during menstruation if you want to have it and unnecessary if you don't want to. Of course a woman who has cramps or feels bloated will probably not feel very sexy.

Some people have practical objections to sex during menstruation; it can be messy and even a bit smelly. You can minimize these concerns by showering first, putting a towel on the bed, or using a diaphragm to catch the menstrual flow. Of course, such preparations require that you acknowledge, rather than deny, what's going on.

It's entirely different if you or your partner believe that menstruation makes a person dirty. You might want to ask yourself exactly what bothers you. Start by talking about the issue with your partner. A discussion with a physician or nurse will probably be helpful too.

At present, most educators believe intercourse during menstruation without a condom is *not* "safer sex."

Remember that tampons can dry out the vaginal lining, so a lubricant may be necessary.

52. Why do religions seem so uncomfortable with menstruation?

According to historian Gerald Larue in *Sex and the Bible,* "There are a number of references to menstruation in the Bible, and all are negative." A woman is portrayed as unclean during and for a week after menses; everything she touches is unclean, including *any* man who has sex with her. In fact, Leviticus (20:18) demands that such a couple be excommunicated, in the same paragraph that it prescribes this penalty for brother-sister incest.

Declaring menstruating women unclean is a potent way of controlling them; indeed, writes Larue, the Roman Catholic Church invoked this ancient law in 1970 when it prevented women from serving in the sanctuary as lectors or commentators during Mass.

The Bible's radical position on menstruation was written by men representing the cultural ideals of a group of people who lived thousands of years ago. Clearly, they feared the power and magic of women, who could bleed and yet not die. The taboo against sex during a woman's least fertile time was also highly functional for a community working hard to increase its population.

Our modern religious beliefs are an inheritance of these very old ones. They also express our contemporary discomfort with women's bodies, which explains the obsessive flood of consumer products designed to sanitize and disguise normal female bodily functions.

53. What is menopause?

Menopause is the permanent cessation of menstruation,

signaling the end of a woman's ability to reproduce. As the amount of hormones produced by the ovaries declines, so does ovulation (the production of eggs). This reduces the need for the uterine lining's monthly buildup of nurturing tissue. Thus, there's less for the body to flush out—menstruate—at the climax of each month when pregnancy does not occur.

In most American women, menopause occurs between ages forty and fifty-five. According to *Taber's Cyclopedic Medical Dictionary*, natural menopause occurs in 25 percent of women by age forty-seven; 50 percent by age fifty; and 95 percent by age fifty-five. It occurs due to surgical removal of the ovaries in almost 30 percent of American women past age fifty.

In some women periods stop suddenly. In others, the process can take several years. The menstrual flow may decrease each month, or the interval between periods may increase until they stop altogether.

Menopause often brings hot flashes, chills (sometimes both, in alternation), depression, fatigue, headache, and insomnia. Vaginal tissue and lubrication may dry up somewhat during this time, making an external lubricant necessary for pain-free intercourse.

54. What is estrogen replacement therapy?

Estrogen replacement therapy (ERT) refers to a low-dose, short-term intake of estrogen. It is usually prescribed to reduce the symptoms of menopause. The hormone progesterone is now frequently included in ERT to reduce the risk of cancer.

Although many physicians hail ERT as a great breakthrough in routine medical care, others do not accept it as safe. Almost everyone agrees that ERT patients must be checked several times each year and that ERT is not appropriate for women with a history of cardiovascular disease or cancer.

55. Do men go through menopause?

There is no reproductively defined event for midlife men as there is for women. As those bizarre supermarket tabloids periodically remind us, a fertile man retains his ability to impregnate a woman until he dies.

Many men do, however, experience a *climacteric* (from the Greek, meaning "rung of a ladder") around age forty-five or fifty. As a man's production of testosterone decreases, so, frequently, do his sexual reflexes and desire. Men at this age also have to start competing with younger men at work, in sports, and for sexual partners, which can be psychologically devastating.

Some men handle this quite well, while others go through the fabled "midlife crisis." This can include manic and/or depressive phases, disrupting their careers and families with job changes, life-style experiments, and new sexual interests.

4

Contraception

There may be some things better than sex, and some things worse. But there's nothing exactly like it.

—W. C. Fields

56. How do you use a condom?

A condom needs to be put on *before* intercourse, because the drops of moisture at the tip of an excited penis are loaded with sperm (and can be loaded with virus, too).

Putting on a condom doesn't have to be a drag. In some countries, such as France, it's considered one of the sexiest parts of intercourse. Some women provide so much pleasure while putting them on that their partners are unaware or unaffected. Many practical people simply shrug and put the damn thing on quickly and quietly so they can continue playing.

To put a condom on, unroll it one turn with a hand that isn't wet from vaginal or penile juices. Squeeze the air out of the empty tip and unroll the condom onto the erect penis. Don't unroll the whole condom first; put it on like pantyhose, not like socks.

57. Why all the fuss—aren't all condoms the same?

No, Virginia, all condoms are not created equal. To start with, American condoms are, arguably, the best in the world—the thinnest and most reliable. That explains why we call ours "rubbers," while the Soviets call theirs "galoshes."

The new generation of American condoms are also loaded with options. Various brands come with lubricants; chemicals (like nonoxynol-9) that kill sperm and germs; raised bumps to increase vaginal stimulation; and a mild adhesive that helps the condom stay on the penis.

Condoms are currently made from either latex rubber or sheep intestines. Because the larger membrane of these "natural" or "skin" condoms allows microscopic viruses to pass through, they are no longer recommended.

Traditionally, condoms have come in a single size. One company is now marketing extra-larges—for, presumably, the man who thinks big. Not surprisingly, no one's marketing a size "small."

58. Why are you supposed to use contraceptive foam with condoms?

Contraceptive foam protects against sperm (or, secondarily, viruses) that might get around the condom. This can happen if the condom breaks during or after intercourse or if semen spills while the condom is being removed.

59. Why are men so resistant to using condoms?

Not all men resist condoms. Most smart ones, in fact, insist on them.

But hating condoms does seem to be a male tradition, like getting drunk and throwing up at fraternity parties. People agree that they shouldn't do it, but somehow they keep doing it anyway.

Men learn the tradition in adolescence. They hear that condoms reduce sexual pleasure so much that using one is like showering with a raincoat on. They hear that real men refuse to use condoms because they're such a hassle, and that besides, contraception is a woman's problem.

In reality, condoms only reduce penile sensation a tiny amount. But they can slip down during vigorous sex, and they need to be removed very soon after ejaculation. If people are embarrassed, putting a condom on can be awkward.

The discomforts most men will tolerate in order to have sex show that there is more involved in their condom resistance than logistical difficulties. One issue, I believe, is the fear of losing an erection while putting a condom on. The other is the fear that a woman will get out of a sexual mood while the condom is being found, opened, and put on.

60. How do you get a guy to use a condom?

Traditional methods include begging, whining, pleading, and threatening. The problem with these is that even when they work (which is only some of the time), nobody feels good about the process. This is a poor way to create an intimate encounter.

Condom use is not something a *man* does, it is something a *couple* does. It's simple: "We do this." We do it because it's the only way to make intercourse safe and healthy. We do it because intercourse requires contraception, and a condom is the form most compatible with my body.

We certainly don't use condoms because you could be a dirty, thoughtless person who might kill me with a disease. We use condoms because I want to feel relaxed and uninhibited when we make love, and condoms make that possible. That is the way you want me to be, isn't it?

61. How do you know when a condom breaks? What should you do if it does?

One partner should periodically check during intercourse to make sure that the condom is still in place and that it hasn't torn. Just reach down with two fingers and gently tug on the open end of the condom.

After ejaculating, hold the condom on the penis and withdraw the two together. Check to see that there is ejaculate collected in the condom's tip.

If you think the condom has leaked, or if you spill semen near the vulva while withdrawing the penis and condom, fill the vagina with contraceptive foam, cream, or jelly *immediately*—an important reason to have some handy at all times. A woman in this situation should *not* douche, which can push the sperm further into the vagina. She *should* see a physician if she misses her next menstrual period.

62. I'm confused. Are birth control pills safe or not?

Like all medications, birth control pills are safe for certain people under certain circumstances. They are safest for healthy women under 30 who have never smoked. On the other hand, most physicians will not prescribe them for women with a health history of cancer, heart disease, stroke, or abnormal vaginal bleeding.

A wide range of oral contraceptives is now available with various combinations and strengths of hormones. Each woman must be evaluated separately to see if she is one of the millions of Americans who can safely use the pill.

Birth control pills have several advantages. These include decreasing the length and severity of menses; improving acne; eliminating ovulation pain; and preventing many STDs (sexually transmitted diseases) from traveling into the uterus and fallopian tubes. In fact, studies suggest that oral contraceptives reduce the risk of pelvic inflammatory disease. On the other hand, they can also reduce the effectiveness of any antibiotics you're taking, including those taken to treat an STD. And high-estrogen pills can increase your susceptibility to yeast infections.

Statistically, pregnancy and childbirth still carry a higher health risk for the average woman than do birth control pills.

63. If I only have sex once a week, why do I have to take birth control pills every day?

Both the condom and diaphragm prevent pregnancy by physically blocking the sperm from uniting with the egg. Birth control pills, however, work by preventing monthly ovulation, or the release of an egg.

The pills do this by controlling the level of the hormones that regulate ovulation. This process goes on twenty-four hours a day, every day of the month, regardless of sexual activity. If pills are not taken every day, they body's natural process of ovulation can break through, release an egg, and make pregnancy possible—all without you knowing it.

64. Why are birth control pills ineffective during the first few months?

It takes a while for control of ovulation to be completely wrested from the body. Because it's difficult to tell exactly what a woman's ovulatory hormone levels are, day by day, using a condom or diaphragm for the first months is a sensibly cautious approach.

65. How do I take care of my diaphragm?

Basically, you should handle your diaphragm with as much care as you would any other piece of medical equipment. Keep it in its case, wash it after each use, dust with a little cornstarch, and hold it up to a light to check for tiny holes. Do *not* use any oil-based products with it (such as vaseline, for lubrication), because they will attack the rubber. In any event, replace it at least every two years.

Have a physician check the diaphragm size if you gain or lose ten or more pounds, or if you give birth.

66. If I have unprotected sex, or a condom breaks, can't I just douche?

No. Douching is not a form of contraception. Sperm travel through the vagina into the uterus much too quickly for a douche to interfere. In fact, a strong surge of liquid will give the sperm a boost and speed them through the vagina and cervix.

67. What is the cervical cap?

Similar to, but smaller than, the diaphragm, the cervical cap looks like a rubber thimble that fits around the cervix at the end of the vagina. Used in Europe for years, the cap was approved for American use by the F.D.A. in 1988. It is used with spermicidal jelly and can be left in place altogether for forty-eight hours. Many women find this more convenient than the diaphragm's limit of twenty-four hours.

The cap must be fitted by a physician and is about 85 percent effective—comparable to the diaphragm.

68. What, exactly, is the rhythm method?

The rhythm method is an attempt to avoid pregnancy by limiting intercourse to so-called "safe" times of a woman's monthly cycle. The idea is that ovulation takes place some six to eleven days after a woman's period ends. Sperm can live up to seventy-two hours; an egg can live—and be fertilized—for a day. Including a few days for a margin of error, this leaves some two-and-a-half weeks per month when some people *think* protection is unnecessary.

One large problem with this method is that ovulation and menstruation are far less predictable than many people think. Patterns can be affected by stress, diet, illness, weather, and other factors. Another problem is that many people do not have the discipline to abstain from intercourse periodically year after year.

For most couples this method is very risky. Ann Landers says that practitioners of the rhythm method are called parents.

69. How do you use a thermometer for birth control?

Because of the ebb and flow of hormones, a woman's body temperature changes slightly during her monthly cycle. Prior to ovulation, there is a slight drop and then a rise for three days. If a woman takes her temperature every single morning *before getting out of bed,* she can actually note these changes and either abstain from intercourse or use condoms while she is fertile.

Obviously, this method requires training, tremendous commitment, a fairly regular lifestyle, and a cooperative partner.

70. What is the Billings Method?

Like body temperature, the mucus produced by the cervix changes during a woman's monthly cycle. The Billings Method involves carefully charting the consistency of the mucus, so a couple can determine when ovulation is about to occur. If a pregnancy is not desired, this would be the time to refrain from unprotected intercourse. Since this requires training as well as checking the mucus several times each day, most couples find it impractical.

71. How does the IUD work? Is it safe?

The modern IUD (intrauterine device) was invented in 1909, although variations of it have been tried on both humans and pack animals (like camels) for centuries with varied success.

About the size of a quarter, and made of flexible plastic with a one-inch string at the end, IUDs seem to work by chemically altering the environment of the vagina and uterus, interfering with conception or implantation. According to the new Kinsey report, only two types of IUDs are currently available in the United States. Because of the high incidence of pelvic infections, infertility, and deaths associated with IUD use, other manufacturers have stopped distributing their product.

Most clinics are currently discouraging certain women from using IUDs because of the increased risk of pelvic inflammatory disease (PID), which can reduce fertility by scarring the fallopian tubes. High-risk women include those with multiple partners or a history of tubal pregnancies.

IUDs do make sense for some women. If you're interested, consult a physician or clinic that specializes in family planning.

72. If women can only get pregnant three or four days a month, why all the hysteria about using birth control all the time?

The question is, *which* three or four days are you at risk? Not only can you not predict these days, you can even affect them through worry or a strong orgasm (each of which can trigger ovulation). For this reason, you aren't even 100 percent safe while menstruating.

Using contraception whenever you have intercourse is a bit like wearing a seat belt whenever you drive: Once you get used to it, it becomes part of the activity. No hysteria, just acceptance and attention.

73. Whose responsibility is birth control—the man's or woman's?

The answer is "C"—none of the above.

Birth control is a routine part of sex. Both partners benefit from its use, both partners should and can be equally well informed about it, and so both partners should take responsibility for it. Equally.

Essentially, this means that each partner should be unwilling to have unprotected intercourse. This decision should only be made once, at the beginning of a sexual relationship. After that, the only negotiation should be about the how, not the if.

Regardless of the method used or its frequency, if one partner is constantly complaining or suggesting unprotected intercourse, the responsibility is not shared.

74. I'm afraid I'm infertile. What should I do?

There are two ways to assess one's fertility: clinical tests and unprotected intercourse. Fertility tests are supervised by a physician. In men they begin with a sperm count, which requires masturbating (privately) into a jar. The woman's test starts by tracking the ovulation process through carefully charting each day's *basal* (on awakening) temperature.

Infertility concerns are voiced by two groups of people: those who want babies right now, and those who don't. Unless someone wants a baby immediately, unprotected intercourse should *never* be used to test fertility. Unfortunately, tens of thousands of women, consciously or not, do so every year to handle their anxiety about the future.

If you have any concerns about your fertility, see a physician.

75. Sterilization sounds so final—and so clinical. How could someone ever decide to do it?

Sterilization is an unpleasant word, isn't it? It calls up nasty pictures of laboratories, medical experiments, and helpless cats. *Vasectomy, tubes tied,* even *fixed* somehow seem more humane, if not completely serene.

More than twelve million Americans have been sterilized, making it the most common form of contraception in the United States. It is essentially 100 percent effective, with virtually no side effects.

The permanence of sterilization accounts for much of its charm. Sterilization is a chance to take control of your life and to decide that the future is here. It can be a very grown-up thing to do—acknowledging that all choices have their costs. Many people get sterilized after their family is the size they want it to be. Others decide to be child-free and see no reason to wait. For both groups, choosing when to end their child-bearing years is a powerful way of launching the next part of their lives.

Because of these implications, all reputable doctors and clinics require patients to have a counseling session before they will perform this procedure.

76. If I get sterilized and change my mind later, can the procedure be reversed?

As microsurgery becomes increasingly sophisticated, more and more sterilizations are being reversed. This is major surgery, however, involving a hospital stay, the risk of infection, and very high cost.

Even if things go well, the ability to conceive a child is still not guaranteed. Success rates for reversing vasectomies range from 18 to 60 percent; for reversing tubal ligations, the range is 20 to 90 percent. Ironically, scarring from the operation can decrease or prevent fertility. For all of these reasons, sterilization should still be considered a permanent decision.

77. Why do many religions think that birth control is a sin?

Many religions regard the function of sex primarily as reproduction, which makes contraception immoral. This is understandable, since these traditions were developed long ago, when communities were trying to increase their size.

In addition, Christianity, since around the third century, has developed a distinct suspicion of pleasure. According to religious scholar Raymond Lawrence, this had a political rather than a theological basis. Since birth control facilitates sex for pleasure, it is considered sinful for this reason as well.

Today, most people have sexual experiences for reasons other than baby-making. Attitudes about birth control reflect this: Most American adults (including Catholics) use birth control at least half the time they have intercourse.

Despite the pronouncements of various religious policy-makers, only a small number of orthodox followers in America truly believe that contraception is a sin.

78. Is it true that in some countries women use abortion as a form of birth control? How do they stand it?

In the Soviet Union, where condoms and birth-control pills are rarely available, people depend on abortion to control the size of their families.

We shudder at the statistic that the average Soviet woman has more than a dozen abortions in her life. But the Soviets see this as a practical, rather than moral, issue. And the fact that women have so many abortions proves that their fertility is not affected.

The major complaints the Soviet people have about this situation are the lack of contraceptive choice and the terrible, assembly-line conditions under which the abortions are performed. The Soviet health-care system is primitive, plagued by inefficiency, and flagrantly unconcerned with peoples' needs.

5

Aging

**I have everything now I had twenty years ago—
except now it's all lower.**

—Gypsy Rose Lee

79. What exactly are the sexual changes I should expect as I approach fifty?

In general, the changes fall into two categories. Most of our body's sexual responses slow down somewhat, and our sexual interests and needs typically change.

Men can expect changes in their sexual reflexes. This means that erection and ejaculation take longer and are more vulnerable to fatigue, emotions, and distraction. Ejaculation is less powerful, with a smaller volume of semen. Women's changes are more hormone-related; breast sensitivity may change and vaginal tissue may be somewhat dryer.

Changes in sexual desire occur in many people of both

genders. In some, libido increases; in some, it decreases; and in others, it remains the same. It's impossible to predict which will occur in a given person.

These changes require new concepts of sexuality and lovemaking. Most older people find intercourse becoming less important, while other aspects of sex, such as cuddling, kissing, smelling, and genital fondling, become increasingly enjoyable.

In general, it's best to relate to your changes not only as a loss, but also as an opportunity to explore and express new aspects of your sexuality.

80. Do men's and women's sexual interest change in similar ways as they age?

That depends entirely on the men and women involved. There is far more difference among all men, and among all women, than there is between men as a group and women as a group. It isn't hard to find couples whose sex drive goes in opposite directions after age fifty; at the same time, it isn't hard to find couples whose changes are well matched, regardless of the direction.

81. Are there health issues that will affect my sexuality in later years?

Because sex is such an integral part of life, virtually *all* health issues affect our sexuality. In older people these include stiff joints, diabetes, osteoporosis, vascular problems, depression, and any condition requiring medication. Areas affected can be erection, ejaculation, lubrication, libido, and the simple ability to enjoy sex undistracted.

The single most important thing you can do in this regard is *talk*: to your physician, your partner, and yourself. Admit that you're having difficulty. Share your difficulty with your mate and ask for support. And bring any problems to your doctor's attention. Since doctors get virtually no training in sexuality, patients have to educate them, presenting information and questions that make them think. A smart, secure physician will respond positively and help you develop a program to cope with and overcome any problems.

82. What's the upper limit to normal sexual functioning? At what age is sex pointless, or defined so differently that it's no longer sex?

However you ask the question, the answer is the same: There is no upper limit to sexual functioning. People who are in good health often desire sex well into old age, and there is no reason they cannot enjoy it.

As for defining and redefining sexuality, this is an exciting lifelong project, not some dreadful event you go through to cope with a deteriorating body. More than one-third of those over sixty who responded to the *Starr-Weiner Report* said that sex was better than ever. Are you going to argue about what exactly these folks meant by "sex?"

83. All this talk about staying sexually active into old age bothers me. Can't I rest now—can't I have a period of life free from having— or thinking about—sex?

Yes, particularly if your partner feels the same, or if you have no partner.

Sex should not be an obligation, like flossing your teeth. Sex is part of life's celebration; if you don't feel that way, it makes no sense to do it. Many people simply can't enjoy sex: They have been traumatized, or have been with insensitive partners, or are extremely alienated from their bodies. To such people, as to everyone else, I say ignore any social pressures about sex. Ignore what other people might think and, sexually, do your own thing. If that means having no sex, fine.

If you have a partner who has a different outlook, you probably have a serious relationship problem. I encourage couples counseling to help you find ways of resolving this conflict.

84. Now that I'm a senior citizen, is it true that I have to "use it or lose it?"

Actually, it's a little more complicated than that. And let's not take the axiom too literally—your penis or clitoris is not going to fall off from disuse.

This expression arose in the sixties as a way of giving

middle-aged (and older) people permission to be sexual. It was based on research showing that the best predictors of sexual activity and satisfaction in old age include activity and satisfaction when younger, and an enthusiastic, positive sexual attitude.

Thus, "use it or lose it" was another way of saying "It's okay to want sex as you get older. It's just an extension of sex when you're younger, so don't feel you need to slow down to get ready for a sexless old age!"

In the nineties, we now discuss this in a more sophisticated way, but the overall concept holds: Enjoying sex as an adult, integrating it into your life, and seeing it as a source of intimacy and a positive way to spend time, are still good predictors of sexual satisfaction when older.

To answer your question, then, you don't *have* to "use it" or do anything else you don't want to do. But the best way to keep your sexual response system in good shape, like any other body system, is to exercise it and pay attention to it. If you're more comfortable alternating periods of sexual activity with periods of abstinence, go ahead and do that. Of course, you'll want to resume sexual activity slowly after a period of abstinence, which we discuss below.

85. I'm thirty-five. I like my seventy-year-old neighbor, but she always holds my hand longer than I like. Is she rude, or what?

Nonsexual touching is important for everyone. Data show that babies who aren't touched enough grow more slowly than babies who are.

Fortunately, most children do get enough touching—even strangers love hugging little ones. As we age, however, things change, and many older people get very little touching. Younger people often dislike the way they look, feel, or smell; their peers are sometimes sick; and social "propriety" discourages us from seeing touching the elderly as wholesome—and crucial.

Younger people take for granted the arm squeezing, hand holding, back rubbing, and friendly hugging of daily life. For older people who aren't getting enough of it, this simple human contact can be profound. Don't do anything you're uncomfortable with, but do understand your neighbor's need.

86. If it's okay for old people to have sex, why don't more of them do it?

First of all, older people *are* having sex. According to the *Hite Reports* on both male and female sexuality, many people over forty (all the way up into the eighties) say they "enjoy themselves more than ever." Just to pick two examples, half of men in the *Reports* over age fifty give, and half of women over age fifty receive, oral sex. And according to the original Kinsey Report, more then one-third of people over age seventy masturbate to orgasm.

After age sixty, sexual satisfaction seems based more on the quality of the relationship (which people can maintain at any age) than on the mechanics of sexual functioning.

People whose sexual frequency or interest declines with age typically cite one or more of the following reasons:

• Social expectations: expressions like "dirty old man," jokes about older people being sexually incapable, and adult children being horrified by the idea
• Personal expectations: the older person's own idea that sex is inappropriate
• Difficulty in finding new partners if a spouse dies;
• Ill or otherwise unavailable partner
• Chronic worry about money or health
• Lack of privacy
• Difficulties in changing the definition of lovemaking
• The belief that if sex can't be like it was, it's not worth doing at all, and
• The belief that masturbation is not normal or healthy

It's difficult to estimate the actual sexual behavior of elderly people. Like adolescents, they tend to hide their sexual behavior to avoid the disapproval and even punishment that sometimes results when it is discovered.

87. As my marriage got worse and worse, sex went down in fre-

quency to practically none. With a divorce and some counseling behind me I'm ready to get out there again, but I'm worried. How do I know all the parts still work?

First of all, let's examine the idea of "practically none." Although you may have been having little or no intercourse, you have probably still been sexual. Fantasy, masturbation, and sensual activities like bubble baths are all forms of sexuality. Thus, your sexuality may have continued active and in good shape during this time.

Long periods without intercourse or other genital sex are not at all harmful, and they don't mean your sexuality has deserted you. You may feel clumsy, you may have forgotten a few things, you may have changed the way you make sexual choices, and you may even discover you have new appetites. All of these remain to be explored. To do so you'll have to trust that your parts still work.

Helpful guidelines? Don't have sex when you're not ready; have it only in ways that reflect who you are and how you feel; let your body express itself however it wishes.

And like any machine that hasn't been used for a while, your body should be warmed up slowly; make sure it's lubricated, and be gentle with it.

88. I'm forty-nine, he's thirty-three, and we've been in love for more than a year. Why does everyone criticize us? Do you agree that this relationship can't last?

There are many reasons that people criticize this kind of relationship. To give friends and family the benefit of the doubt, let's acknowledge their sincere desire to protect you from being hurt. This is not completely unrealistic.

On the other hand, some criticism may simply reflect jealousy. Your situation also challenges people to confront their own beliefs and self-imposed limitations about what is possible. Many people feel threatened by this. Finally, your relationship is a clear announcement that you are interested in sex. Many folks, unfortunately, feel threatened by middle-aged people making such a statement.

Will this relationship last? No one can predict. Your arrangement, like all others, has both strengths and weaknesses. In this high-tech, low-intimacy era, every relationship—no matter how conventional—is an uphill battle. Yours will be as difficult as most others; your passion and satisfaction will make it less difficult than many. Certainly, it will help if you pay more attention to each other's hearts than to your ages.

89. I took a wrong turn while in my dad's nursing home last week and stumbled onto a room where two elderly residents were getting ready to make love. Don't nursing homes have rules against this stuff?

Yes, most nursing homes have rules about this—much to the shame of the rest of us. As Siemens and Brandzel put it in their nursing textbook, "The most sexually disenfranchised members of our society are the permanent residents of nursing homes."

Just as most parents are uncomfortable with the sexuality of their children, children of all ages tend to be uncomfortable with the sexuality of their parents. The older the parents, the greater the discomfort tends to be. Most nursing-home administrators have been clearly warned by bill-paying adult children that "there better not be any hanky-panky around here."

People typically rationalize this prejudice by saying things like "I just don't want Dad to get hurt" or "Aunt Sarah doesn't realize how people are gossiping about her." In truth, we still have a long way to go before we feel comfortable giving everyone the right to his or her sexuality. I hope you will extend this human right to your aging father. He deserves it as much as you do.

90. Let's be honest: Fifty-five-year-old men don't want fifty-five-year-old women like me, they want younger women. So what am I supposed to do?

First of all, let's get the facts straight: Many older men desire women their own age or even older.

In any event, it's important that you don't try to imitate younger women. Instead, be the best *you* you can be. What do you have to offer? The answer to this question is much more important than your age.

Remember, too, that sex appeal goes far beyond having a perfect body. True, society has a limited grasp of older people's sexuality, especially women's. But nothing is as sexy as someone who *feels* sexy. If that's you, you've got it made.

It's easy to be angry about getting older. No one wants to confront his or her mortality. The mirror can be a teller of hateful truths. But the mirror only tells one small part of the story. And if age brings wisdom, the story the mirror tells should get less important year by year.

To make the most of your sexuality at any age, be yourself. Make plenty of friends. Masturbate. Pursue partners you're interested in. And keep in mind that not all men want a sweet young thing. The more grownup ones want a woman with a few years on her compass.

91. My widowed mother and her new boyfriend sleep together five or six nights a week in Florida. Should I let them sleep together when they visit me?

Ah, what goes around, comes around. Our parents used to be uncomfortable with our sexuality, and now we're uncomfortable with theirs.

Your mom is probably as confused about this as you are. If one or both of you need to deny that there's sex going on (and, of course, there may not be), that's sad, but she and her friend should sleep separately. People can always find reasons to justify this: the kids shouldn't know (why?); it's embarrassing; it's immoral; it doesn't look right.

The truth is, we don't like to be confronted with our parents' or kids' sexuality. It challenges our assumptions about sex and confronts us with the realities of our own sexual situation. Most people would rather structure things so they can simply avoid their discomfort.

Should they sleep together? If you're interested in participating in reality, yes; if you're more interested in maintaining illusions and avoiding your feelings, no. If you choose the latter, it's best to acknowledge the real reason, rather than resorting to rationalizations that insult everyone.

To paraphrase Pogo, we've turned out to be the people we warned our parents about.

92. I'm a single, middle-aged man. When can I stop using condoms for birth control?

Unless you have a vasectomy or a negligible sperm count, the answer is simple: never. Men manufacture sperm—by the millions—their entire lives and are able to father children long after they can't do much else.

Women, on the other hand, only ripen eggs during the fertile era of their lives. This usually ends in their mid-forties, as the interval between menstrual periods gets longer and longer. A woman should use some sort of contraception until one year after her last period.

Of course, birth control is only necessary if you have intercourse. Consider other forms of sexual expression as well. And remember that condoms are critical for reducing the risk of catching STDs—at *all* ages.

93. Now that I'm approaching menopause, do I have to have a hysterectomy? Will this make me less interested in sex?

Approaching menopause does *not* automatically mean you need a hysterectomy.

Hysterectomy is the removal of the uterus, with or without the cervix. This operation renders a woman sterile and eliminates her menstrual periods. It usually does not involve the removal of her ovaries, and thus does not induce menopause.

While some women experience great psychological or sexual distress as a result of this procedure, most do not. In fact, many women report improved sexual relationships after a hysterectomy because they no longer fear becoming pregnant.

Good reasons for hysterectomy include cancer, fibroid tumors, uterine collapse, and advanced pelvic infection.

But there is serious evidence that a huge number of hysterectomies in America are done unnecessarily. As with all surgeries, a second opinion should be sought before proceeding.

94. I have a friend going through the change of life, and she says it's no big deal. Does she have a special trick, or is she simply fibbing?

The "change of life," or menopause, affects different women differently. While for some the loss of estrogen initiates a confrontation with aging and mortality, for others it merely signals the end of contraceptive worries and menstrual cramps.

One aspect of your friend's "special trick" may simply be her lucky genes. The other may be her attitude—that menopause is not a dramatic "change of life" but merely a minor event in a much longer, richer journey.

6

Sexual Health

Doctors must go to school for years and years, often with little sleep and with great sacrifice to their first wives.

—Roy G. Blount, Jr.

95. How do prescription drugs affect a person's sex life?

The level of current medical knowledge about the sexual impact of drugs and other treatments is shockingly low, but one thing is clear: Dozens of the most commonly prescribed medications can produce sexual side effects. These include drugs for the treatment of heart disease, high blood pressure, arthritis, convulsions, and gastrointestinal disorders.

The most common sexual side effects of drugs (with an example of each) are: reduced desire (tranquilizers, like Xanax); erection problems (antihypertensives, like Inderal); ejaculation problems (antipsychotics, like Thorazine); impaired orgasm (antidepressants, like Tofranil); and testicle, breast, and menstrual disorders (cancer drugs, like Leukeran).

Practically no funding exists for research on these issues. Either no one in the medical establishment or government thinks sexual side effects are important, or those in medicine and government are simply too uncomfortable with sexuality to raise the question. This tragic situation is reinforced when patients don't raise sexual concerns with their physicians, allowing doctors to remain ignorant of (and uncomfortable about) these issues.

96. My brother said his medication was causing impotence, and when his doctor changed the kind of medicine, the problem went away. Why?

Probably because the second kind belongs to a completely different class of drug than the first; that is, it operates by a different mechanism. While a particular body may not "like" one kind of drug, it may tolerate another quite well.

This is true, for example, with high blood pressure medication. To accomplish the same result, physicians prescribe such different drugs as beta blockers, calcium channel blockers, ACE inhibitors, and diuretics. If one causes problems, another often works fine.

The moral of the story is to discuss the possible sexual impact of any drug your doctor prescribes. Your brother was smart to do so. The results speak for themselves.

97. Why the big fuss about lubrication? Sometimes we're so excited we don't want to stop; other times we just don't have anything handy.

Lubrication during insertion and intercourse is not just a luxury, it's a health issue. Insufficient lubrication creates irritation, which can cause tiny vaginal or penile tears and infection.

The most common cause of insufficient lubrication is insufficient arousal. It isn't enough to want sex or to want to please a partner. A woman's body has to be ready, which can take as long as thirty minutes or more.

Some women think they "should" secrete as much lubrication as they need and that they aren't "real" women if they don't. And others assume that if they are ready for sex mentally, their bodies are ready, too. These are myths, not facts.

Many couples benefit from external lubrication before and during intercourse, and many more could. If you have any friction-type discomfort or irritation, if insertion is ever uncomfortable or painful, or if you simply don't feel moist enough during lovemaking, you probably need something wet and slick. Try K-Y, Sylk, Astroglide, Foreplay, or any other well-known water-soluble product.

98. Am I crazy, or do I really get a vaginal infection as soon as I get over the flu?

Actually, you're pretty sharp to notice this pattern. The explanation probably has to do with *how* you get over the flu.

Antibiotics, you see, affect the bacterial balance of the vagina, killing the good bacteria as well as the bad. This allows the candida fungus, which is always present in the normal vagina and mouth, to increase. The result is what we call a yeast infection.

To prevent the flu-yeast sequence next time, treat your flu without antibiotics. Or get some Monistat or Gyne-Lotrimin, and take it to inhibit the yeast as soon as you finish taking the antibiotics. A common home substitute for this medication is a teaspoon of *plain* yogurt inserted in the vagina twice each day. Because yogurt contains the same vaginal bacteria that antibiotics kill, it restores the vaginal environment that keeps yeast in balance.

Whatever you do, don't douche. As noted elsewhere, this typically causes more problems than it solves.

99. Why are we always told to drink cranberry juice for a bladder infection?

Believe it or not, it isn't the cranberries. Here's a hint—organic cranberry juice won't work.

The prepared cranberry juice we buy is loaded with benzoic acid, which is used as a preservative. It helps fight the bladder infection by increasing the acidity of the vaginal environment.

Then why not drink citrus juice, you ask? Because it isn't acidic *enough*. In fact, the relative weakness of citric acid can trigger an alkaline response by the body, leaving you more vulnerable to a bladder infection than before.

When you have a bladder infection, remember to drink plenty of water, and to urinate frequently (to clear out the germs), even though it's uncomfortable.

100. **What is honeymoon cystitis? Can single people get it too? How?**

Cystitis is inflammation (infection) of the bladder, which can also involve the urethra (the tube that carries urine out of the body). It is typically caused by bacteria, which are often transmitted during intercourse.

Cystitis is one of the most common reasons women seek medical attention; its main symptom is the continual feeling of having to urinate (whether you can or not), accompanied by a burning sensation. A physician will typically prescribe antibiotics. As we've seen (see question 98), this presents problems of its own.

"Honeymoon" cystitis refers to the increased likelihood of getting this disease when the frequency of intercourse increases dramatically; when sex resumes after a long interval; or when you have sex with a new partner. It's just a nickname; anyone can get it.

The best way to avoid cystitis, or bladder infections, is to urinate frequently, which flushes bacteria out of the urethra. Drinking plenty of water will encourage this, especially right before and right after intercourse. Also, avoid chemicals that irritate the vagina and urethra such as douches and "feminine" sprays. Finally, apply as much lubrication as necessary before, during, and after intercourse to prevent irritation by friction.

101. **For years my mother and aunts have douched. Shouldn't I?**

No, not unless your nurse or physician has specifically told you to do so. The vagina is a self-cleaning organ, like the eye;

a healthy vagina is as clean as a healthy mouth. For years, however, the advertising industry has implied that there is something wrong with the normal smell, taste, and texture of a healthy vagina. This is ignorant and destructive.

A persistent foul odor, of course, should be checked by a doctor. It often indicates an infection needing treatment. But for most women, showering once a day is sufficient vaginal hygiene.

At best, douching is a waste of time. Unfortunately, prepared douche products contain chemicals that upset the vagina's bacterial balance and irritate its delicate tissue. Users frequently acquire vaginal problems this way, try to remedy them by douching, and get into a frustrating downward spiral.

Before assuming your vagina smells or tastes bad, ask your partner how he or she feels. Some people consider their partner's juices an aphrodisiac, you know. Wouldn't it be nice to know that about yours?

102. What exactly does my doctor mean by "always wipe from front to back?"

When you wipe yourself after urinating or moving your bowels, it's important to keep the bacteria in your rectum out of your vagina and urethra. Carelessness about this causes many vaginal infections. So wipe from your vagina ("front") toward your rectum ("back"), not vice-versa.

By the way, if you don't feel comfortable asking your doctor what he or she means by something, consider finding a doctor you can talk to.

103. What is the prostrate? Why do old men talk about it so much?

First of all, it's "prostate," not "prostrate." The real mystery is why this word is mispronounced by practically everyone.

The prostate is a gland about the size of a walnut surrounding the urethra and the neck of the bladder, like a fist holding a drinking straw. The gland contributes 95 percent of the volume of the ejaculate.

If a diseased prostate swells (*prostatitis*) it can squeeze and even shut off the bladder neck or the urethra itself, making urination painful or even impossible. This requires immediate medical attention. If the problem is caused by infection, antibiotics can generally cure it.

For the majority of men, prostate swelling is a natural part of aging. The usual recommendation is surgery, which scrapes away part of the tissue to relieve the pressure and restore comfortable urination. For more serious problems, such as cancer, more serious surgery is necessary.

Because conventional prostate surgery affects the urethra, subsequent ejaculations typically go back into the bladder rather than out the penis. This does not affect orgasm itself, although it takes some getting used to. In unusual, serious cases the surgery can damage the genital nerves, creating erection problems.

104. Why does the doctor have to check my prostate that awful way? What is he doing?

Theoretically, your doctor is inserting a gloved, lubricated finger into your rectum to feel the various surfaces of the prostate for any abnormalities. It should take only a few seconds; be glad he or she is conscientious enough to insist on doing this.

During the prostate exam, the combination of arousal, irritation, and the urge to urinate can be even more unsettling than the temporary physical discomfort. Men sometimes get erect (from the stimulation) and/or embarrassed, which is understandable but unnecessary. Rather than ignoring how you feel, go ahead and discuss it with the doctor.

By the way, breathing deeply and slowly can make the exam less uncomfortable.

105. How do you have intercourse when your back and knees are stiff?

First of all, try to avoid being stiff. An hour before you think you might have sex, take some aspirin or other anti-inflammatory drug, such as Motrin or Naprosyn. A warm shower or bath will also help make you more comfortable. And getting a short massage from your partner not only feels good but can itself evolve into erotic play.

Don't be afraid to experiment with various positions that take the stress off joints. A side-by-side position, for example, or woman-sitting-on-man may be more comfortable than the more traditional missionary position. Don't be afraid to stop one or more times and stretch a bit.

And, of course, remember that lovemaking doesn't have to include intercourse. There are plenty of less stressful ways for you and your partner to enjoy yourselves.

106. For a monogamous couple, are there any rules for making anal sex safe?

Yes, several. The first is, use tons of lubrication. The second is, use subtle motions instead of long, hard thrusting. The third is, don't go from anal to vaginal intercourse without washing the penis, finger, or vibrator (or whatever) *thoroughly*.

Anal sex does have drawbacks, including discomfort. It's probably the easiest sexual way of transmitting HIV (the AIDS virus); couples who aren't strictly monogamous should simply not do it. On the other hand, anal sex can be intensely pleasureable for one or both partners and can also be extremely intimate.

Anal sex is practiced by a substantial minority of Americans. If it doesn't particularly appeal to you, just forget it. If you aren't monogamous and still do it, use a condom.

7
....

Sexually Transmitted Diseases(STDs)

Herpes, unlike love, lasts forever.

—Fortune cookie

107. How exactly should I talk with a partner about sex diseases?

The same way, one hopes, you talk about anything really important with someone you're close to—clearly, directly, and with a sense of purpose. No apologies are necessary; be wary, in fact, of any sex partner who *doesn't* want to discuss health and disease.

Many people find that conversations about STDs are easier outside of the bedroom. Set up a situation that helps you feel comfortable: a walk in the park, a long drive, maybe a special meal together. Explicitly say that you're not trying to protect yourself from a thoughtless person who's trying to infect you; rather, you're trying to create the circumstances in which you feel safe enough to relax and be uninhibited. For sample conversations, see chapter 18.

You and your partner might also enjoy listening to the new audiocassette "How to Talk About Safer Sex" by sex therapy pioneers Bernie Zilbergeld and Lonnie Barbach.

108. Now that I have a sex disease, I can barely face myself in the morning. I feel so dirty; who will ever want me?

You don't have a sex disease, you have a disease. It just so happens that it's transmitted through sexual contact rather than some other way.

Calling STDs "dirty" is the result of fear and ignorance. No disease is any dirtier than any other; certainly, the body doesn't make those kinds of moral judgments about itself. The judgments come from social pressure, the kind that used to cause people to hide their cancer, and before that,their leprosy.

So long as you feel dirty you will attract partners who treat you accordingly. Instead, get involved in therapy or a self-help group, or read. When you accept yourself, you will present yourself to the world as someone who has a lot to offer and who deserves respect. You will then attract people who can see past your disease to the special person you are.

109. When should I tell a potential partner I have an STD? I want to be responsible, but I don't want to scare someone off.

Telling someone too soon can make you appear anxious and rude, which makes everyone uncomfortable. On the other hand, a potential partner should be told before actually deciding to have sex with you. This can be difficult, of course, because many people become coy or noncommunicative when they're in the middle of sexual decision-making.

When you start to sense some sexual energy in the air, suggest that you both share some relevant information about yourselves. Most people will appreciate the integrity you show by raising the issue. Explain that you want to be honest, which means giving a potential partner full information with which to make an informed choice.

Remember that your goal is to facilitate communication. One guideline is, when and how would *you* like to be told?

110. Exactly how do you ask someone about his or her sexual history?

In *Safe Encounters,* Beverly Whipple and Gina Ogden offer these suggestions about discussing STDs with a partner:

- Slow down
- Ask questions
- Feel good about yourself
- Exercise your right to safe sex

In asking about someone's history, you want to find out his or her overall attitudes, as well as specific practices relevant to your sexual health. This is different from just being nosy, and it requires a combination of sensitivity and straightforwardness. No, nobody said it was going to be easy.

Here are some things to say after you've raised the subject. You can do these in any order that feels natural.

- Ask about your partner's concept of "sexual history"
- Make it clear that you're not critical or judgmental
- Explain your concerns
- State that your concerns are not "personal"—i.e., not triggered by your partner's looking sleazy or untrustworthy
- Say that this conversation is uncomfortable for you, too
- Ask how this conversation could be more comfortable for your partner
- Offer information about yourself, and invite your partner to ask you questions
- Explain that you are interested in having sex together, and that you both need information to help you decide what *kind* of sex you're comfortable with

111. How do you tell if someone has an STD?

This is a complex question, because there are many different STDs, with a wide range of symptoms. One thing is certain, though—you *can't* tell by someone's social status, manners, or education. Lots of perfectly nice people get these diseases.

Many STDs have symptoms that can be seen on the surface of the skin: Warts have raised bumps, for example, and syphilis is accompanied by genital sores. But many diseases exhibit no outward symptoms (e.g., chlamydia); exhibit symptoms only during an outbreak (herpes); or exhibit symptoms that disappear when the disease gets worse (syphilis). So things are pretty complicated.

Certainly, any discharge from the penis or vagina should be checked, particularly if it smells bad or is painful. Open sores around the genitals, anus, or mouth are also a reason for extreme caution. So are rashes anywhere on the body.

Without carrying a laboratory around in your purse or briefcase, there is no real way to be sure that someone does not have an STD. Because it is so difficult to know the state of someone else's health, caution is always called for in sexual situations. Condoms and safe-sex behaviors (see question 114) are always appropriate with anyone other than a long-term, strictly monogamous partner.

112. What is the connection between STDs and sterility?

Unfortunately, many STDs don't just cause pain and discomfort, they also damage people's reproductive systems, frequently without their knowledge.

Examples of STDs that can compromise or destroy fertility are chlamydia, herpes, gonorrhea, and the viruses that cause genital warts and AIDS.

113. Exactly what does "exchanging body fluids" mean?

The human body manufactures many liquids, such as tears, saliva, and spinal fluid. Those that are most likely to carry the AIDS virus are blood and semen; vaginal secretions and mother's milk are currently suspect, too. "Exchanging" these fluids simply means that there is contact between yours and someone else's, such as blood-blood exchange (as with sharing drug needles), or blood-semen exchange (as often happens during vigorous anal sex).

114. What is safe sex? Is it different from safer sex?

"Safe sex" refers to forms of sexual expression that do not involve the exchange of body fluids. It includes, for example, masturbating together, telephone sex, and sensuous eating. It also includes any activity with someone who is absolutely, without question, free of any STD.

"Safer sex" describes activities with a risk factor that is being addressed. The limitations of science (often complicated by lack of knowledge about a particular partner) make it impossible to know the exact level of the risk. Such activities include intercourse with a latex condom and tongue ("French") kissing.

Some people use the terms "safe" and "safer" interchangeably; some say "safe" when they mean "safer." Although using latex condoms reduces a person's risk of disease substantially, it does not make intercourse or oral sex 100 percent "safe."

115. I seem to have yeast infections all the time. What gives?

Yeast lives in the vaginas of millions of healthy women, causing no problems. Under certain circumstances, however, this fungus grows too fast, causing a common infection called *candida* or *monilia*. It causes a white, curdy vaginal discharge, and itching and swelling. When men get it through intercourse, it causes burning and itching in the urethra.

Frequent yeast infections can be caused by diabetes, pregnancy, birth control pills, antibiotics, and a diet heavy with dairy products, artificial sweeteners, or sugar. Wearing tight jeans or nylon pantyhose prevents the air circulation that keeps yeast under control, too.

Treatment usually takes a week or two and involves a vaginal cream, tablet, or suppository. Because yeast can be passed back and forth between partners in a "ping-pong" manner, both partners must be treated simultaneously until each is cured.

116. What is chlamydia, and why is it such a problem?

Chlamydia is a microscopic organism that can infect the cervix, uterus, fallopian tubes, and male and female urethra. It can live in humans for years, damaging the reproductive organs, with or without symptoms. For example, only one-third of women with a chlamydia infection of the cervix have any symptoms; this makes it especially easy to pass on to a partner.

The symptoms of chlamydia include vaginal discharge and burning, and frequent urination. According to the Kinsey Institute's 1990 report, chlamydia is now the most common sexually transmitted bacterial infection in the United States. The report estimates that there are at least 4 million new American cases each year.

Because it so frequently shows no symptoms, and given that a reliable new test for it exists, an annual chlamydia test for all sexually active women is a good idea.

117. What is herpes?

Herpes is a common disease caused by a virus. It produces skin sores and flu-like symptoms such as headache, fever, and fatigue. It can be treated but not cured. Apparently, millions of people have herpes without any symptoms.

Herpes doesn't look like anything most of the time, because the majority of people with the disease only have outbreaks periodically (three times a year, say, is not uncommon). Unfortunately, the virus can be spread even when a person shows no symptoms.

An outbreak usually begins with one or more very small raised bumps on or near the penis or vulva. These blisters, which are filled with clear, very infectious fluid, eventually break, leaving painful, open sores. If undisturbed, they gradually scab over and heal some five to ten days after appearing.

Apparently, herpes is an old disease, known to the Greeks, Romans, and Louis XV.

118. When is herpes communicable?

It is certainly communicable when sores are present and very probably during the *prodromal* stage (a day or two before sores appear), when most people recognize a characteristic tingling or even pain. Professionals disagree about the extent to which herpes can be spread at other times.

Herpes is most easily transmitted by contact between one person's infected area and another's mucous membrane or skin break. It can also be transmitted during pregnancy and birth.

119. What's the difference between herpes 1 and herpes 2?

Primarily the location. Although both types can infect a person anywhere, herpes on the lips and mouth is generally said to be type 1, while herpes on the genitals is called type 2.

120. What is the treatment for herpes?

The herpes virus lives in the body's nervous system, and so it responds to a person's stress levels. Thus, stress-management activities such as rest, meditation, exercise, and good communication are important prevention and treatment tools.

Foods high in the amino acid arginine seem to promote outbreaks, so you may find it beneficial to reduce your intake of nuts, chocolate, alcohol, and caffeine. For many people, the drug acyclovir (Zovirax) helps reduce the duration and intensity of outbreaks. A common side effect of this drug, unfortunately, is headaches.

121. What exactly is AIDS?

AIDS stands for *a*cquired *i*mmuno*d*eficiency *s*yndrome. These words mean you don't inherit it, you acquire it (infected mothers may pass it along during the birth process, but this sharing is mechanical, not genetic); that the immune system becomes too weak to fight other diseases; and that it is characterized by a group of symptoms, including unusual cancers and infections.

122. What is HIV?

HIV stands for *h*uman *i*mmunodeficiency *v*irus, which causes

AIDS. A person who has been exposed to this virus is called HIV-infected. As many as 50 percent of those who are HIV-infected develop AIDS within five years. People who are HIV-infected can transmit the disease even if they have no symptoms of AIDS.

123. What is ARC?

ARC stands for AIDS-related complex and refers to various symptoms that HIV-infected people show before developing AIDS. One such symptom is persistent swollen glands in two or more places other than the groin.

ARC is reclassified as AIDS when a person develops unusual cancers or infections that are not dangerous to noninfected people.

124. How do I tell if I have AIDS?

Most of the symptoms of AIDS also occur in healthy people: fatigue, weight loss, diarrhea, night sweats, confusion. Less common are white spots in the mouth and purplish blotches on the skin or mucous membranes.

The diagnosis begins by testing a sample of your blood. But the test cannot measure whether or not you have the disease, only whether or not you have been exposed to the HIV. It takes your body several months to react to the virus by producing antibodies (which is what the test measures), so you need to take the test some three to six months after your latest possible exposure.

That means there should be no unprotected sex or sharing of needles whatsoever for at least three months before the test. Otherwise, the test is not evaluating your health as it is, but only as it was.

125. Why does AIDS mostly strike gay men?

This is no longer the case. It was true in the early years of the disease in America because the virus was being transmitted through anal intercourse, a form of sex then popular with gay men. The delicate lining of the rectum would tear, allowing contact between one person's blood and the other's semen.

In Africa, however, the majority of people with AIDS are heterosexual. And in America in the nineties, drug use and multiple partners among heterosexuals (as well as safer-sex practices in the gay community) make heterosexuals the fastest-growing source of new AIDS cases.

126. Why does drug use lead to AIDS?

The AIDS virus is frequently transmitted by blood. A hypodermic needle that carries a few drops of one person's blood right into another person's blood can easily carry the virus.

Because needles can be expensive or hard to get, some drug users share them. Thus, not all drug use is AIDS-risky, only drug use that involves needles ("intravenous" drug use), specifically the sharing of needles among those who use them.

The use of other drugs, such as alcohol, marijuana, and cocaine, can indirectly lead to the transmision of AIDS by temporarily reducing people's commitment to safer sex behavior, such as the use of condoms.

127. Why can't science cure herpes or AIDS?

Both herpes and AIDS are caused by viruses, which antibiotics cannot kill. The best way to control a viral disease is to develop a vaccine and vaccinate those at risk, as has been done with polio.

Several things about HIV make this difficult, including the odd fact that laboratory rats don't get AIDS.

128. What is the treatment for AIDS?

Presently, there are drugs that help restore some immune functions and prevent the virus from spreading, prolonging the lives of certain AIDS patients. One such drug is AZT. Unfortunately, it has a number of side effects, costs an average of $10,000 per year, and must be taken for the rest of a patient's life.

To boost their immune systems, many AIDS patients improve their diets, get as much rest as possible, and make other lifestyle changes, which can also increase the length and quality of their lives.

129. Is it my imagination, or do some TV commentators actually seem glad to have AIDS and other sex diseases to complain about?

It is not your imagination. Many right-wing commentators are saying that the spread of AIDS and STDs proves that "immoral" sex (meaning sex they don't like) offends God and should be illegal (as it is in many dictatorships).

Such people are cynically manipulating the shadows of illness and death to promote their own agendas. Around the country, they are preventing young people from getting life-saving information through school sex education and contraceptive advertising on radio and television.

130. All this talk about AIDS has just about ruined sex for me. How can I relax? Will sex ever be fun again?

You have the symptoms of EFRAIDS: Exaggerated Fear Reaction to AIDS. It's understandable nowadays, but it's destructive to both individuals and to communities.

For some people, AIDS and other STDs offer a good excuse to avoid or criticize sex. But sex is not the problem: certain sexual behaviors are.

So stay away from high-risk behaviors: anal sex, unprotected intercourse, sharing needles. Develop a taste for safer sex: intercourse with a condom and nonintercourse activities such as satisfying each other with your hands.

AIDS is forcing people to realize that talking intimately with each other is part of sex. This is, in fact, a good thing. Talk with your partner(s) about your concerns, and get their support for safer sex. And get the facts: Two excellent paperbacks are *The Complete Guide to Safe Sex* by Ted McIlvenna, et al, and *Safe Encounters* by Beverly Whipple and Gina Ogden.

Once you decide what kinds of sex are safe and appropriate for you, do them—enthusiastically and joyfully.

Part II

Turn-Ons and Arousal

8

Desire

Anyone who eats three meals a day should understand why cookbooks outsell sex books three to one.

—L. M. Boyd

131. What is considered a normal level of sexual desire?

Do we want to judge the sexuality of a seventeen-year-old boy, a thirty-five-year-old woman, and a fifty-year-old man using the same standards? There is no such thing as "normal" sex drive.

Not only does desire vary from person to person, it also varies for each individual from week to week and year to year. Stress, emotions, and general health change our desire level constantly; for example, do you feel like having sex right around tax time? Having a notion of your one "normal" desire level is asking for trouble.

When discussing sexual desire, we must also ask, desire for

what? For a partner who is bathed, smiling, and ready for you? Or for one who is critical, selfish, and rough? A person's "normal" desire level for each would be quite different.

132. Why does everyone seem more interested in sex now than they did, say, forty years ago?

Are Americans more interested now than forty years ago? Even if they weren't, our contemporary permission to talk about sex would make it appear so. But we are, I believe, more interested now. Reasons for this include:

- Television, which brings sexuality into everyone's home
- Mixed-gender workplaces, in which people spend most of their waking time nicely dressed and interacting with people of the other sex
- Increased privacy, contraception, and cures for the traditional STDs, which make sex less difficult and scary
- A decline in the influence of religion and in the prevalence of the nuclear family, both of which have been dedicated to preventing sexual information and activity
- A dramatic decrease in the age of puberty, leading to sexual discovery at a far earlier age, normalizing the experience of sex without marriage
- The current social ideal that pursuing "sexiness" is within almost everyone's grasp and that, along with money, it is the hallmark of adulthood, and
- The advertising industry's sexualization of virtually every part of American life, which results in our being bombarded with sexual connotations that never existed before

On the other hand, "Our ignorance of history makes us libel our own times," wrote Flaubert over a century ago. "People have always been like this."

133. What is the role of "chemistry" in sexual desire?

Poets, philosophers, clergy, biologists, and psychologists are still not sure. Neither are sex experts.

Many people feel that love is the source of sexual desire.

For them, "chemistry" only counts insofar as it helps create love. Others, however, observe how frequently we are attracted to people who would be completely inappropriate as mates. Many of us have been wildly turned on by someone we didn't belong with, or even like. Part of the explanation probably involves pheremones, discussed in question 12.

One nice thing about this kind of attraction is the way it allows us to explore our fantasies. Not bound by the requirements of "proper" partners, we can feel attached without having to "pay" in the real world. Who cares if our fantasy object has a bad temper, poor parenting skills, etc?

Although the price is frequently high, most of us yearn for the things that come with "chemistry." These include the willingness to ignore consequences; the experience of being in the moment; the ability to appreciate the perfection of our bodies; and the experience of feeling like a teenager. Zoom!

Biologist James Weinrich describes the difference between love and chemistry this way: "Love is blind; lust is blond."

134. Why are some people simply not all that interested in sex?

Different people are born with different levels of sexual interest. There are, in addition, factors that accentuate or lessen a person's inborn interest level.

One common factor is early traumatic experiences. These can range from molestation to date rape to terrible first experiences with clumsy, ignorant, or selfish partners. Another common factor is the belief that sex is bad, dirty, or dangerous. This is a lesson taught and learned in most families, religious traditions, and communities.

Other reasons for low desire include:

- Discomfort with passion
- Fear of losing control
- Fear of intimacy
- Fear of pleasure
- Generalized anger at members of the other gender
- Anger at one's partner, and
- Dislike for a partner's technique, needs, or attitude

The concept of *low desire*, by the way, is always relative. Without a partner who desires sex more, a person wouldn't have the "problem" of low desire, regardless of his or her actual desire level.

Recall the scene from the film *Annie Hall* in which two partners are each asked by their respective therapists how often they have sex. "Hardly ever," whines Woody Allen. "About three times a week." "Practically all the time," complains Diane Keaton. "About three times a week."

135. Why are some people almost always interested in sex?

Sexual desire, like the desire for swimming, Barbra Streisand records, and Chinese food, is not distributed equally among all people. While some of us can't get enough of one or another of these, to others, *any* is too much. Tragically, such people usually seem to find each other and pair up. But that's another story.

In a sex-crazed/sex-phobic society like ours, it's impossible to tell how much sexual desire is "normal." Is being "almost always interested in sex" healthy or not? Judgments about this usually say more about the person doing the judging than about sex or human nature.

Certainly, most people would have more interest in sex if they were less afraid of passion and of temporarily losing control of themselves. If we were comfortable with our bodies and felt that pleasure was a legitimate way to spend time, we'd also have higher sex drives.

On the other hand, some people are always ready for sex because they're starved for touching or affection, and sex is the only way they can get either one. Sex is also used as a way of getting nonsexual rewards, such as a sense of power, belonging, adulthood, or general validation.

136. How important should sex be in a relationship?

Various authority figures will be happy to tell you exactly how much. Some churches, for example, say people shouldn't focus on sex much at all. *The Joy of Sex* puts sex at the center of a healthy relationship.

I strongly believe there is no "should" in this matter. Some couples are intimate with little or no sex. Others have lots of great sex but no other ways to connect or communicate. Still others use sex as a way of periodically cementing an already satisfying love. And the length of the relationship is a factor, too: Sexual frequency tends to decline as a relationship continues.

While there are many exceptions, sex is often a small part of a relationship when both partners are satisfied, and a large part of a relationship when one or both are dissatisfied.

137. Why are sexually active men called "studs" (positive), while women who act the same are called "sluts" (negative)?

Paternalistic, Western societies like ours have very different sexual standards for men and women. Our culture still finds it difficult to imagine women with the kind of independent sexual desire men are expected to have.

In the absence of any wholesome model of female sexual interest, we condemn sexually active women. The insult translates as, "This female will have sex with many people whom she doesn't romantically love."

When a man wants to do this we understand (and even applaud), because he is expressing a basic part of his masculinity. A sexually free woman, on the other hand, contradicts the classical definitions of femininity. It is this threat that propels the hostile judgments by both men and women.

138. Does talking about sex mean you want to do it? There's a guy in my office who never shuts up about it.

People talk about sex for different reasons. I suspect that your coworker is sexually dissatisfied, and so he sexualizes his conversations to compensate.

On one level, I suppose he wants to have sex more or differently than he is having it. On another, talking may be the psychologically safest form of sexual expression for him. If you don't want to participate in this with him, don't judge him or whine about it. Tell him in a simple, direct way that you feel his bringing sex into your conversations is inappropriate, that you feel intruded upon, and that you want him to stop.

139. Does having an affair spice up the desire for one's spouse?

"I know what this looks like, Mabel, but I was just trying to improve our marriage . . ."

Some people do find that indirectly adding others to their sexual relationship enhances it. There are husbands who get aroused knowing their wives are desired and made love to by other men. Some even get turned on by hearing all the details. Women seem not to share this taste; I rarely hear of a woman who asks her husband to bring another woman home.

Sometimes an affair unlocks previously unknown parts of a person's sexuality. More than a few women, for example, have their first orgasm with someone to whom they aren't married. Some of these women then take their new skills and awareness back to their marriage, thereby enriching it. Others find their partner unwilling to change, and divorce has been known to follow.

In any case, having an affair simply to enhance your marriage is not very practical. There are too many unknowns involved, and there are other, more practical tools available, such as marriage counseling and books on sexual enhancement.

140. I guess I know that older people are sexual, but why does the whole idea sort of give me the creeps?

I think we're uncomfortable with older people's sexuality for two reasons. It reminds us that our parents are sexual, which few of us like to acknowledge. It also takes away a crucial distinction between "us" (non-old) and "them" (old): we're sexual, *they*'re not.

You'd better get comfortable with the idea of senior citizens moaning with pleasure, though. Eventually you'll be one, and you'll want the same opportunity.

141. Sometimes what I really want is some touching or hugging. Is this the same as wanting sex? How do I know which one I really want? What if my partner wants sex for a different reason?

Desiring the nurturance of touch is not the same thing as wanting sex. We take it for granted that babies need plenty of cuddling; in a more perfect world, adults would also get plenty of hugs, back rubs, arms around the shoulder, and massages.

For many people, unfortunately, sex is the only way to get touching. This is sad. It leads to people having sex when they don't want it and to both partners feeling cheated.

Once you believe that wanting to be touched is totally legitimate, you can tell when that's what you want. For one thing, you won't think of touching as a preliminary—it will be satisfying in itself.

We should all learn to ask our partners for touching when we need it, and we should be able to get it without having to pay for it with sex. If your partner isn't interested in more touching, at least suggest lovemaking positions that will give you the body contact you desire.

142. My wife complains that I don't want sex with *her*, that I just want sex. What's wrong with that? Don't women ever feel that, too?

The desire for "just sex" seems to be more common for men than for women, although this is gradually changing.

You and your wife are wasting your time arguing about whether "just sex" is good or bad. Instead, you need to discuss what each of you wants from sex, so you can explore forms of sexual expression that satisfy both of you. There is no substitute for sharing such information about your respective sexual desires. Arguing about right and wrong prevents that crucial exchange.

Your wife, for example, may want more affection, which you can satisfy with more eye contact during intercourse, by saying her name, stroking her face, etc.

While there is nothing wrong with wanting "just sex," there is also nothing wrong with wanting to feel connected to a partner during sex. The challenge is to satisfy both kinds of needs with the same lovemaking. If that doesn't work out, couples should at least attempt to satisfy each other's needs periodically without being asked or pushed.

143. I'm dating two different people right now, and I'm much more interested in sex with one than with the other. Is this normal? Does it mean I care for one more than the other? To be fair, should I try to make love with each one about the same amount?

Your situation is a common one. While it may mean that you are more emotionally attached to one person than the other, it may also mean that you simply enjoy the sex more with one than with the other. Only you can determine which it is. Each is understandable.

Sexual desire, of course, is a function of many different things. You know you get aroused by the way someone smells, tastes, feels, and so on. But there's more to it. All things being equal, for example, it's easier to desire a mate who says "Let's go out to eat" then one who says "It's your turn to cook."

But there's still *more* to desire, because in truth, we ultimately turn *ourselves* on. Clearly, you're doing that more with one partner than with another. Unless you're misleading someone, there's nothing wrong with that.

You don't need to make love the same amount with each person. But if you want to increase your desire for partner B, ask yourself what you're doing with partner A that you aren't, but could be, doing with B. Examples might include making time for sex, communicating what you want, and anticipating a positive outcome.

You might also want to ask yourself why you behave differently with your different partners. Do you have feelings about one or the other that you've been denying?

144. I've heard a lot about "nymphomaniacs." What exactly does this mean? What causes someone to be like this? If these women are really so interested in sex, where do I find one?

Some say that a nymphomanic is a woman who wants sex one more time than her partner.

Actually, the "nymphomaniac" is an ever-popular cultural image, like the "poor little rich girl" and the "whore with a heart of gold." The myth of the nymphomaniac is that such a woman loves sex so much, she can't get enough. Many men think this would be ideal but find actual high-desire women intimidating.

The term "nymphomania" is now used only by the most traditional psychiatrists. It refers to a woman who cannot experience sexual satisfaction regardless of the number of orgasms or partners she has. This is not the same thing as loving sex. Clinically, it is rare, and is often associated with manic-depression. What is far more common is the sexual frustration that results when women can't or won't tell their partners what they need.

145. What is frigidity? How is it diagnosed? How is it treated?

"Frigidity" used to be the diagnosis given to any woman who wanted sex less than her husband. The possibility that the husband was rough, narrow-minded, or in desperate need of a shower was rarely considered.

Sex therapists today do treat many cases of inhibited sexual desire and arousal. In contrast to the bad old days, this diagnosis is used for both men and women, and it is not a criticism of the person's adequacy.

Therapists treat inhibited sexual desire by exploring the feelings that the sexual blocks are indirectly expressing. Sometimes the feelings are long-simmering resentments about the relationship. Sometimes people have been wounded earlier in life and have not resolved their emotional pain.

Occasionally, inhibited desire is a symptom of another disorder, such as depression or thyroid dysfunction.

146. I'm against sex education because it makes kids want sex. Why don't people realize this?

They don't realize it because it simply isn't true. I am deeply distressed when people who say they understand children falsely claim that kids have little or no natural sexual interest.

Even the youngest infant experiences sexual pleasure and demands the enjoyment of sucking. Babies experience erections and vaginal lubrication, and they touch their genitals as soon as they can control their tiny hands.

Whether they want to masturbate or play doctor, children are interested in sex for the same reason adults are: It feels good. Besides, kids are curious. How does my body work? How does the other sex relate to me and my sexuality?

Sex for children, of course, has little to do with intercourse. Healthy kids touch themselves, wrestle, ask each other sexual questions, and sometimes touch or kiss each other. They do that whether or not there are adults around, although the more they are punished, the better they learn to hide it.

Sex education doesn't create sexual interest in children. Their bodies do that quite well, with a boost from the advertising and popular-culture industries. Good sex education simply helps kids understand their sexuality, the pros and cons of sexual relationships, and how to take care of themselves once they get into one.

147. Why do I get hornier in the summer? Do other people?

Many people experience this, and for good reasons: We get more sunlight, which makes us feel more alive; we get more exercise and eat better, which makes us feel more alive; and everyone walks around wearing less clothing, which makes us glad we feel more alive.

9

Technique

In sex, macho doesn't count for mucho.

—Zsa Zsa Gabor

148. How important is sexual technique?

I think poor technique is more important than good technique. That is, you don't need good technique to make sex enjoyable, but poor technique—say, biting someone too hard, trying to have intercourse with insufficient lubrication, or insisting that lovemaking follow the identical formula every time—can get in the way of satisfaction.

The best insurance against poor technique is attending to our partner's preferences ("less teeth, please") and our common sense (yelling "I'm coming!" in someone's ear is never pleasant).

Technical expertise is less important than honoring your body's own rhythms. Think less about what's "right" and more about what feels good. Ultimately, physical and mental relaxation will lead to enjoyable sexual behaviors far more quickly than following a program of "good technique."

149. If technique isn't everything, what else is there in sex?

Technique involves what you do to create arousal or satisfaction. There are many other, less tangible aspects of creating or maintaining an environment in which you and your partner can enjoy those physical sensations.

These include relaxation, a sense of humor, respect for limits, visual stimulation, a nonjudgmental attitude, and encouragement to explore self and other. How do you contribute these things? By being yourself and by communicating.

150. What do you mean when you say "there's no such thing as foreplay?"

Author Warren Farrell says we call it foreplay because it's what comes before the big play—intercourse. That was certainly the male attitude when I was in high school: Foreplay was stuff you did to get a girl hot for sex. Since you were looking forward to something much more exciting, you mostly just put up with it.

Both adults and adolescents, however, need a broader view of sexuality. Intercourse and even orgasm are *optional* parts of a sexual experience. Describing everything else as "getting ready for sex" robs us of the deep satisfaction available from kissing, caressing, teasing, and oral and manual stimulation.

Calling something foreplay diminishes its value and meaning. No wonder some people rush through it. If a sensual or sexual behavior is worth doing at all, enjoy it fully: Savor it, lose yourself in it, forget that there's anything else you could be doing at that moment. It's not foreplay, it's sex.

151. How can I learn better sexual technique?

The drive for self-improvement is commendable, but is this trip necessary? You many not need to learn better technique.

If you don't feel quite comfortable with sexuality, work on that—through therapy or reading—and the technical improvement will take care of itself. If you're in a relationship, you and your mate should talk to each other about what helps you relax and what feels good. You can also read sex books together and discuss them.

Cultures around the world provide us with theories, manuals, and techniques for better sex. There's the Kama Sutra of India, the Quodoshka system of the Cherokee, the pillow books of China. The Indian mystic Rajneesh taught a philosophy and detailed practice of sex. There are books about tantric and ecstatic sex in most languages.

Today's X-rated films offer another approach to technique. As with most sexual disciplines, you need to see some of it as metaphor, rather than taking it all literally. No one should expect to have a ten-inch erection, nor to climax from simply looking at one. With that limitation in mind, you can pick up a few ideas from the better films.

A local sex therapist can be a valuable resource on what's available. He or she can also discuss various local workshops that may be worth attending.

152. I try to have really great technique, but sometimes I don't. How can I make sure I'm great all the time?

You can't—but that's all right, because you don't have to be.

Sexual satisfaction doesn't depend on you being "great." It's more a matter of being relaxed, emotionally present, comfortable with your body, and eager to enjoy yourself.

In normal life, worries, disappointments, and physical pain all compromise our sexual feelings and behavior. There will always be occasions when you don't even care about being great. So don't worry about being great "all the time." As Jonathan Winters says, "Only the mediocre are always at their best."

153. What makes a person a great kisser?

You don't need to be a great kisser. Just express yourself

in a way that feels comfortable, paying attention to the breathing, sighs, and other signals you get from your partner.

For those who insist on how-to-be-a-great-kisser advice, okay. You need:

- To have a clean, fresh mouth
- To have a true enjoyment of kissing, with very little concern about what happens next
- To arrange your body so you're comfortable
- To be aware of your partner's needs
- To convey the feeling that there's nothing you'd rather do, and no one else with whom you'd rather do it, and
- To be unconcerned about how you're being rated as a kisser

Perhaps Chico Marx had the right technique. "I wasn't kissing that woman," he once told Groucho. "I was whispering in her mouth."

154. How can you tell in advance if a person will be good in bed?

You can't, partly because what makes someone a great lover to you may bore or annoy someone else. There are, however, clues that suggest someone may be, er, unsatisfactory. These include:

- Selfishness
- Discomfort with his or her body
- Lack of a sense of humor
- Believing that sex is dirty
- Being phobic about dirt, mess, or smells
- Thinking that sex is basically a waste of time, and
- Constantly apologizing for everything

155. My husband says I need too much foreplay. How do I tell if that's true?

Your question speaks eloquently about the problems in your relationship involving power, trust, and self-esteem.

By "foreplay," you and your husband probably mean the caresses and other sensual behaviors that lead to intercourse and whatever else you do to have an orgasm. If you're both enjoying this, you can't, by definition, have or need "too much."

But it's easy to be critical if "foreplay" is considered a waste of time, like warming up a car before you can actually go somewhere. Why might it feel like a waste of time? Either because it isn't enjoyable, or because someone is more interested in having an orgasm than in sharing pleasure and intimacy. The first problem can generally be solved through communication. The second is a lot more complicated and usually requires professional help.

Moving on, let's assume that, for whatever reasons, you and your partner disagree on the desired amount of "foreplay." Appealing to an expert, or to a notion of what's "normal," suggests that your needs don't matter very much in shaping this sexual relationship. "I want it" should be a good enough reason, or at least an acceptable starting point for negotiating.

Explain to your husband that when you feel your needs are not taken seriously, it's even harder for you to relax and feel sexually available. What kinds of kissing and touching can you discover that you both enjoy?

156. Are there really a lot of positions for intercourse? Why do people use different ones? Which are the best? Which ones should I use?

Yes, there are dozens of positions for intercourse. They offer varying amounts of eye contact, clitoral stimulation, depth and angle of vaginal penetration, degrees of comfort during pregnancy, etc. Varieties include woman on top, man on top, side by side, and "doggie style" (woman on hands and knees, man behind her).

No position is "best"; couples should simply do what feels good at the moment. If and when the moment passes, they can casually switch to another position.

Unless there are medical considerations such as recent pelvic surgery or obesity, there are no positions you "should" use. Simply arrange your arms, legs, and body, and those of your partner, in whatever ways feel comfortable—keeping the vagina within easy reach of the penis.

That well-known cynic Billy Wilder says that more and

more Americans are making love doggie-style so that both partners can watch TV during sex.

157. What do you do if your mouth or jaw gets tired during oral sex?

Sooner or later, everybody has this experience. The easiest
thing to do is give your mouth a rest and switch to another
enjoyable activity. To keep from getting tired right away, make
sure you're comfortable before you start, even if it takes an
awkward moment or two. Don't be afraid to discuss this with
your partner, either before or during lovemaking.

158. Last week we tried "69" for the first time and almost suffo-cated? How are you supposed to do it?

The term 69 is slang for two partners giving and receiving
oral sex simultaneously. Depending on the height and anatomy
of the people involved, it can be easy or difficult. There are
several ways to do this: person A on top, person B on top, and
side by side. You may find that one is easier than the others.

Participants sometimes get so excited that they forget they
have someone's head between their legs. Don't be afraid to tap
your partner on the behind or big toe to remind him or her to
ease up. Also, feel free to rest for a few moments and enjoy
being pleasured (and catching your breath) whenever you like.
Substitute your hand for your mouth if you want to keep stimulating your partner.

159. What are these sex therapy exercises that improve people's tech-nique?

They fall into two categories. The first involves communication—teaching people to talk about what feels good and what
doesn't, what they like and what they don't like. A typical assignment might be, "This week, tell your partner three things
you like about his or her hugs and one thing you'd like to be
different."

The second group of exercises involves structured touching. Developed by Masters & Johnson in the sixties, these "sen-

sate focus" exercises are designed to help people really *experience* touching and arousal, instead of thinking, watching, and judging their bodies and performances. They also provide a convenient laboratory for people to see how they respond to change. A sample assignment might involve partners giving each other a two-minute hand massage without any goal whatsoever.

These exercises often sound simplistic, nothing you couldn't do at home on your own. But therapists provide the context, the supervision, the follow-up discussions, and the fine-tuning that make these exercises valuable tools for individual and relationship change.

160. My partner keeps saying I need to be more "in the moment" during sex. What does this mean?

First, you must ask your partner.

"In the moment" can mean several things. Perhaps you are uncomfortable with some aspect of your body or sexuality, and your experience of sex is partly diluted by guilt, shame, or fear. Perhaps these feelings make you easily distracted by noise, extraneous thoughts, undone chores, and the like.

Another way we may not be present is through frequent judgments of our sexuality: our technique, performance, desires, sounds, and fantasies. Worrying about what we're doing instead of enjoying what we're doing can really undermine closeness and satisfaction.

161. It's been ten years, but I still can't get my first boyfriend out of my mind. Why can't I find anyone who turns me on like he did?

One of the saddest things in life is that we only get one first lover. If you had a good experience with yours (and of course, not everyone does), nothing will ever be quite that sweet again.

Why can't anyone turn you on like he did? Ten years ago, you were younger and far more impressionable. You had no basis for comparison. You appreciated this man as your personal guide into a special world, into adulthood. Ten years later, his kiss and touch have become legendary, larger than life. You've forgotten everything but the fire. How can any contemporary experience match that?

There are plenty of warm, sexy, single men in the world. Are you as open to them as you were ten years ago? As free to say, "Yes, this feels good?" Are you allocating as much time for sex, and preparing for it with as much enthusiasm, as you did then? It's fine if you aren't, but these are some factors that influence your current experiences.

Think hard about what you want and how open you are to having it. And think about the woman who spent twelve years looking for the perfect man. When she finally found him, he was looking for the perfect woman.

162. What do you do with a condom after you've finished using it?

Condoms are not like flowers; you don't press them in a book and save them after they wilt.

Your friendly neighborhood plumber asks that you *please* not flush a used condom down the toilet. Instead, put it in the wastebasket, ashtray, or other receptacle you've cleverly put by the bed prior to making love. Yes, that's the trick—taking care of it beforehand.

If you haven't done so, however, there's no need to get awkward or to pretend that this soggy rubber dropped into your hand out of the sky. If you're friendly enough with someone to use a condom, you're friendly enough to get rid of it without embarrassment.

163. Is it actually dangerous to blow into the vagina?

As funny as it sounds, blowing into the vagina during oral sex can be dangerous. Air bubbles can be picked up by blood vessels and create an embolism (blockage) that could be fatal, especially during pregnancy. Be reassured, though, that kissing, licking, sucking and biting are safe in this regard.

164. What kind of touch is appropriate on the clitoris? On the penis? On the testicles?

All of these questions have the same answer: It depends on the person. Some people like a light feathery touch, others like a medium touch, and others like being pummeled. Also, desires change depending on excitement, mood, time of day, time of month, and, it sometimes seems, the phase of the moon.

In general, women prefer a light stroke on the clitoris, with pressure increasing as excitement builds. Men seem to prefer medium pressure with an up and down movement on the shaft of the penis. Most also like a light cupping or stroking of the testicles; hard squeezing, however, can be very painful.

The important thing is to know your partner's preference. And how do you know? All together now: "communicate!"

165. Why is oral sex called a blow job?

To tell you the truth, I don't know. But the name is misleading—you don't blow. You lick, suck, and nibble. If all you do is blow, you'll have one disappointed partner.

166. Why do some people like you to blow in their ear?

This "blow" is also a bit misleading. What people really like is having you *breathe* in their ear. Why? The ear is flooded with little nerve endings exquisitely sensitive to pressure and temperature. A partner's breath is warm and moist, which can provide intense stimulation. You can also gently explore this area with your tongue or nibble around the edges with your teeth.

Another enjoyable aspect is that in order to breathe in someone's ear, you have to get very, very close.

167. I don't like the way my husband kisses. What can I do?

What some people do is they stop kissing their husbands. Big mistake.

Explain to your husband how much you want to enjoy kissing him, and ask if he wouldn't like that, too. Of course he would. Without focusing too much on what you *don't* like, demonstrate what you *do* like. Kiss him the way you want to be kissed. Show him how to move his tongue, how to use his teeth, how to have a relaxed jaw, and how to stroke your leg (or whatever) at the same time (might as well ask for everything).

Feel free to introduce new, fun elements into your kissing: fresh fruit, a blindfold, ice cubes alternating with hot tea. By the way, does your husband have any ideas for making your kisses more enjoyable? Ask and listen.

168. My husband says I don't make love in a "feminine" way. What does he mean?

Everyone's definition of femininity is different, so you'll have to ask him.

Some people's picture of "femininity" is fairly passive: responding rather than initiating; controlling noises, smells, and movements; and not needing to feel strong or powerful. This may be what your partner means. Or perhaps he'd like you to respond more, with quicker, more vocal orgasms and greedy kissing.

Maybe he'd like his ego stroked more, with frequent words of admiration for his technique and style. It would be nice for him to express his needs without resorting to labeling and criticizing you. This would probably make you feel sexier—which you might want to point out to him.

169. I heard about these people who like leather and chains. Do they actually like pain?

Like so much about sex, the answer is not a simple yes or no. The question itself, in fact, is actually quite complex, because the leather-and-chains set is only a fraction of the larger number of people who enjoy *erotic power play*. This term, used by therapist Bill Henkin, describes the conscious use of power games to enhance sexual experience. It covers sexual activities such as spanking, blindfolding, verbal domination, role-playing, and yes, leather and chains.

Pain is generally not the focus of these activities. Rather, players are aware of the heightened threshold of pain that comes with sexual arousal, and they play with that threshold instead of avoiding it. You may have done that yourself when deliberately biting someone a little harder than usual in the midst of passion.

Unquestionably, some people do enjoy sexual pain. They like it under controlled, emotionally safe circumstances, with boundaries agreed upon in advance. Most other people who play with erotic power exaggerate normal relationship dynamics, challenge their limits and those of their partners, and enjoy expanding their vocabulary of sexual arousal.

170. Anal sex both interests and scares me. How do you prevent it from being painful?

There are three keys to enjoying anal sex: lubrication, lubrication, lubrication. Since the anus does not lubricate itself like the vagina, you must use an external preparation like K-Y, Sylk, or Astrolube. Saliva is inadequate because it is so easily absorbed and has no slickness to it. Besides, you'd need a lot more spit than anyone can easily muster.

Anal sex can be enjoyable, intimate, and adventurous. Set your speed for "barely moving," as the muscles need time to adjust to the shape, angle, and direction of the penis or other object involved. Rather than tensing in anticipation of pain, use your breathing to consciously relax the rectal muscles.

A condom is absolutely required for all but totally monogamous couples. If you feel any sharp pain, stop immediately. Wash the penis thoroughly before inserting it in the vagina or mouth afterwards.

171. How do you kiss and breathe at the same time?

First, let's get our priorities straight: Breathing beats even the best kiss on earth. As you suggest, it would be nice to do both together.

One way is to breathe through your nose. Another is to widen your mouth slightly so you can breathe around the edges, while you use the middle for kissing. Ultimately, really serious kissing requires you simply to stop and breathe periodically. While you're at it, drink some water, too.

172. Why do men always want to go faster than I do?

Perhaps because they're more focused on intercourse, while you're more focused on kissing and caressing. Or because many women take longer to get aroused than many men. Experts disagree about the roles of biology and culture in creating these contrasts. Everyone agrees that both men and women complain about them.

As clearly as you can, tell your partner that you really want to enjoy every bit of your physical time together, not just the intercourse. Together, make those activities as gratifying as possible. We tend to rush less when we're enjoying ourselves.

173. My partner sometimes laughs during sex. Why? How do I stop this?

If you can't laugh in bed, why make love?

When we're really self-conscious, it's hard to believe that others' laughter is not directed *at* us (as opposed to *with* us). Instead of being defensive or critical, ask him or her what the laughter is about, and believe the answer.

Some people, feeling inadequate, try to keep sexual situations tightly controlled. To them, a partner's laughter can be an interruption, a distraction, a scary, nonscripted event of ambiguous meaning. To put it in technical terms, such people need to lighten up.

Maybe your partner is simply delighted to be making love with you. Enjoy the music.

174. Sometimes my partner interrupts right in the middle of sex because something doesn't feel exactly right. How do I get her to cut this out?

Why do you want her to stop?

On the one hand, you should be pleased to have a partner who takes sex this seriously—not just doing it, but perceiving the power in sexuality and the need to be comfortable with it. On the other hand, if the interruption seems to follow a pattern over time, she may be worried or self-conscious. Discuss your discomfort with her interruptions, and ask if the routine can be changed.

175. When you're in the middle of sex, with teasing and play-acting and everything bouncing around, how do you say something for real?

All sexual couples need special ways to say "Stop," "Don't," "I'm okay," and "Are you okay?" that can be immediately understood. They can be "code" words, gestures, even a certain tone of voice. Like sports-team signals, they should be created and taken for granted for an entire year unless changes are necessary.

Setting up such a code is one more step on the road to being sexually powerful. It lets you know when "Stop now!" means "Stop" and when "Stop now!" means "Whatever you do, *don't* stop."

176. What is the effect of alcohol on sexual technique?

Alcohol has the same effect as all central-nervous-system depressants:

- Motor coordination is clumsier
- Sensitivity to touch is reduced
- Sensitivity to communication is reduced
- Erection and orgasm reflexes are less reliable

Drinking may look sexy in the movies, but our bodies actually get less sexy with it.

10

Play and Experimentation

I believe in nothing—everything is sacred
I believe in everything—nothing is sacred

—Tom Robbins

177. I'm willing to try new things, but what if my partner misunderstands, thinks I'm more experienced than I am, and gets upset?

This is a common question. Recent surveys indicate that many people deliberately understate their past sexual experience to their current partners. One way to do this, of course, is to inhibit your willingness to experiment.

Clearly, if you're pretending to be relatively inexperienced, experimentation is dangerous. That's a good reason to be honest about your past.

It sounds as if your partner needs you to be a very particular way in order to accept you. Going along with this will help create a relationship in which control and power issues will surface again and again. If your partner needs to be the only source of good things in your life—or needs to dictate how much sex is the "right" amount—the sooner you know, the better. You need to see and confront the destructive potential of this situation.

What if your partner thinks you're "too experienced?" The appropriate response is, "too experienced for what?" If the answer is "too experienced for me," parting company is the healthiest thing you can do. Any other answer should be negotiable. Just don't apologize or defend yourself.

178. How much of my past experimenting should I reveal, and how much should I keep hidden?

That depends on two things. First, what are the present consequences of hiding this information? Typically, keeping sexual secrets results in isolation, inhibition, resentment, and sexual dissatisfaction.

Second, what would be your reasons for revealing the information? Certainly, wanting to end or limit the above consequences is a good reason; desiring more intimacy, communication, acceptance, sexual satisfaction, and sense of freedom are other completely appropriate reasons. On the other hand, reasons such as wanting to test a relationship or hurt a mate always lead to trouble.

Has your mate said "I don't want to hear it?" Does your mate feel he or she has the right to dictate your past behavior? We're frequently better off honoring such clear requests for silence. On the other hand, if you need to share, share.

For a more detailed answer, see my book *Your Sexual Secrets: When to Keep Them, How to Share Them.*

179. My girlfriend says "Come on, let's do this new thing!" and I want to, but I'm afraid if I do, she'll hold it against me later. What should I do?

This question raises the issue of trust, which is crucial to safe and satisfying sexual experimentation. Trust is built by explicit agreements and successful experiences of shared risk-taking.

Like faith, trust cannot be forced. Do what you can to feel that a particular risk makes sense. Review the history of your relationship concerning exploration and experimentation. Discuss various possible outcomes, your and your mate's probable reactions to them, and what you each want and need in such situations. Ask as many questions as you can think of, and then take the plunge—or don't.

180. Several times during sex, I've done some daring new thing and loved it—only to feel ashamed or regretful the next day. What should I do?

Examine this dynamic from both sides. On the one hand, how do you feel about the way you make sexual decisions? If you are impulsive, self-destructive, or drunk, your decisions will probably be questionable.

On the other hand, how do you decide what to regret the next day? If you are moralistic, judgmental, pleasure-phobic, or unable to accept your sexuality, even the healthiest decisions will appear bad.

To get a reality check, you might want to speak with a therapist, physician, or close friend. Don't seek a definition of what's "normal," but rather get a sense of how reasonable your rules of decision-making and self-criticism are.

181. Experimenting during sex sounds great, but my big belly really inhibits me. What should I do?

Hey, easy on the belly; it's an innocent bystander here. Your *feelings* about your belly are inhibiting you, and that's what you need to change.

Our culture is aggressively clear that big bellies, small breasts, and various other-sized body parts disqualify us from sexual experimentation. If our bodies aren't perfect, we imagine that we look bizarre, laughable, or pretentious moaning, sweating, or straining during sex. Wrong, wrong, wrong.

Sexuality is who we are, not what we look like; and it's

what we do, not the shape of what we do it with. If you feel inhibited because of your belly, you must take responsibility for your beliefs and not blame your flesh. There are millions of large-bellied sexy people in the world. Their secret? They simply don't believe that fat-and-sexy is foolish or impossible. Take some of that life-affirming energy and rub it onto your beautiful body.

182. My husband wants to explore *everything* sexual that anyone does or mentions. Isn't this impractical?

Apparently, you're married to a "trisexual"—someone who will try anything.

Impractical? Yes and no; it's important to ask *why* he has this attitude. Does he feel inadequate? Is he desperately afraid of missing something? Or is he just enthusiastically open to new ideas?

That's the issue to settle first, and your tone suggests you think there's more to it than just enthusiasm. Do you feel pressured to go along with things? Are you weary of experimenting? Are you afraid you're being pushed further and further out from conventional sexuality? Such feelings should be respected—which requires that you discuss them with your mate.

183. I'm tired! How do you know when you've experimented enough?

Enough for what? If you're tired, that's enough.

184. What if I try something new and I don't like it?

In at least one regard, sex is like vegetables—if you try something that you don't like, you can say "I don't like it" and never taste it again.

Actually, there are several other ways in which sex is like vegetables, but that's the subject of another book.

185. Our experience is pretty limited. Where can we get ideas for sexual experimentation?

The ideas are the easy part, since they're everywhere. The

harder part, I think, is finding the time and the courage to explore and change your ideas about sexuality and yourself. If you have those, you can enjoy picking up ideas from:

- Erotic films and magazines
- Fantasies, both your own and your partner's
- Books of erotic fantasies, such as *My Secret Garden* by Nancy Friday and *Little Birds* by Anais Nin
- Your friends, if you hang out with people who talk about such things
- Past experiences you enjoyed with others, and
- Your senses; think of delighting your nose, your tongue, and so on, using your sexuality. That's certainly how the idea of kissing with fruit in your mouth got started.

186. My wife is willing to experiment—for *me,* not for her. How can I get her to be more enthusiastic and to enjoy it more?

Most people who are uninterested in experimenting are either very satisfied or skeptical about ever being satisfied. Thus, it can be difficult or impossible to change such people.

If anything works, it will be gentle acceptance, not steady pressure. So ask if there are any changes your wife would like in your sexual relationship. And lay off the demands for a month or two.

187. Once you get into experimenting, don't you have to do more and more just to get excited?

Or, to put it another way, don't kicks just keep gettin' harder to find? In a way, yes—and that's not all bad.

The good news is that our sexual vistas are neither limited nor dangerous—which is *not* true of many other forms of pleasure-seeking. Thus, a program of continual sexual change does not necessarily threaten our well-being. On the contrary: It can be a healthy form of self-exploration and expression that unfolds over time.

On the other hand, kicks *don't* just keep gettin' harder to find. Many people keep coming back to their favorite things and eventually settle into a repeating, if varied, repertoire. Remember, you're aiming not for kicks but for satisfaction. And when we're satisfied, the desire to experiment isn't a drive but just an interest.

188. On a lark, my wife and I tried something offbeat a few months ago. She enjoyed it much more than I did and now wants to make it part of our regular routine. I only want to do it occasionally. What should we do?

Remember Klein's Second Law of Sexuality: If it doesn't feel good, don't do it.

Your question is not about experimenting but about courtesy and respect. Tell your wife you want a month's moratorium; you'd like her to forget about the new behavior unless you initiate it, which you may or may not do. You'll both be pleasantly surprised at how much this reduces the tension in your sexual environment. Meanwhile, encourage new sexual adventures. Perhaps you'll find new things you *both* want to add to your routine.

189. I like sex, but when I don't want to experiment with something new, my partner criticizes me and says I'm uptight. How do I prove I'm not without just giving in every time?

People shouldn't have to "prove" that they're not uptight. Intimacy is not well served by constant threats of judgment if you don't act the way your partner wants. Besides, your partner's definition of "open" may be someone who never says no to anything. If so, you could never meet this unrealistic standard.

Your mate's occasional disappointment is understandable, but he or she must handle it in a more responsible, flexible way. Calling you names and trying to coerce you into doing things you don't like undermines trust and creates resentment.

What's needed here, I believe, is a more cooperative approach to sexuality. If you do indeed enjoy sex, there must be plenty of adventures you can share together. While your mate should lay off criticizing you for your limits, this isn't enough.

You must change as well, demanding to be treated with respect, and interrupting sex when you aren't.

Presumably, this will be uncomfortable for both of you. Working through this as a team instead of as adversaries will make the transition easier, quicker, and more productive.

190. I try to be more creative in sex, but how do I shake this feeling that my mother is watching me, which inhibits me terribly?

Bad news—your mother *is* watching. Like most of us, you've internalized your mother's critical judgments and taken over her job. An effective, joyful adulthood requires that you spend far less time on that job.

People who accomplish this are amazed at the amount of emotional energy it frees up. For example, instead of struggling with yourself about sexual experimentation time after time, you could simply choose to do some things and not to do others.

Therapy is an excellent way to change this dynamic. Reading can also be helpful. I recommend Nancy Friday's *My Mother, My Self*; Virginia Satir's *The New Peoplemaking*; and Bernie Zilbergeld and Arnold Lazarus's *Mindpower*.

191. It's not that my partner isn't adventurous, he just doesn't like *me* initiating anything new. What should I do?

First, you need to find out what he objects to. This will help you figure out ways you could initiate that he can handle. Also, see if you can move away from the sense that one person is teaching the other, toward the sense that two people are exploring together. This may defuse some of his discomfort.

When you're feeling close, explain how this situation is affecting you. In a noncritical way, discuss your resentment, decreased desire, and so on. Suggest that he might feel the same if you couldn't handle him initiating.

If he says he "just can't help it," that "this is just the way I am," individual or joint counseling is called for.

192. I'm afraid. What if we discover some kinky thing we really like, and we become addicted?

There are two fears behind this common question. The first is that we might discover that we're not who we thought we were, that we're one of those people we thought were bad or dirty. What's at issue here is our judgments of various aspects of sexuality, not any goodness or badness intrinsic to sex.

The second fear is that sex will take us over if we give in to it. But there is no sacred, hidden aspect of sexuality that we cannot handle. Assuming that you're not hurting yourself or someone else, base your sexual decisions on how something feels. You can have any sexual satisfaction you like and can refuse any you dislike.

193. Can we really try whatever we want, or are there certain lines we just shouldn't cross?

Although our culture provides many strict judgments about which sexual boundaries must not be crossed, I think there are only two that deserve serious thought.

The first boundary is physical damage. How far, for example, should people take erotic punishment? I believe the limit is physical *injury* that remains after the session, such as a sprained ankle or broken finger. That's because while the stimulation that creates such injury may feel good at the time (remember, our pain threshold changes dramatically during any intense excitement), highly aroused persons cannot make rational judgments about what they're willing to pay for that excitement.

The second consideration is permanent relationship damage. We all know how sex with a friend can damage a friendship, even though both people felt it was a great idea at the time. Unfortunately, the same can be true with a mate. Some people say they have "lost respect" for a partner who was willing to engage in sex that seemed acceptable at the time but turned out not to be.

This is not to say you shouldn't sleep with your friends or take chances with your mate—just that doing so can have an impact beyond the sexual moment. This, I think, is the signal to be careful—and that exhilarating emotional growth may lie ahead as well.

194. My spouse periodically talks about threesomes, and lately the idea seems exciting, though scary. How should we get started with this? Will we be threatening our marriage?

Communication is the key to protecting your relationship. It is vital that there be no coercion involved. Threesomes are potentially explosive emotionally, so do it only for yourself, *not* to please your mate. Discuss "checking in" with him or her during the action; know what your respective limits and boundaries are; and think about what might make each of you uncomfortable.

Threesomes come in many different shapes and sizes. They can be spontaneous or planned; queen-size (two men), king-size (two women), or same-sex; you can toss all the bodies into a pile or create various pairs watched by the third person.

It sounds like you've already taken the first step, which is to talk about it together. Share your fantasies of what you'd like and how it would feel. Discuss the logistics: Do you want to invite a friend to join you? Go to a nightclub and pick up a stranger? Hire a prostitute experienced at this?

First-time "dont's" include:

- Don't drink so much that you can't communicate clearly
- Don't invite a third party about whom one of you feels jealous
- Don't invite a third party whom you don't trust to handle him/herself
- Don't try anything just to prove you're cool
- Don't persuade anyone to do anything
- Don't continue if you don't like the way things are going
- Don't start unless everyone understands one anothers' expectations

Keep in mind that your experience may be quite different from what you see in porn movies. And don't forget to smile and even laugh—if you feel like it—while you're experimenting.

195. I'm male, and I've been toying with the idea of letting another man touch me. Does this mean I'm gay?

It may, but it probably doesn't.

Many men are curious about how it would feel to be stimulated by another man. This curiosity is reinforced by the fact that masturbation is frequently more satisfying than intercourse or oral sex.

Sexual orientation is usually developed during childhood, and gay people generally discover their homosexuality before age twenty-one. Many people, however, worry about it to the point where thoughts about homosexuality are disrupting their lives even though they're completely heterosexual.

Don't judge your thoughts and eroticism. Enjoy the fantasies, and act in whatever way makes sense to you.

196. How do I get my partner to loosen up and experiment a little?

When we want our partners to grow or change, it's always helpful to be gentle, patient, nonjudgmental, and playful.

In a real sense, however, there's very little we can do to "get" others to loosen up. At best, we can create an environment in which they may feel more comfortable exploring themselves; some people will accept this invitation, while others won't.

So share your vision of sexuality with your partner: sex as an arena for self-expression, spirituality, bonding, and pleasure. Describe how you see this kind of sex contributing to your life and how experimentation fits in. Explicitly note your acceptance of your partner's body, smells, sounds, etc.

Whisper that there's a special place you want to share with your partner; then tease and seduce and play so he or she is curious about following you there.

197. I'd be willing to experiment more if the "regular" sex were more satisfying. Why can't my partner understand this?

There are several possibilities:

• Your partner may simply not know you're unsatisfied

• Your partner may think that experimenting is the way to increase your satisfaction
• Your partner may be dissatisfied with the "regular" sex you share
• Your partner may not define "regular" and "experimental" sex the way you do

Whichever of these is the case, communication is essential. The anger and frustration you both feel will make it difficult, but do it anyway. Start by making sure your partner knows you're eager for more "regular" sex.

198. Last year I got involved with a very experienced woman who introduced me to a lot of new things, like exhibitionism. When she turned out to be a liar and cheat I ditched her, but now I feel foolish, dirty, and used. What should I do?

This is not about sexuality, it's about interpersonal integrity. Someone ripped you off, so you feel angry and hurt. By all means, vent those feelings. But keep in mind the important difference between *feeling* angry *now* and *being* dirty *then*. You didn't do anything that you regret, you just regret the circumstances under which it all evolved.

The consequences you're so hurt over are not about your *sexual* choices, but your *relationship* choices. Don't condemn your sexual decisions simply because of the defects you discovered in your sexual partner.

199. Do many people like to make love in elevators and parking lots? I don't want to get caught, but I must confess that the possibility excites me.

This is actually very common. People like you are not quite exhibitionists, who compulsively expose their sexuality to others and can't reach satisfaction any other way.

Enjoying the *risk* of discovery is different. It is one of the ways we inject mystery or excitement into our sexual experiences. According to sexologist Dr. Jack Morin, some version of this process is important for good sex once people pass a relationship's early "lust" stage.

Other common ways of doing this include taking contraceptive risks, picking up strangers (especially ones who don't seem quite safe), having sex that could, if discovered, damage one's career or marriage, experimenting with sadomasochism, and even talking "dirty."

The dynamic itself is part of being human, but you should keep the following concerns in mind: You should never exploit anyone along the way; and erotic adventures should be pursued consciously and thoughtfully, so that you don't take risks that can, in fact, hurt you.

200. What are jack-off parties? Should I go? How do I get invited?

Jack-off (or "JO") parties are a form of safe sex that started in the gay community in the mid-eighties. Some expanded to include straight men as well, and a few now even welcome women. These last are called "jack-and-jill-off," or "JJO," parties.

The parties consist of people who share safe sexual activities, such as masturbation, massage, voyeurism, exhibitionism, and latex-protected genital play. Parties are held in several large cities with established gay communities. Without knowing someone who already attends, it is extremely difficult to get invited; for starters, contact your local gay hotline or swinger's newspaper.

Should you go? If you can imagine good sex without intercourse, can handle rejection, have a good sense of theater, and can be comfortable in a sexual situation you're not controlling, *perhaps*. If not, no.

201. I hear that some couples share their fantasies, which sounds like fun. Just how might we do this?

Have a brief chat *outside* of bed to make sure you're both interested. Start with some pretty low-key fantasies, such as dancing with a stranger and getting excited, or flirting with your seat-mate on an airplane. If you enjoy it, just keep going. Discuss it again afterwards or several days later to make sure you're on the same wavelength, and then you're in business.

For more about this, see chapter 13.

202. What is autoerotic asphyxiation? Should I try it?

It is masturbation with a very serious gimmick. Practitioners typically stand on a chair, rig a noose overhead, and put the rope around their neck. They stimulate themselves, and when they are close to orgasm, they step off the chair, momentarily hanging themselves. The combination of sexual excitement and loss of oxygen is supposed to be exhilarating, especially if the orgasm is timed correctly. The person plans to return to the chair to interrupt the hanging before losing consciousness.

Of course, we often flail about during orgasm and lose control. Sometimes the orgasm is so powerful that people forget to return to the chair. Occasionally someone kicks over the chair and can't reach it. In these instances the person can die. It's a grisly sight for someone to discover. As Johns Hopkins University sexologist Dr. John Money says, "Those who do this do it with great frequency, so the odds of something going wrong increase with time."

Periodically a well-intentioned parent will try to scare the nation into believing that every teenage boy is at risk of killing himself through this practice. The FBI puts the figure at 500 to 1,000 deaths each year.

Should you try it? It may sound interesting, but people do sometimes die from it. I wouldn't try it. This is one kind of dangerous sex that isn't made safer by condoms.

11

Masturbation

Masturbation: The reason Neanderthal got off his hands and learned to walk upright.

203. How much time do most people spend masturbating?

This varies tremendously, depending on age, health, emotional state, and other life circumstances. Many people masturbate almost daily, some two or three times a day. Other men and women masturbate once a week or once a month. And plenty of people don't masturbate at all. Depending on the person's emotional state, each of these can be considered "normal."

Ideally, we would all enjoy masturbating whenever we wanted, for as long as we wanted. In reality, most people masturbate in a furtive way, trying to finish before they're "caught" by a spouse, parent, or child.

If you can, experiment with different styles and rhythms of masturbating. While many people hurry to "take care of business" in just a minute or two, it's also nice to make love to yourself for, say, twenty minutes.

Clearly, you're spending too much time masturbating if it frequently makes you late for work or school, keeps you from getting your chores done, or prevents you from telling your friends about any great new sex books you're reading.

204. What does it matter what our culture teaches about masturbation?

It matters in two ways: in the way we treat our children, and in the way we treat ourselves.

Antimasturbation hysteria peaked in America around 1910. At that time, children were frequently handcuffed at night to prevent them from touching themselves. Eighty-five-year-old pioneer sex educator Dr. Mary Calderone recalls that as a youngster she was forced to sleep in elbow-length metal mittens. "It humiliated and frightened me," she recalls grimly. "I always wondered what I'd done to deserve this torment, and no one would talk about it."

While we no longer torture children in this way, many parents still punish their kids for absentmindedly touching themselves in public, or for intentionally doing so in private. As a result, many of us grow up fearing our own sexual desire.

We carry this legacy into our adult relationships, where we inhibit, criticize, or fear our sexuality. Decades after childhood, we still believe we shouldn't masturbate; we still want to; and we still hope no one finds out that we do.

The word *masturbation* comes from the Latin "to pollute with the hand." Don't you think it matters that that's how society describes the most basic sexual pleasure?

205. I heard my fiancé tell a buddy that "of course" he'd continue masturbating after we married. How can he be so sure? Should I worry about this?

Married people masturbate for the same reasons that single

people do. It's a reliable way to nurture oneself; it's the source of many people's most explosive orgasms; it's a way to have more sex if you're not getting enough; and it's a form of sexual independence, through which you can enjoy satisfaction even when your partner is uninterested.

Your fiancé sounds as if he has a healthy enthusiasm for solo sex. Not to worry; your best response is to let him know you know and explore with him the role that masturbation will play in your marriage.

206. Okay, there's nothing wrong with masturbating. But how much are you supposed to get into it? I start out calm, but I wind up pinching my nipples, moaning, etc.

Moaning and other expressions of passion are normal during sex; since masturbation is sex, those expressions are appropriate during self-pleasure. Need more encouragement? Take it from Ron Koertge, in *Erotic by Nature*:

This is for every man who licks his shoulder during solitary
      sex,
rubs his beard against the stripey deltoid muscle
or bites himself hard.

This is for the woman who at the body's buffet touches
      her breasts
one at a time,
then reaches for the place she has made clean as Mother's
      kitchen.

And please don't jump up afterwards and rush for the wash-
      cloth
like all the relatives were on the porch knocking,
their hands hot from casseroles and a cake with God's name
      on it.

Rather lie there, catch your breath, turn to yourself
and kiss all the nimble fingers, especially the one that has
      been

you-know-where, kiss the palms with their mortal etchings,
and finally kiss the backs of each hand
as if the Pope had just said that you are particularly
blessed.

207. Does masturbation have any ill effects that we know of?

Only that you eventually learn to distrust anyone who's
ever told you that masturbation is dangerous.

For hundreds of years, medical books have offered quasi-
scientific "proof" that masturbation is harmful. Although
such theories have been widely distributed and taken very
seriously, none has ever been substantiated. The fact that
mental patients can be observed masturbating led to the myth
that self-stimulation causes insanity. If scientists' masturbation could be as easily observed, our beliefs might be quite
different.

As recently as 1950, popular sources such as the *Boy Scout
Handbook* were repeating myths and religious views as scientific
"fact," all without any basis whatsoever.

Scientists now agree that masturbation does not harm us
physically or emotionally. In fact, many say that the pleasure,
physical movement, and stress reduction we get from masturbation offer clear health benefits. Fortunately, a prescription is
not necessary.

208. If sex with me were better, would my partner masturbate less?

Only your partner knows the answer, which I urge you to
find out. I sense it might be the relationship's first honest sexual
conversation.

In general, masturbation isn't a substitute for sex, it *is* sex—
albeit a different kind than you get with a partner. Don't get
trapped in the myth that one replaces the other. Actually, some
people feel sexier and desire their partners more when they
masturbate regularly.

Unless your mate masturbates so much that you can't find
time to have a conversation, don't focus on it. Instead, com-

municate about the kinds of sexual attention you want and negotiate with your partner about the kinds of sex you can enjoy together.

209. How do I convince my partner that masturbation is okay?

Yours or your partner's?

If it's yours, explain what you get from masturbating. Discuss your partner's objections, including the possibility that he or she may feel rejected.

If it's his or her own masturbation your partner can't accept, there's a limit to what you can or should do. Certainly, we hate to see our loved ones suffer, especially unnecessarily. Explain that you masturbate as well and that mental health experts now agree that it's healthy and normal for both men and women. If appropriate, encourage your partner to seek out a sympathetic professional.

Ultimately, we have to let our partners struggle with their own inner conflicts, even when we've resolved those conflicts ourselves.

210. Don't think I'm stupid, but do women really touch themselves? Do they use their clitoris, vagina, or G spot?

Yes, women masturbate almost as frequently as men. In addition to their hands, women also use running water, pillows, dildoes, and vibrators. And fantasy. According to the *Hite Report,* most women favor either the clitoris or vagina; a few enjoy both equally.

211. I read a book suggesting that spouses masturbate in front of each other. How can I tell if we should do this?

There's no "should" here. Instead, regard this as an opportunity—to enjoy yourself, to arouse your partner, to expand your sexual options, and to share with each other who you honestly are.

You can either discuss it ahead of time or just go ahead and do it when it feels right. You can even put your partner's hand on his or her genitals to silently say, "It's okay," or "Please do—I think it will be a turn-on."

212. Why can't I enjoy masturbation without lubrication?

Why should you? Friction is a big part of sex, and lubrication is the way we adjust that friction to make it enjoyable. Too much friction on any part of the body—genitals, foot, throat, scalp—is uncomfortable. Lubrication isn't a burden—it's a gift.

213. I hear lots of great things about vibrators. If they're so great, don't people get hooked on them?

Yes and no; mostly no, because most women feel there's a lot more to sex than climaxing as soon as possible.

Yes, some women do start to depend on their vibrators, which are reliable and always available. This can be very liberating; it can validate a woman's sexuality, and even lead to reevaluating a frustrating relationship.

On the other hand, a small number of women find that once they get used to the hard mechanical "buzz," they get impatient with the softer stimulation of a penis, hand, or tongue. Therapists advise such women to gradually decrease their vibrator use while explicitly educating their partner on how they like to be touched.

214. I have wild fantasies when I masturbate, but I'm embarrassed and even a little scared of them after I'm done. Is this normal?

Wild fantasies during masturbation are very common and make perfect sense. While you're pursuing solo arousal and satisfaction, there's no one around to require your emotional presence. Thus, you can focus your attention on making your (imaginary) sexual encounter as rich as you like.

Why do these images trouble us later? We first envision them in the heat of passion, when they make sense on an emotional level; when we reflect on them later, they've lost that context. Aspects such as aggressiveness or voyeurism stand out and are suddenly jarring.

These fantasies may also trouble you because you fear they reflect what you *really* desire. They don't. Most people enjoy fantasies of activities they have no interest in doing. Fantasy does *not* predict behavior in reality.

215. Intellectually, I know that masturbation is okay, but I just can't get rid of my guilt about it. What should I do?

So long as Americans teach their kids to feel guilty about masturbating, therapists' offices will never be empty. For that matter, neither will the jails; crimes of violence or sex are typically committed by people from repressed homes that instill sexual guilt, not by people from progressive homes who have learned to honor sexuality.

Different schools of psychology attempt to heal sexual guilt differently. All agree, however, that such guilt is self-destructive and that it can be reduced.

One way to reduce the guilt is to think of masturbation as a form of self-love, like sticking to a diet, exercising regularly, or getting a shoeshine. You deserve self-love and the pleasure of accepting it.

An excellent book you may find helpful is *Sex for One*, by Betty Dodson.

216. Since I enjoy making love, why are my strongest orgasms from masturbation?

Your experience is quite common. Shere Hite reports that a majority of both male and female respondents said their most intense orgasms were from masturbation.

Why do so many people have the experience you do? It makes sense that our own hand has a surer touch than a partner's. We are the best lovers for ourselves because, as Woody Allen says, we practice a lot when we're alone.

217. Sometimes I masturbate simply because I'm frustrated and I want a quick high. Is there anything wrong with this?

Many people use masturbation in the way you describe—

although few will admit it. There is nothing wrong with doing so, as long as it isn't the only way you have of feeling good. Total reliance on *any* such method—whether it's eating, watching television, or calling Mom—is unhealthy.

The lone voice disagreeing with this is Sexaholics Anonymous–type groups. They say that using masturbation simply to feel good or to escape from problems indicates sex addiction. I don't believe this.

218. I heard that too much masturbation means you have a sex addiction. I'm worried—how do I know if I'm a sex addict?

You can't be a sex addict, because there is no such thing. "Addicts" have a disease that has invaded them, instead of a pattern of poor decision-making that can be changed. They are never cured, only "in recovery."

You *may* be masturbating compulsively. That means you are doing it in a way that interferes with other parts of your life; or you are doing it even when you get no satisfaction, be it sexual, emotional, or even the simple satisfaction of escape.

If neither is the case, your masturbation is almost certainly not a problem. If one or both of the above apply, you could have a problem, which may reflect some deep guilt about sexuality. Reducing this guilt (through, say, therapy or education) can frequently reduce the compulsive aspect of masturbation.

219. Sometimes when I want to masturbate, it just doesn't work. Either I can't get erect, or I lose my erection, or I'm too sore from having recently masturbated. Why is this? What should I do?

Each of these is a message from your body, and that message is "I'm not interested in sex right now."

Most of us are used to ignoring or denying our bodies' messages, whether they're about food, exercise, stress, or whatever. The body always defeats the mind when the two conflict; if the issue is sexual, erections and orgasms often disappear.

You need to recognize when your body is saying no. And you need to learn new ways of dealing with this when your mind protests and says yes. When your mind wants to masturbate and your body says no, what do you really need—a hug, a sense of well-being, someone to talk to? Or something else?

220. Will masturbation deplete my sperm count? Will it undermine my virility?

No. Sperm is manufactured in the testicles twenty-four hours a day, every single day. You can't possibly ejaculate enough to deplete your available sperm seriously.

Erection and orgasm are caused by involuntary reflexes between your brain and blood vessels, and your brain and pelvic muscles. Except for any accompanying guilt or anxiety, masturbation has no effect on these reflexes.

221. I enjoy masturbating so much that I've just about lost interest in finding partners to have sex with. Is that wrong?

This question may or may not be about sex. It might be about isolation, poor social skills, fear of intimacy, anger toward or mistrust of people, and so on.

Certainly, sex with a partner is more complicated than sex alone. You have to find an interested partner, bond with that person, consider his or her needs, communicate, and stay connected after the sexual encounter ends. You have to deal with fear, anger, anxiety, sadness, mistrust, and expectations.

Our society defines partner sex as more mature and satisfying than masturbation. Is there anything about partner sex that makes the hassles worthwhile to you? If not, you either need a different, more positive experience of partner sex or you need to resolve the emotional issues that prevent partner sex from being satisfying.

Keep in mind that you don't have to choose. You can have partner sex *and* solo sex in your life.

222. Why do some men masturbate in public? What should we do about it?

Public masturbation is a form of exhibitionism—a compulsive act of inappropriately exposing the genitals, which the exposer finds sexually arousing and gratifying. Exhibitionists are almost invariably men.

Also known as *indecent exposure* or *flashing,* this is typically a harmless activity; the exposer rarely molests or even talks to his "victims." He is hoping to shock or offend; a nonreaction is the easiest way to discourage such a person. One well-known feminist once told a flasher dryly, "If that thing were mine, I wouldn't show it to *anyone.*"

Why do people expose themselves? Probably some combination of anger and terrible insecurity about their masculinity. Flashing is a rather sad way of telling a world that seems hostile, "Oh yeah? Well, screw you."

The best training children can get in handling flashers is the understanding that sex is not bad. Children need to know that they do not cause this unusual behavior in others and that they are not harmed simply by seeing a strange man's penis. If they say they've been flashed, tell them the guy has emotional problems, is stuck at an immature stage of life, and so is best left alone. We'd all be better off if these people were given therapy instead of jail time and criminal records.

223. Why do men like to look at *Playboy* or X-rated videos while they masturbate? Do women look at this stuff? Why the difference in men's and women's use of pornography?

Some 20 million men consume one or more X-rated magazines or videos each year. The pictures support fantasies that make masturbation more exciting. Viewers enjoy getting aroused as they imagine having sex with the women and men they see.

A smaller number of women also enjoy magazines and videos. Explanations of this gender difference vary widely. Is it because women are less interested in sex? Certainly not. Because they're less visually oriented and more context-oriented about sex? Probably. Is it because any woman admitting she's interested in erotica has to grapple with criticism of her "nonfeminine" attitude? Definitely. Is it because women are concerned that their male partners will misunderstand, resent, or punish their interest? Sometimes.

Finally, many women consume a different kind of pornography: romance novels, full of the same sexy scenes, stereotyped gender roles, and unrealistic pictures of women that make up "men's" magazines and videos. And women can read the stuff without feeling they're being "too sexual" or "immoral."

224. Doesn't the Bible condemn masturbation?

Not really. The actual story in Genesis (38:7–11) says that when Judah's son Er died childless, Er's brother Onan was required to impregnate Er's widow to carry on the family name. During sex, however, Onan withdrew and "spilled his seed," which displeased God, who eventually killed him.

Some people claim that Onan was punished for masturbating. Reflecting this confusion, the dictionary defines onanism as both "male masturbation" and "coitus interruptus" (withdrawal during intercourse before ejaculation)—which are obviously not the same thing. The social norms of Onan's time make it clear that his crime was either contraceptive behavior or direct disobedience of God.

We should be wary of religious leaders who use this story to damn something as normal as masturbation. The Catholic Church's position was reaffirmed as recently as 1975. While it acknowledged the sociological and psychological evidence that masturbation is part of normal human development, it was still declared "an intrinsically and seriously disordered act."

225. Occasionally when I know my man will be horny and I'm not, a quick masturbation session gets me in the mood for sex with him later. Is this weird?

No, it's both clever and loving. Clearly, you enjoy being on the same sexual wavelength as your partner. Arousing yourself is a good way to get your juices flowing—literally! Some people maintain their interest by stopping short of orgasm. Others enjoy the climax and keep the sexy feelings around to share with their partner.

This illustrates one more of the many healthy reasons that people masturbate.

226. How are you supposed to get any privacy to masturbate? Do I have to announce it to everyone so I won't be disturbed?

Every home should have at least one room whose door closes and locks. We all deserve a chance to be alone in private, without having to give an explanation. Whether you use your time there to masturbate or ponder the meaning of life is not important. A locked door says "please don't bother me for a little while." Some families have a little hotel-style sign that says the same thing.

Such boundaries are uncommon in American families, where people frequently interrupt each other and rudely violate each other's space. Establishing healthy boundaries and a positive respect for them is a critical task in responsible families. Shaping your family's attitudes in this regard will make privacy more available and "announcements" unnecessary.

12

Orgasm

Orgasm: the perfect compromise between love and death.

—Robert Bak

227. What is orgasm?

Orgasm is the climax of a period of sexual excitement, generally marked by the release of sexual tension and other involuntary physical responses.

Actually, we don't quite understand how it all works. A mysterious combination of physical and emotional factors leads to the brain signaling the nervous system to set off the reflexes we call "orgasm."

These reflexes include increased heart rate and breathing; reddening of the skin, especially on the face and chest; clutching of the fingers and toes; pelvic throbbing; erection of the nipples; and contractions of the muscles around the anus, vagina, and prostate. The penis usually spurts semen; a small number of women "ejaculate" from their urethra as well.

228. Why does orgasm feel so good?

For the same reason that chocolate, sunsets, and great music feel so good. It's just the way the human nervous system is wired.

Orgasm does offer some special feelings. The increased blood flow leads to a sense of warmth radiating from the pelvis to the rest of the body. Emotionally, orgasm usually brings a sense of release and satisfaction. The bonding that often takes place if you're with another person also feels good.

Finally, many people enjoy a spiritual dimension in orgasm. It's a chance to experience the perfection of our bodies and our divine connection to the entire universe.

For all these reasons, "no one has yet succeeded in describing orgasm properly," says sex educator Michael Carrera. "The pleasure is so intense that it seems there are no words subtle enough or strong enough to describe it."

229. Do all people have orgasms?

All people, except for those who have certain birth defects, or have suffered certain accidents, have the capacity for orgasm. However, some men and more than a few women find climaxing difficult or impossible, a condition called *anorgasmia*. Occasionally, this is caused by improper or insufficient stimulation. It can also be caused by a lack of familiarity with one's body or the process of orgasm. Even more rarely it's caused by problems in the vascular or nervous system.

Generally, anorgasmia has psychological roots, reflecting one or more unconscious fears. These can include fear of losing control; fear of being taken over by sex; and fear of being overwhelmed by one's partner (who may be a psychological stand-in for "all men" or "all women"). These fears can be the result of neurotic or critical parenting, traumatic early sexual experiences, rigid religious training, rape, or sexual abuse.

Teaching a child that sex is bad or dangerous is the easiest way to create anorgasmia in a future adult.

230. How do you know if you've actually had an orgasm?

Men rarely ask this question because it's pretty obvious: Satin ribbons of sticky white stuff usually come spurting out of you, and your penis goes from big (or medium) and hard to small and soft. And if the man is like me, Chinese food suddenly becomes intensely important.

So this is primarily a women's question. The popular wisdom used to be that if you're asking, you haven't had one. But this isn't necessarily true. If romance novels and your sister's stories have made you expect skyrockets, and all you keep having is entertaining sparks, you could be having hundreds of orgasms and not know it.

There are the common signs of orgasm discussed in question 227: the contractions, skin flush, etc. But everyone's orgasm is different. And we shouldn't expect orgasms to involve thunderous crashing and soul-draining intensity, although some people do occasionally experience that.

You can best determine whether you've had an orgasm by how you feel. Although some are less satisfying than others, most orgasms leave people with a sense of completion, satisfaction, wholeness, and appreciation of themselves. A smile is common, too.

231. At what age do people usually start having orgasms?

Orgasms begin in infancy, when the sexual response system is periodically triggered by hormones. They continue in babies and toddlers and are one of the motivators for developing motor coordination. Young kids have orgasms as a result of sex games and of masturbating. Boys and girls climax in adolescence, of course, through involuntary wet dreams and voluntary self-pleasuring.

Some parents try to discourage children from having orgasms, but they only pique their kids' curiosity and make them feel dirty, guilty, and ashamed.

232. Is there a difference between orgasm and ejaculation? Which do men prefer?

Ejaculation is a physical event, consisting of rhythmic contractions around the prostate gland and anus, and the resulting spurts of semen out of the penis. Orgasm is a psycho-physical phenomenon that includes ejaculation and the feelings of relief and satisfaction that typically accompany it.

While many therapists and physicians note that there is a difference between ejaculation and orgasm, the majority of men do not, either in conversation or their experience.

Researchers involved in documenting male multiple orgasm feel very strongly about this issue. "Ejaculation and male orgasm are *not* synonymous," say researchers Bill Hartman and Marilyn Fithian. "It is time to lay this insidious idea to rest forever." For more on this, see question 235.

233. What exactly is the difference between a clitoral and a vaginal orgasm? Which is better?

Whereas men almost invariably report their penis as being the center of sexual pleasure, women have two such centers: the clitoris and the vagina. Most women prefer one to the other, while a few enjoy both. Some even enjoy a third, the G spot.

Some women climax through stimulation of the vagina alone, while about twice as many (according to the *Hite Report*) climax through stimulation of the clitoris.

In the bad old days, psychiatrists (almost all men) were sure that the clitoral orgasm was immature, inferior to the vaginal orgasm. This view has been completely discredited by modern sexologists, physicians, and social critics.

Women describe the difference between clitoral and vaginal orgasms in various ways. Most women feel that one is more intense than the other; many find that after they have their preferred kind they can enjoy the other one but get impatient with the opposite order.

This contrast is highly subjective, however. Devices registering the body's response to each type of orgasm (heart rate, vaginal contractions, etc.) record virtually the same data. This is not surprising, since all orgasms result from activation of the sympathetic nervous system.

234. What exactly is a multiple orgasm? How do you have one? Why can I have one at some times but not others?

The typical orgasm is followed by a resolution period, during which breathing and other physical aspects of sexual arousal return to their normal, resting levels. A multiple orgasm occurs when you climax again—usually within half a minute—without completely returning to those resting levels and going through the entire arousal process.

What makes this possible? The most important factors are believing that it's possible and being open to the pleasurable feelings. Trusting that both you and your partner can handle it is important too. Breathing deeply (instead of unconsciously holding your breath) while you climax keeps the sexual energy moving, instead of containing it.

In 1953 Alfred Kinsey and his research team estimated that 15 percent of the population was capable of multiple orgasm. With women's increasing knowledge of and comfort with their bodies, the percentage today is no doubt substantially higher.

While some women can have multiple orgasms during most of their sexual encounters, others are only able to have them occasionally. This may be a trick of nature; why do we sneeze at pepper some times, but not others? Why do some people sneeze so much more than others? The contrast may also reflect psychological, emotional, and contextual issues. A person may feel more open one day than another, less afraid, sexier, etc.

Pressuring yourself to have a multiple orgasm generally decreases your chances of having one. Do not make this an "accomplishment," the focus of your entire sexual interaction, an opportunity to fail at sex. Besides, it's not always practical—no one wants to be late to, say, the Inaugural Ball.

235. Do men have multiple orgasms?

This is a controversial question. The answer depends in

large part on your definition of orgasm; if no ejaculation is involved, how does a man know he has climaxed? All men have peaks and valleys during sexual arousal. When is a peak an orgasm and when is it just a peak?

Then there's the definition of multiple orgasm. Does this mean ejaculating, losing an erection, becoming aroused and hard within seconds, and ejaculating again? Does it mean several orgasms before ejaculating? Or does it include either one?

The truth is, most American men have little idea of their sexual capabilities. We rarely experiment with breathing, moving sexual energy, visualization, spirituality, or disciplined techniques. Most of us learn that sex ends the second we finish ejaculating. But there may very well be more.

As researchers Bill Hartman and Marilyn Fithian say in *Any Man Can:*

• Ejaculation and male orgasm are *not* synonymous
• You can't tell the difference between the physiological data recorded from multiorgasmic women and multiorgasmic men
• The male multiple orgasm is a learned response, like other sexual behaviors, and almost everyone can learn to have one

236. What do therapists mean when they say that orgasm is not the point of sex? Doesn't everyone think it is?

You're probably right when you suggest that most people think orgasm is the point of sex. But this creates an awful sense of pressure for many people and focuses sex much too narrowly.

When you were younger, remember how much you enjoyed kissing, hugging, smelling, teasing? There was a whole sexual world out there to explore. It's still there, available whenever we let go of the idea that the only sexual activities worth doing are things that lead to orgasm.

On various occasions, the "point" of sex can be closeness, intimacy, pleasure (which may or may not include orgasm), self-expression, a sense of competence or power, and a chance to give or share. These pleasures help put orgasm into perspective.

237. How do you tell if a woman has had an orgasm?

You can ask, but many women say they are tired of being asked. If she *truly* wants to end an enjoyable sexual encounter (as opposed to stopping because she thinks you want to), that's a pretty dependable signal. There are other signs, too (see question 230), but remember that each person's orgasm is unique.

In the ideal situation, two things will help you know: being with a woman enough times to learn her particular pattern; and believing you can trust a woman to let you know if she's not satisfied—and trusting her.

238. Is it true that some women can feel satisfied without climaxing? How? How do I know when this is the case?

Yes, it's true. And although I've heard this explained roughly 8 zillion times, I *still*—along with most other men— don't understand it completely. That's because the dynamic is so different for men, who want to ejaculate after virtually every state of arousal. Perhaps it has to do with the pressure of semen that builds during excitement.

Many (not all) women can, at times, feel complete as their arousal subsides without orgasm, particularly if they feel physically and emotionally connected to their partner. Such women don't say that they don't care about climaxing—they generally do—only that they don't need it to happen every time.

So how do you know if a woman is okay about not climaxing? Experience with the same woman eventually teaches little signals (winks, sighs, smiles) that say "no problem, I'm fine." If you're with an assertive woman who talks about her needs, you can simply trust that she's fine if she doesn't say anything.

With women you don't know well, you can either ask or trust. The difference between trusting and simply being a jerk is that jerks aren't attentive to the verbal and nonverbal cues that say "I'm not done, can you/we please do more?" A sensitive, trusting man is.

239. I always strive for us to climax at the same time, but sometimes it takes a lot of work! How do I accomplish this more easily?

Note the words *strive, work, accomplish.* You're putting a lot of effort into something that could, instead, transport you away from the pressure to perform and achieve.

You already know that coming together is extremely difficult to pull off—sort of like singing underwater. Yet many people think of simultaneous orgasm as the ideal sexual experience. Why? After you get beyond the myth that "it's the best sex," you're left with only two possible reasons: it creates a special sexual intimacy; or it's the most competent sexual performance.

That special sexual intimacy can be created in many different ways—without giving up what you lose in simultaneous orgasm. And using sex to gain a sense of competence is *always* problematic. What do you lose by trying hard to come together? A sense of spontaneity, the feeling that anything goes, the confidence that you and sex are perfect no matter what you do.

Don't try so hard to climax together. Work less, think less, *do* less, and you'll get more of what you want from sex. How many other human activities promise such a deal?

240. My husband seems to fall asleep seconds after he climaxes. Is there some sort of sleep hormone that gets released in men after they ejaculate?

Although it's a great excuse ("Honest, honey, I really wanted to keep going, but those darn hormones . . ."), there is no actual "sleep hormone." Some scientists speculate that the burst of brain chemicals at orgasm causes a special kind of physical fatigue, but this is still conjecture.

Several factors do account for your all-too-common experience. For one thing, orgasm provides the most relaxation some people ever experience. It releases not only sexual tension, but many other kinds of stored-up tension as well. Combine this with the time of night that many people have sex, and going seems the logical step after coming.

For men who fear intimacy, the moments after orgasm feel scary. There's the expectation of cuddling and closeness, without the distraction of sexual arousal. Words like "I love you" invariably seem appropriate. If two people have very different needs in the afterglow department, sleep can be, consciously or not, an ideal solution to a tricky situation.

If you're bothered by your man's tendency to snore before the last sounds of your lovemaking have stopped echoing, discuss it *before* you get into bed together again.

241. Why do men always ask if I've come after we make love? How do I get them to stop?

Part of women's irritation with being asked, I think, is the sense that "if you don't know, you must not have been paying attention." This is frequently not true. Determining if a woman has climaxed can be difficult, especially since different women do it so differently.

Men generally ask for one of two reasons: they're concerned about whether or not you're satisfied; and they're concerned about whether or not they've done an adequate job. Fairness suggests that you respond gently if you sense that your partner is asking for the first reason. It does not require you to show as much patience with the second.

To men who seem genuinely concerned, simply reply, "Everything's great . . . let's talk about it later." Do, in fact, later discuss the various ways your partner can observe your orgasm and the fact (if it's so) that there are times when not climaxing is totally acceptable.

To men who seem to regard your orgasm primarily as a badge of their accomplishment, also reply, "Everything's great . . . let's talk about it later." Later, discuss your partner's seeming detachment from you, his concern with performance rather than experience or emotional contact.

At the same time, be aware that even the most sensitive man also learns that a woman's orgasm is the key symbol of his masculine adequacy. It's tough to ignore blithely decades of that training.

If you haven't climaxed when asked, and you'd like to, feel free to smile and encourage your partner to keep going.

242. I feel like I can hold off my ejaculation pretty well—until a certain point. After that, an earthquake couldn't interrupt me. Why is this? How do I change it?

You're referring to the point of inevitability. This is caused by the pressure of the semen collecting in the ejaculatory tubes. If anything about sex is normal, this is it; you can't change it.

And there's no reason to. If you like, you can learn to recognize this point sooner, so you can either back away from it (delay ejaculation) or choose the way you ejaculate (change from mouth to hand, for example).

243. I didn't know that girls had orgasms until I was in college. Is there something wrong with me?

No. The average American male grows up learning only one thing about girls and sex: They've got it and we want it. We learn practically nothing about female sexual pleasure, and what we do learn is that a "real man" "makes her love it." That is, the female orgasm is merely an indication of male sexual prowess.

How are young men supposed to learn about female physiology and sexuality, anyway? Until very recently, most of us received no school instruction on this. We watched the girls hustled off to learn some mysterious female thing around sixth grade, and that was it. *Playboy* wasn't much help, and who could ask his mother or father?

The situation hasn't changed much at all: Most schools offer little or no sex education. Families and churches teach very little—or worse, they teach fear and distortions.

In some native tribes, adolescent males are judged on how well they please their female partners—not on how well they can "score." *They* know about female orgasms early in life.

244. My wife can have one orgasm after another, but I have to rest

after ejaculating before I can get erect again. Why? What can I do about this?

Men require a waiting period in between ejaculating and becoming erect again. This *refractory* period varies from minutes to hours; in elderly men, it can be as much as a day.

Physiologically, women do not require a refractory period; they can go from orgasm back to excitement without a resolution or nonaroused phase. This contrast doesn't need to be a problem; your wife can have plenty of orgasms courtesy of your hand or mouth either after you ejaculate or before you have intercourse.

The only way you can avoid the refractory period is by not ejaculating.

245. Is it okay to be sort of animal-like while you climax? If I let myself go, I moan and sweat. I try not to, but it keeps happening.

Yes, it's great to be "animal-like"—in the best sense of the word—while you climax. Americans rarely use the expression in a positive way, however, reflecting our preference for experiencing passion in a controlled way—which is a contradiction in terms and a common source of sexual problems. Orgasm is a release of sexual energy; the more you let it explode unconfined, the more intensely it can release. It's a sad commentary on our civilization that we criticize letting go as "animal-like."

There's a reason you find inhibiting yourself during orgasm difficult—it's contrary to the way our nervous systems are built. It's like wanting to exercise without sweating, or crying without shedding tears.

If your partner is uncomfortable with your sweating and moaning, gently confront him or her with how crucial this is to your sexual satisfaction. If you are uncomfortable with it, confront yourself. Good ways to do so would be through therapy or books such as David Ramsdale and Ellen Jo Dorfman's *Sexual Energy Ecstasy* or Alex Comfort's *The Joy of Sex*.

246. My new girlfriend tells me I should breath more while I come. Why?

It sounds like she wants you to relax more. Breathing un-blocks the flow of sexual energy, which leads to longer, deeper orgasms. It also helps you be more present with your partner.

Chapter 21 also talks about breathing and sexual energy.

247. Some people like to be stimulated right after orgasm, while others don't. Which is right?

Whichever the person wants. Some people feel postorgasm touching or movement provides a gradual, gentle ending to sex. Others experience it as a physical or emotional intrusion.

With new partners you can gently inquire before or at the time, or you can do what you prefer and carefully observe the reaction. With long-time partners just do what you've learned they like, unless you specifically want to experiment. Whatever partners prefer, it's right—for them.

248. What are Kegels? How do they affect orgasm?

Developed by Dr. Arnold Kegel in the 1950s, Kegels are exercises that strengthen the muscles surrounding the female pelvis. Because these muscles contract during orgasm, strength-ening them makes a woman's orgasm stronger, more pleasur-able, and more easily triggered. Some women find the exercises themselves arousing and use them to help get excited with a partner.

To identify the *pubococcygeus* ("pew-bo-cok-*sih*-gee-us") muscle that encircles the vagina, stop the flow of urine. You may be able to feel the muscle contract. If you insert a finger into your vagina you can also feel the muscle contracting.

There are three Kegel exercises:

1. Contract and relax the muscle as quickly as possible, breathing regularly

2. Contract the muscle, hold for a count of three, then relax, breathing regularly

3. Bear down on the muscle as if pushing something out of the vagina, or as if trying to urinate in a hurry, breathing regularly

Do exercises 1 and 2 twenty-five times each, twice daily, working up to fifty times each; do exercise 3 ten times twice daily, working up to twenty-five times. Kegels become easier to do with practice and take only a few minutes per day. A woman should notice changes after two or three weeks and can expect the optimal effect after three months.

Men can also do Kegels, but little research has been done on their effect.

13

Fantasy

If your sexual fantasies were truly of interest to others, they would no longer be fantasies.

—Fran Lebowitz

249. My fantasies sometimes scare me. What should I do?

Many aspects of our sexuality can be scary: the loss of control, the sounds we make, the desire to bite or dominate, etc. Some people handle this fear by inhibiting their sexuality. Others find ways to trust themselves and learn to enjoy the uncertainty.

Our sexual fantasies can be scary if: we feel we shouldn't find these images sexually arousing; we fear we desire the things we fantasize; or we fear that we'll attempt to do what we fantasize.

The first feeling reflects a misunderstanding of sexuality;

people are excited by a very broad range of images, much broader than the range of *behaviors* that excite them.

The second and third fears are rarely justified. People do occasionally become compulsive about their fantasies, however, and find that the line between fantasy and reality begins to blur. If you feel that you're in danger of acting out your fantasies, seek professional help *immediately*. A county mental-health clinic or local hospital's psychology department would be good places to start.

Ultimately, the fantasies we fear will recur. So put less energy into the scary ones, and they will fade a bit. At the same time, remember that as long as you aren't completely dependent on one particular fantasy, your fantasies are not a threat and they don't reflect deep problems.

250. What actually determines the kind of sexual fantasies we have?

The real answer is, no one knows.

There seem to be two factors—psychological and social. Various psychological theories suggest that sexual fantasies are symbolic expressions of hidden emotions; a way of resolving Oedipal-type conflicts; a way of taking power over part of one's life; or a fairly harmless form of entertainment.

The media are the prime social influence, with their seductive, repetitive messages about youth, beauty, and deep feelings of competence and power. One's family and religious background often provide the archetypes and symbols of our fantasies.

Or is it just the phase of the moon and what you had for lunch that day?

251. Is it common to fantasize about one person while making love with another?

Yes. In fact, this is the most common sexual fantasy—sex with someone other than our regular partner. Some people imagine elaborate scenes with B while making love with A. Others simply imagine they're with B.

Rodney Dangerfield describes the time he and his wife

wanted to make love but were very slow making things happen. "What's the matter?" he asked. "Can't you think of anyone either?"

252. In a monogamous marriage, is it unfaithful to have sexual fantasies about someone else?

Monogamy means different things to different couples. Some people feel it even excludes masturbation; others feel it can even include sex with another person as long as it's an unplanned one-night stand, not an ongoing relationship.

Only you and your partner can decide exactly what your agreement means, and only you can decide what it means to you as an individual. We cannot control our fantasies completely. If you believe your monogamous agreement prohibits certain fantasies, sooner or later you're going to be powerless—and feel guilty—about violating your agreement. That would be unfortunate.

Discuss this with your spouse, underlining your marital and sexual satisfaction. Very few people believe their wedding vows eliminate their partner's fantasies.

253. Don't most people want to try out their fantasies? When people do, is it usually as good as the fantasy or not?

Most people do *not* want to act out their fantasies. When young, some people do try out a few of their fantasies, with mixed results. Sometimes it's as good as or even better than the image. Other times people realize that they never wanted to *do* the thing, just to fantasize about it.

Also, remember that in fantasy we're relaxed and self-confident. In real-life sex we may be anxious, self-conscious, self-critical, or feeling pressured. This alone can make fantasy better than reality.

Part of fantasy's appeal is that you get to enjoy *some* of the benefits of doing a thing without *any* of the negative consequences of doing it. Thus, many people do not wish to play out their fantasies, feeling they already have the best deal possible.

254. I'm happy with my wife, but sometimes I think about other women while we're making love. Does this mean I don't love her?

No. For one thing, we can't completely control our fantasies. For another, fantasy isn't only a means of escaping a negative situation; it's also a way of enriching a positive one.

Trust your own judgment about whether or not you love your wife. Don't criticize the harmless things you do that make the experience of love more lively. Besides, do you think she would prefer that you make love with her and fantasize about another woman, or make love with another woman and fantasize about your wife?

255. Do some couples actually share their fantasies? Why? How can people share such intimate information with anybody?

Yes, some couples share some or all of their sexual fantasies. This *is* very intimate, and for some people that's the point—to open up in such a deep way. In addition to enhancing closeness, the sense of freedom can also make sex better.

Sharing fantasies is also a way for couples to try on or rehearse things they may want to do at some future time; for example, anal sex, or threesomes, or play-acting different scenarios (like the bishop and the scullery maid).

Of course, fantasy sharing should be consensual. While it isn't necessary for both people to share, both do need to agree that sharing will take place in a safe environment.

256. Is it a good idea to share my sexual fantasies with my husband?

People have varying results with fantasy sharing. The key factors, I think, include good reasons for sharing, comfortable partners, and a supportive relationship. To help you decide, ask yourself a few questions:

- What is my goal?
- Do I want to do this, or am I doing it just for him?
- Has he expressed an interest in my fantasies?

• What kind of relationship do we have—supportive, exploratory, critical, attacking?

One common reason for sharing fantasies is to make sex more exciting. Many people do get this result.

257. I try not to think of my ex-wife during sex, but I just can't help myself. Any suggestions?

First of all, why is this a problem? Your recurring thoughts don't necessarily mean you want your ex-wife back. (If you do, that's a different problem.) If the fantasy is entertaining, you can simply enjoy it. At some point, it will probably go away by itself.

What might this fantasy be about? You may not be done with your ex. There may be things you enjoyed in that sexual relationship that you want to duplicate now. These might include comfort, trust, playfulness, creativity, and self-expression. Do you need to make changes in your current sexual situation?

258. Sex is sort of blah unless I focus on my favorite fantasy. Then it's great. Is there anything wrong with that?

There is nothing wrong with using fantasy to enrich sex. When preferences become requirements, however, they limit you. Many experiences become unavailable when you have to have them a certain way, whether you're interested in lingerie, fantasies, or army camouflage.

Choice and flexibility play key roles in satisfying sex. If someone feels coerced—either by self or partner—the resulting sex cannot be positive and life-affirming. Whether the reflexive or rigid behavior involves doing something unwanted, or not doing something wanted, it's difficult to relax and let the sexual energy flow.

If you'd like to expand your horizons, try something new. Instead of summoning the fantasy, focus on how much pleasure you're feeling—gently tell your partner how else you'd like to be touched; and the things about your partner that arouse you, such as hair, voice, body, and smell.

259. You say fantasies are harmless, but my church says that mine are sinful. I've tried, but I can't seem to change. What should I do?

The primary question here regards the church's role in your life. Is it advisory or absolute? If you decide it's absolute, you must believe what your church says.

On the other hand, you may use the church as a guide to living a moral, spiritually wholesome life. In that case, you take its counsel—seriously—and say "I'll accept the responsibility of making my own choices."

You then factor in your values, experience, and intelligence in making decisions. You have the option of finding a place for sexual fantasies within a life that is devoted to honesty, intimacy, and service. I deeply believe that using your values and judgment to make sexual decisions in this way is exactly what God intended.

260. Although I'm not the least bit sexually interested in people of my own gender, I sometimes fantasize about them, and it excites me. Does this mean I'm a latent homosexual?

Educator Sol Gordon used to answer this question by asking, "If you sometimes think about your dog, does that make you a latent dog?" "Latent homosexual" is not a category I find useful. The human mind and emotions are far too complex to be accurately described by narrow categories like "straight" or "gay." Besides, under the right circumstances, we're all latent *everything*—homosexual, musical, etc.

It is natural and very common to fantasize about members of the same gender. Attractive, interesting people can be found in both sexes. And anyone who has been frustrated about not being touched *exactly* right must wonder if a person of the same sex would touch them better. Bisexual men, for example, often report that other men know how to give them oral sex better than many women do.

Sometimes, same-sex fantasies are about ease and comfort, a contrast to the "battle of the sexes" many people have experienced in heterosexuality. For some people, in fact, the gentleness and conflict-free playfulness is the central theme. The homosexuality is almost incidental.

261. With AIDS and other diseases so common, should I try to have fantasies that feature safe sex?

No, that's not necessary. Just as our fantasies don't have to be free of racism or ageism, they don't need to reflect principles of physical or mental health. That's the beauty of fantasy—all eroticism, no consequences.

That said, let's note that fantasies can be used as a way of learning to eroticize today's requisite realities. An example is a man learning to enjoy a woman putting on a condom.

262. My wife says she never has sexual fantasies. Can that be? Why?

Although unusual, this is entirely possible. Maybe your wife is one of those people who interrupts her sexual thoughts subconsciously, before they even bubble into awareness. Alternatively, perhaps she has exactly the sex life she wants and enjoys it as is instead of speculating on how it might be.

Or maybe your wife doesn't consider her interests "sexual," preferring descriptions like "love" or "romance." *That's* what little girls are allowed to think about, you know, not "sex."

263. Don't you think people get warped if they constantly fantasize about the same thing all the time?

Fortunately, this does not happen too frequently. *Warped* is a strong word, but I do agree that such behavior isn't healthy. And I think this is true whether the fantasy involves money, power, or anything else, not just if it involves sex.

Ours is a culture that encourages sexual obsessions. The average American sees and hears tens of thousands of sexual images every year, which is itself astounding. These images are all pretty similar, featuring young, beautiful partners with enthusiastic, unwavering desire. In this environment, *not* being overinvolved with sexual fantasy is hard to explain.

264. The people who look up to me would flip if they knew about my violent sexual fantasies. I hate hiding, but I just can't let anybody suspect. What should I do?

No one is required to discuss *everything* about themselves, not even with their mate or best friend. Sexual fantasies are among the things we reveal the least.

There is a big difference between secrecy and privacy. The former means we feel obligated to hide something because we find it unacceptable. The latter means we choose to not share something even though we find it acceptable, because it is simply no one else's business.

You sound like you feel guilty, fearful of being exposed and accused. If you can accept your fantasies, you will feel less uncomfortable hiding them. Your reduced guilt will decrease your fear of exposure. The problem here is not your fantasies but your relationship to them.

265. My sexual fantasies of being rough and dominating don't fit with my self-image as a warm, gentle person. How do I reconcile this?

You said it—you're a warm, gentle person. As long as you're comfortable behaving this way, the self-image sounds appropriate. Besides, even gentle people play consenting power games in bed. As long as such behavior is consenting, it can still count as gentle in the larger sense.

266. How do I get my new partner to stop telling me her fantasies?

Say, "I feel hurt and unhappy. Please stop telling me your fantasies." If that doesn't work, say, "I don't want to hear this. I'd like to know why you insist on doing something you know is distasteful to me." Finally, explain that her behavior is unacceptable and that if she won't change it, you'll leave. If she doesn't, do so.

267. Is it true that some people can climax by fantasy alone?

Apparently. In her Rutgers University lab, Dr. Beverly Whipple and colleagues recorded seven female subjects going through the entire erotic process—becoming aroused and eventually climaxing—without ever touching themselves. Their physiological responses—both subjective and as recorded on instruments—were identical to their responses when actually masturbating genitally.

In a way, this makes sense. You can trigger the salivation reflex by thinking of lemons, and the shiver reflex by imagining fingernails on a blackboard. The body thinks orgasm is just one more reflex. Presumably, many more people are capable of this "fantasy orgasm." Makes you want to sit home and practice, doesn't it?

268. My partner asked about my fantasies. After I shared them, he called me names and said he'd have to "rethink" our relationship. Why?

The intriguing question here is whether or not your partner had these thoughts for a while before this conversation. Sometimes people get their mates to "admit" things they can then use against them.

Some people think they have the right to judge their partners' emotions, fantasies, and thoughts. (They are perfect mates for those who grew up with alcoholic or very critical parents.) The solution is to be clear about how you intend to be treated and to stick to these boundaries. It may be painful, but you may be much better off without this negative, energy-draining influence in your life.

14

Sex Toys, Erotica, and Aphrodisiacs

She was so wild that when she made French toast she got her tongue caught in the toaster.

—Rodney Dangerfield

269. What are the best aphrodisiacs?

For thousands of years people have searched for aphrodisiacs—substances that enhance sexual desire and/or ability. Around the globe, hopeful people have tried powdered rhinoceros horn, mandrake root, extract of sheep testicle, ginseng tea, and just about everything else.

There is only one substance that can truly increase sex drive without altering consciousness or behavior: the hormone testosterone. But it only works if the body's testosterone level is low, and it will not work if the sexual problems are psychogenic or disease-related. Side effects can be serious for both men and women. This is not a street drug to play with casually.

Sexually speaking, many people would like to develop greater intimacy, self-confidence, and creativity, while reducing anxiety and guilt. Introspection, honest confrontation, and straightforward communication can do that. Drugs, on the other hand, often interfere with a sexual relationship and the body's functioning.

270. You say there are no true aphrodisiacs, but what about alcohol?

Many people use alcohol before or during sex because it reduces anxiety and inhibition. Unfortunately, it can also undermine sexuality by making you less sensitive to the stimulation you're getting. And it makes closeness difficult by reducing your ability to communicate and to take your partner's needs seriously.

If you're nervous, do something about it rather than just pushing it—and your partner—away. Talk about it. Tell your partner what you want—closeness and a sense of adequacy—and how you feel—perhaps distant or inadequate.

Shakespeare had it right, you know. Alcohol, he said in *Macbeth*, inflames the desire but diminishes the ability.

271. Movies, songs, even comedians say sex is better with drugs. Is that true?

"Drugs" covers a lot of ground, from caffeine, nicotine, and alcohol (all of which undermine sex), to marijuana and cocaine (whose effects vary depending on dosage), to amphetamines, barbiturates, crack, and PCP (all of which kill sex, then kill the user).

In small amounts, marijuana and cocaine make people feel good, which makes them more open to their sexual feelings. More serious users, however, have trouble connecting with others, and they often lose interest in sex. They also lose their judgment about how the drugs are affecting them, and they tend to mistrust others' opinions about this.

Unfortunately, the government refuses to support the serious study of either sex or recreational drugs, so there are no good data on how one affects the other.

272. Who said "the ultimate aphrodisiac is power?" What does this mean?

Former Secretary of State Henry Kissinger said it years ago. Presumably, he was talking about himself.

273. Why do some women enjoy vibrators so much?

The clitoris is the primary female sex organ, and intercourse does not usually stimulate it enough for orgasm. Vibrators are a handy way to get that clitoral stimulation. As sex therapist Lonnie Barbach says, "If most couples made love by rubbing the testicles against the clitoris, women would climax most of the time and men would have trouble."

Unlike hands or mouths, vibrators don't get tired, don't desire communication, don't need to be in the mood, and don't request reciprocation. They're *almost* perfect. But they can't replace human beings. They can't kiss, they can't make you laugh, and they can't warm your feet.

And that's why they're not dangerous. You can get very used to the pleasure they give you, but most people periodically want more from sex than they can provide.

Vibrators can be a temporary aid—they're an effective way to learn how to climax—or a permanent addition to your sexual repertoire. In the latter case, they are like oil or candles or satin sheets—a toy that nourishes the energy of your erotic life.

274. I recently started seeing this girl. When we got to her bedroom, it was like a hardware store—vibrators, handcuffs, all kinds of stuff. Weird! What gives?

And they say romance is dead.

It's hard to know what's going on there. She may be a fun-loving, adventurous sort who doesn't take sex too seriously and likes to play. You know, "Girls just wanna have fun." Of course, it's important to say "This is over my limit" if something is. Let's hope she can enjoy making love without props.

If she can't, that's an important clue that there's something wrong. Maybe she uses the equipment to create distance or prevent intimacy. That doesn't make this stuff bad, you know. People create psychological distance with all kinds of things, such as fine china, cigar smoking, and compulsive cleanliness.

When you feel distanced by a partner for any reason, talk about it, whether she's using leather or silk. Don't criticize her for being wrong, just tell her how you feel. Try, for example, "I feel distant from you, and I'd like to be closer. Some of these toys are getting in my way. Can we use them less, or differently, or not at all?"

275. How do I ask a sex partner about using a vibrator or other toys?

First, don't apologize. Make sure *you* feel okay about it, and then share your excitement, inviting your partner to go on a little adventure. It may help to underline that this is not about him or her being inadequate but about the two of you exploring new things.

It's just sex, after all, so keep your sense of humor about the whole business. People can handle almost anything if they're approached playfully—as in, "Look what I have for us!"

276. Where do I buy things like vibrators?

Ah, when the going gets tough, the tough go shopping. Your local adult bookstores (assuming self-righteous crusaders haven't chased them out of town) generally carry a decent selection of toys.

We do live in an era of specialization, of course. So the nation's best sources for sex toys are:

• Good Vibrations (1210 Valencia Street, San Francisco, CA 94110; 415/550-0827), and
• Eve's Garden (119 W. 57 Street, New York, NY 10019; 212/757-8651)

You can visit them in person or order by mail or phone. Then, like Julius Caesar, you can say *veni, vidi, visa:* I came, I saw, I shopped.

277. Can you explain this whole leather/whips/S&M/spanking thing?

It's a lot more than one single thing. For example, some folks like to dress up in leather, talk mean and get very excited, and have more or less regular sex. Others like to hit or be hit, experiencing most of their sexual arousal or release mixed with pain. There are dozens of "scenes" in between.

What all of these have in common is erotic power play; that is, the conscious manipulation of the power aspects of eroticism and the thresholds of stimulation and pain. And they experiment with surrender and control, a profound part of sexuality little discussed in the West.

Erotic power play should *always* be consensual. In reality, two people do it together, rather than one doing it to the other. And as one expert says, "It feels totally different from what it looks like." See question 169 for more information.

278. My husband wants me to wear lingerie around the house. What does he think I am, a slut?

What's wrong with that? All *slut* means is a person—no, a woman—who's interested in sex and willing to enjoy it—and who admits it. That's a turn-on for men, you know. It could be for you, too. It involves no disrespect at all.

Most men are more visual about sex than most women. They enjoy seeing a woman dressed up, as well as dressed down. Brevity, of course, is the soul of lingerie. It's not practical. It's the opposite of sensible shoes. It says "Let's play." It flatters your body while showing it off.

Your husband is saying he wants to enjoy looking at you and wants to enjoy knowing you're interested in sex. This can be delightful. Enjoy—indeed, cooperate with—the intention and attention. If you don't want to play with lingerie, use whatever toys are comfortable for you.

279. What is pornography?

The word *pornography* is derived from the Greek "the writings of prostitutes." Its main goal is to stimulate sexual interest or arousal. Millions of people use it to enhance masturbation. Many also use it to heighten lovemaking with their partners.

Pornography typically shows people having sex or getting ready to have sex. Some say it also includes pictures of nude women (or men) doing nothing but posing for the camera. Like all other forms of human expression, it can be artistic or trashy, creative or tasteless.

Our culture's ambivalence about sex makes the act of deliberately arousing someone else questionable. No one challenges artists who make us feel sad, angry, happy, silly, or confused. But making us feel sexy!! That is given a special name with special restrictions.

Pornography is not a legal definition. The Supreme Court has ruled that something is obscene, and therefore illegal, when it violates community standards and has no redeeming social value. No other form of expression is subject to such stringent and arbitrary standards, not even demonstrations by the American Nazi Party. Clearly, some people are more afraid of sex than of anything else.

280. What is the difference between erotica and pornography?

I am sometimes told that pornography is stale and distorted, that it manipulates sexual fear, is always about control, and dehumanizes both viewer and subject. Erotica supposedly provides arousal intimately, honestly, and playfully.

Frankly, I don't find this a useful distinction. What's honest to one person can be gruesome to another. And what's dehumanizing to one can be liberating to another. The debate makes me nervous because it seems intended to separate "good" arousal from "bad."

Is there a limit to acceptable erotic materials? Sure: taste. If something turns someone off, I'd rather they just say so (and keep away from it), instead of pronouncing the material morally inferior or dangerous.

In a free society there will always be stuff floating around that someone dislikes. I feel that way about slasher films and the *National Enquirer*, which are violent and distorted, and which promote stereotypes. But the danger of repression is far worse, particularly when the message is that sex is bad.

Particularly when I'm not the one who gets to decide what's okay.

281. What exactly is the difference between soft-core and hard-core films?

In hard-core films, the viewer actually sees genital insertion (into mouth, vagina, and/or anus). The camera proves that the actors are having sex.

In soft-core films, genital insertion is not shown. These films portray intercourse by simulating or implying it, rather than showing it. Lovers are shown humping and moaning, and the viewer is supposed to imagine the details. Soft-core films also show nonintercourse eroticism, such as spanking or mud wrestling.

The difference is relevant only to people who insist that explicit sexuality can harm viewers. This, in turn, reflects a more fundamental problem—the way our society defines sex according to some formula of body parts, orifices, and movements, rather than as a combination of energy, feelings, and experience.

282. I'm curious about this new "women's erotica." How does it differ from traditional pornography?

These books and films attempt to appeal to women by including more affection, humor, story, character, and a gentler approach than traditional porn. They present situations and feelings most women can relate to better than simple lust and anonymous encounters: delight about the colors in a room, for example, or the curve of a man's wrist.

Women and men who enjoy more explicit, single-minded stuff often find this material a bit slow and tame. Some men tolerate it with their female partners on the grounds that it's better than no erotica, perhaps with the hope that it's a steppingstone to more intense fare.

283. What "women's erotica" is actually available? How does it fit into the bigger picture of commercial sex?

You're referring to films by women like Candida Royalle and to books edited by women like Lonnie Barbach (*Pleasures*), and the Kensington Ladies Erotica Society (*Ladies' Own Erotica*).

Without question, we should welcome the new women's erotica into the marketplace. It encourages both healthy sexual conversation and healthy sexual arousal. It supports a more realistic vision of what normal sexy people are like. And it challenges the conventional idea that there is something immature or dangerous about people who deliberately choose to get turned on.

Of course, the *old* women's erotica is still enormously popular: Romance novels and soap operas are giant commercial successes. Although both forms center on sexual relationships, producers and consumers alike pretend that sex is only a minor part of the appeal. What's the difference between these forms and what society calls pornography? Only respectability. Both are distorted versions of sex and power.

For information about films, contact Femme Productions in New York City (212/226-9330). For information about books, contact the Sexuality Library in San Francisco (415/550-7399).

284. You say pornography is harmless, but what about all the violence in it?

No one, of course, is in favor of violence (except in television, mainstream films, and romance novels). That's great, because according to the Meese Commission, formed by President Reagan to destroy the pornography industry, fewer than 1 percent of the images in the top-selling X-rated magazines contains "force, violence, or weapons." Films may have a touch more than magazines, but the old "sex-and-violence" argument just isn't backed up by reality.

Do X-rated materials cause violence? The Meese Commission could find no evidence that consuming dirty pictures and words, even violent ones, causes people to behave dangerously.

285. How can anyone look at pictures of other people having sex? They must be sick.

Not according to dozens of surveys of "normal" people. To note just a few:

• *Redbook* magazine (100,000 women): 46 percent use pornography "often or occasionally"
• *Psychology Today* magazine (20,000 readers): more than 75 percent have used X-rated materials
• United States Commission on Obscenity and Pornography (2,500 randomly chosen adults): 75 percent have used pornography

Clearly, it's primarily "normal" people who enjoy X-rated materials. Just as clearly, if you don't enjoy them, you shouldn't use them.

15

What Is Normal?

I haven't had sex in so long I've forgotten who ties up who.

—Joan Rivers

286. Why is the most common sexual question "Am I normal?"

Because unlike other important activities, we don't observe others having sex, don't hear anyone discussing their sexual feelings or experiences seriously, and don't have access to reliable information about what other people feel and do.

This fact, coupled with the pressure to be as sexually liberated and satisfied as the Joneses, leads many people to wonder if they are sexually normal.

287. There must be some people who don't worry about being sexually normal. What is sex like for them?

For such people, sex is an experience rather than a performance. It is something to enjoy rather than something to evaluate. While it may not always be satisfying, it isn't an opportunity to fail, either technically or morally.

288. I see all these magazine surveys, and the sexual behavior of their readers never sounds like me. Does this mean I'm abnormal?

It may mean that you express your sexuality differently than those readers do, which is not the same as being abnormal.

Consider, too, that people lie on sex surveys, generally in the direction of what they think the survey takers want to hear. People also shade their responses in the direction that they like to think of themselves. You may do this yourself when the doctor asks you your weight; we tend to answer a little closer toward our ideal than we actually are.

Sex surveys are usually designed by statisticians, not sexologists. They use expressions like *make love, foreplay,* and *how many times,* which are much too simplistic to describe real people's sexuality. Though they do the best they can, respondents usually paint a simpler picture of their sexual experiences than really exists.

Finally, remember that only a small fraction of any group answers surveys, and it is not a random sample. Thus, large segments of most groups are underrepresented by surveys, mail campaigns, and the like. This is obviously what happens, for example, when a small unhappy group protests sex on television, while no one from the satisfied majority writes in praising it.

289. My church seems pretty clear on what's sexually normal and abnormal. Are you saying it's wrong?

No, because only an ideological organization like a church can actually believe in normality. Believers are supposed to accept their church's definition of normality on faith, rather than thinking about what the church says.

Churches, of course, do not admit that their judgments of sexual normality are ideological. Rather, they insist they are simply interpreting sexuality's inherent qualities. Sincere peo-

ple can disagree about this, particularly since the disastrous results of the church's sexual interpretations are evident everywhere.

290. What about morality? Doesn't that figure in deciding what's normal?

Morality and *normality* are similar concepts. They are judgments, not facts; they cannot be disproved or refuted; anyone
can decide how they should be defined for everyone; and those
who don't agree are frequently criticized as inadequate human
beings.

As a human activity, sexuality, by definition, has a moral
component. Too frequently, however, sexual morality has stood
for rigidity, limitations, and the social and political status quo.
It has had less to do with honorable relationships between people and more to do with which body part goes where, and with
the gender, race, age, and class of the people to whom the body
parts belong. This is, at best, well-intentioned paternalism and,
more commonly, bigotry. It is not "morality."

I believe the basis for a moral sexuality is simply an extension of the Golden Rule: Do not do unto others as you would
not have others do unto you; and don't do it to yourself, either.
The specific way you choose to implement this is up to you
and is virtually irrelevant.

291. I'm concerned about too many things being considered normal. Doesn't "normalizing" a sexual attitude or behavior give it society's endorsement?

Yes and no. Mostly no.

Sexuality is so basic a part of our lives that people express
it despite society's rules. For example, between one-third and
two-thirds of all marriages experience at least one extramarital
affair, even though society frowns on it. Despite the lack of
social support, people have sex before marriage, they have oral
sex, they go to prostitutes, and so on.

The main result of society stigmatizing these and other
forms of sexuality is that people do them and feel guilty, not

that they don't do them. It can't be good to have large segments of a population feeling guilty, particularly about private, consenting behavior.

Finally, normalizing forms of sexual expression does put forth a message. It empowers people. It undercuts isolation by helping people talk with one another about a formerly taboo subject. And it allows people to celebrate their sexuality if they want to. It doesn't tell them they should, it simply allows them to if they want to.

292. You say "Don't focus on numbers," but isn't that what tells us what's normal?

Only if you define "normal" as "most common." If you do, blue eyes would have to be considered abnormal. So would orgasm from intercourse and using birth control 100 percent of the time.

Statistics can only tell us what other people do (or say they do, which in sex is definitely not the same thing). Statistics don't tell us why people do what they do or what their activities mean to them. This is the real story behind the numbers.

Let's say that several different people report that they made love three times in the previous month. How similar would those experiences be if one respondent was a fifteen-year-old who had sex one night while his girlfriend's parents were gone; if the second respondent was a career woman who made love with three different men while on a two-week vacation; and if the third was a fifty-year-old newlywed with erection problems, cuddling with his wife most Sunday mornings? Numbers do not tell the whole story.

"Most common" is only one way to define normality. People also use "normal" to mean "morally correct"; "physically healthy"; "whatever supports our view of the world"; and "according to tradition."

293. I rarely hear the media talk about what's normal, so why do you say they are so important in defining it for us?

The key message the media send us about sexual normality

is their remarkably uniform vision of sex. On television, in movies, and on magazine covers, sexy people are almost invariably young, beautiful, and eager. They have no communication problems, no concerns about birth control or disease, and they have wildly responsive bodies. No erection problems either, no sir.

The advertising industry also shapes our sexuality with a single theme, repeated millions of times during each of our lives: We are all in danger of being sexually inadequate; this is terribly painful, and there's only one dependable cure.

If we believe the advertising industry, this cure is not communication, nor resolving fears of intimacy, nor correcting early teachings or negative beliefs about sex. The solution to sexual inadequacy is buying things! Whatever the product, advertising can sexualize it—by making it a solution to a problem.

Ads tell us that what's normal is to worry about sexual adequacy and to resolve that worry by buying things. If you don't worry, you're not normal. And if you don't buy, or don't want to buy, you're also not normal.

Finally, let's remember that there are rules about what sexual images the media is willing to carry. Many women's magazines won't include information about real female sexuality—for example, the fact that women use vibrators or touch themselves during intercourse. Radio stations won't carry even tasteful ads for condoms. And television programs rarely show us gay people, except as fools or psychopaths. The trend is so uniform it can only be called censorship. Censorship of the real in favor of an invented concept of what's normal.

294. What are "lovemaps"?

Sex researcher Dr. John Money of Johns Hopkins University coined this term. It describes the unconscious organization of our concepts of what is sexually arousing. Each of us has a unique lovemap; for some, blond hair and blue eyes are preferable; for others, black high heels and leather garter belt are an absolute must.

Looking at the way people's sexual preferences develop helps us see the similarity between common turn-ons and uncommon ones. This perspective helps us investigate sexuality without the need to decide what's "normal."

295. Why are some groups so obsessed with defining what's sexually normal and punishing those who aren't?

The people who most want to control others' sexual feelings and behavior are generally those who are most frightened of their own. This gives them a heavy investment in controlling people's sexuality.

Why? In the case of some churches, creating sin gives them a market for forgiveness. In the case of the government, it gives politicians a chance to prove to their more frightened constituents that they favor "wholesome family values," want to protect children, and are against "perverts."

Most people who are concerned with others' sexual normality claim that they are concerned with sexual crime and antisocial impulses. But even if no one acted or felt this way, they'd have to invent something like it. It's the perfect rationalization for their own frightened, irrational sexual attitudes.

296. Why does society's vision of sexual normality seem to change every decade or two?

Because the concept of sexual normality is an arbitrary social invention, with no intrinsic attachment to anything of substance—sort of like paper money that isn't backed up by gold.

Look at what was considered abnormal only forty years ago: vibrators; touching oneself during intercourse; couples masturbating together; women enjoying oral sex. All are now considered fairly routine in many parts of the country. As the mass media reach deeper into every corner of our nation's consciousness, the cycle time for such changes grows shorter.

Who knows what currently "kinky" things will be considered normal by the turn of the century? Be wary of anyone who describes anything as "obviously" sexually abnormal.

297. Is our vision of sexual normality changing as women's sexual needs and experiences are taken more seriously?

Yes. For example, multiple orgasm, female lust, and pre-marital sex have all become more legitimate as society has recognized the realities of female sexuality.

Society's concept of sexual normality is being similarly expanded as the voices of other sexually disenfranchised groups are finally being heard. These include older people, gays, and the disabled.

298. My partner says I'm kinky, but I disagree. How do we decide who's right?

What does "kinky" mean? To various people, it means creative, dangerous, good-humored, corrupted, scary, and experienced. What does your partner mean by kinky? What do you mean?

More importantly, what is the disagreement about? Presumably, there's something you enjoy or want to do that your partner doesn't. If so, he or she should have the right to say "no, thank you" without having to give a "good" reason (such as "there's something wrong with what you want"). If you and your partner cannot agree on enough sexual activities to satisfy you both, professional help is indicated.

If, on the other hand, this is just a friendly intellectual disagreement, you can both be right. Since there's no standard definition of kinky, there's no way of telling who is and who isn't.

To some people, a feather is kinky; to others, only the whole chicken is.

299. So how do I know if I'm sexually normal?

This, of course, is the most common sexual question. It's also the saddest, I think, because it reflects modern Americans' loss of trust in their own sexuality.

Unfortunately, most of us do not *know*, deep in our bones, that our sexuality is okay. Understandably, we feel continual pressure to figure out if we're sexually normal.

But healthy human sexuality has a dark side—not a bad side, just a dark one. In addition to its lighter side, our sexuality includes greedy, aggressive, lusty, controlling, amoral (not *immoral*) aspects. This dark side can scare people who don't trust themselves sexually, making them wonder how they can be "normal" when they have thoughts, feelings, and even behaviors that seem "bad."

How do you know if you're sexually normal? You decide. You understand that healthy sexuality is a vast, complex web of light and dark that is not dangerous. You realize that "normal" is simply a judgment and that you are as qualified to make that judgment as anyone else. So make it.

And if you commit part of your existence to expressing your sexuality in life-affirming ways, and if you really experience yourself when you do that, you don't have to decide. You feel it, and that's how you know.

300. Why are professionals such as physicians, lawyers, and the clergy willing to say what's sexually normal? Why are you so reluctant to do so?

In answer to the first question: (1) Because these professionals are not in the business of empowering people in the area of sexuality; (2) Because they rarely have a crosscultural overview of human sexuality; and (3) Because when it comes to sex, they look more at body parts than at what's in the hearts and souls of the people involved.

In answer to the second question: (1) I am; (2) I do; and (3) I don't.

Part III

Love and Intimacy

16

Turn-offs

A man has missed something if he has never left a brothel at dawn feeling like throwing himself into the river out of sheer disgust.

—Gustav Flaubert

301. What are the most common turn-offs?

Broadly speaking, the most common turn-off is being with someone you don't want to be with. This can be a new partner you don't really desire; or a regular partner when you're angry, sad, or otherwise not in the mood.

Other reasons people get turned off from or during sex include:

- My partner has poor hygiene
- My partner won't do what I want
- My partner acts selfish
- My partner does not respond or is unenthusiastic
- My partner compares me to other men or women

- My partner drinks a lot
- My partner judges me
- My partner doesn't accept my refusal to do certain things
- I don't like the way my partner looks
- I don't trust my partner

302. Why should the things mentioned in the preceding answer turn someone off? Shouldn't our bodies just respond to sexual stimulation, regardless of how we feel?

Although our body's sexual responses are essentially reflexes, our thoughts and feelings can easily block those reflexes.

Periodically, for example, a man will come into my office and complain that he's having erection trouble. When I ask about his relationship, he'll often say he's been angry at his wife for years, doesn't like her body, and hates the way she refuses to have oral or manual sex. "Good news," I'll eventually respond. "Your penis works fine."

Penises are not meant to function under these circumstances. Imagine putting molasses into the washer instead of soap. The clothes wouldn't get clean—but you wouldn't blame the washer, would you? It isn't designed to work with molasses. And penises aren't designed to work with the many turn-offs people with stress-filled lives frequently experience.

303. Why doesn't my spouse listen when I talk about what turns me off?

People don't listen either because of the way they're spoken to or because they don't want to hear what's being said to them. Your first task is to find out which is the case. Is there a way that you could talk to your spouse that would make it easier for him or her to listen? If so, try it—a different tone of voice, not using certain "hot button" words, a more playful approach, better timing, whatever.

On the other hand, your partner may feel so sexually insecure that he or she hears any request or suggestion as a com-

plaint. This can make listening just too painful. Such a situation calls for professional help.

304. Why can't my partner remember what I like and don't like from one time to the next? Believe me, I'm clear enough about it.

If this has been going on for a long time, it could be pretty
serious. I imagine you've told your partner you're unhappy
about this many times.

Either your partner doesn't much care about your satisfaction; your partner is so anxious about his or her own sexual
adequacy that your satisfaction gets lost in the shuffle; or this
is the way the two of you are playing out a larger power struggle.

If this is a new problem, discuss how the two of you can
resolve it together. If it is an old problem, explain exactly how
distressed you are and what you want. If you don't see even
the smallest sign of change in four weeks, seek professional
help.

305. Why does my partner take it so personally when something turns me off?

This is a perennial problem. Our partner sincerely wants
to know how we feel. We say so, and our partner gets hurt,
angry, or sad. It's the main reason people give for not sharing
more.

Most people's sense of sexual adequacy is pretty fragile.
And in America, men learn they're supposed to be sexual experts, while women learn they're supposed to be sexual mind
readers. Hearing that a partner is turned off means, then, that
someone has failed as an expert or mind reader. For these reasons, many people feel threatened when presented with a turn-
off.

Talk about this with your partner outside the bedroom.
Assure him or her that if you have a complaint, you'll present
it in a clear, unmistakable way. Until then, your partner doesn't
need to take your turn-offs so personally.

306. What's the best way to say, "Yuk, I don't like that?"

What's your goal? If it's to wound your partner, then wrinkle your nose, stick out your tongue, and say "Yuk, I don't like that." If your goal is to enhance your sexual relationship, then do something else. For starters, keep that goal in mind and remind your partner of it as many times as necessary.

You have an opportunity here, not a problem. Touch your partner's hand or shoulder while you talk, and smile. Keep the conversation positive, explaining what you like rather than what you don't like. For example: "It's nice when you nibble my arm. I'd like it even better if you went slower and didn't squeeze my breast at the same time. After I get real excited, squeezing my breasts feels better."

Family therapy pioneer Virginia Satir used to say that if you can tell someone they smell bad in a way that makes them feel you've just improved the relationship, you have communication figured out.

307. When I don't like something, how do I know if I'm being reasonable or just too picky?

When it comes to sex, I think everyone should be picky. Sex offers limitless vistas; why be less than picky?

There is no formula to help you distinguish between what's sexually sensible and what's sexually picky. Certainly, if you lack a sense of entitlement—a sense that your needs are usually reasonable—your judgment about these things cannot be trusted any more than if you were terribly selfish and greedy.

If you generally like your partner, your body, and sex; if you can be sexually satisfied in several ways; and if you aren't using sex to prove something, or to wield power over others, then deciding you don't want a particular kind of sex is probably reasonable. You can always discuss this with your friends or consult popular books (see Bibliography), but keep in mind that their standards may be different from yours.

People who ask this question frequently learned, as children, to mistrust their judgment about themselves and others.

308. Everybody's turn-offs seem to be different. How are you supposed to know what people like and don't like?

Everybody's turn-offs *are* different. To know what people like and don't like, you need to ask, usually several times. Don't make a grim interrogation out of it, though. Look at it as a delightful chance to find out how to please someone you like. Remember to use nonverbal as well as verbal methods.

309. Why is it that I dislike certain things with one partner but don't mind them at all with another?

In sex, the thing you're doing and the person you're doing it with tend to melt together. So oral sex with Harry may simply be oral sex, which may or may not move you. But oral sex with George may be Oral Sex With George. The things you generally don't like about it (say, you get claustrophobic or you dislike the ejaculate) either don't occur or don't seem so bad.

Why is that? George's relaxed attitude may help you feel sexier and less inhibited. He may be clean, attentive, and funny, which helps you take things less seriously. And he may communicate a love for your body that makes it difficult to dislike anything that feels good.

It's still a great human mystery—how can one person's kiss be so profoundly different from another's?

310. "Uptight." That's how my husband describes the fact that certain things turn me off. How do I change his mind?

If you and your husband were in counseling with me, I'd say, "You two are focusing on whether or not Susan is uptight. Since your sexual dissatisfaction is a couple problem, let's focus on what kinds of sexual activities you both enjoy." By approaching sex as partners rather than as adversaries, healthy people can usually create good sex.

On the other hand, this conflict may reflect personal issues that are interfering with your sexual compatibility. For example, can your husband accept you being turned off to *anything* he likes? Do you sometimes set the sexual rhythm, or is he always in charge? Many couples run into problems when one partner has a strong need to control the sex.

Do you have a sense that you could enjoy sex if you weren't being criticized? Can you enjoy a variety of sexual activities? If so, you're probably not "uptight." On the other hand, if sex for you is loaded with embarrassment and danger, your attitude may be a serious obstacle to a good sexual relationship.

311. My husband is a wonderful man, but he just isn't very romantic. Do we *have* to talk about sex every time we do it?

Of course not. On the other hand, talking about pork-belly futures is no aphrodisiac either. What's wrong with talking about sex? It can be tiresome if done with the wrong words or wrong tone of voice, at exactly the wrong time, or for the wrong reason. But talking about sex—what we're going to do, how good it's going to feel, how pleased we are to be doing it, how delightful it is to be doing it with each other—can help create a sense of play and enhance the whole experience.

The point of not discussing sex while we're doing it is often denial. Actually, that's what "romance" is all about: focusing on some idealized image of sex and love to avoid experiencing the realities of sex and love.

312. Please explain this: I'm eager to have sex, and then something happens to turn me off, and I just can't get interested again.

It sounds as if your state of arousal is fragile; that is, being aroused has little power to keep you aroused.

Some people can get and stay aroused under a wide variety of circumstances. But others are only able to maintain their excitement under very precise conditions. In an odd way, this allows them to ignore the reality that they're actually having sex. When that spell is broken, they've lost a key condition. Eliminating the distraction or the turn-off cannot then re-create that key condition.

I suggest you examine your need for the perfect sexual situation. Is this a denial of your sexuality? Does it reflect insecurity about the power of your sexuality? Do you fear the intimacy that comes from losing yourself in sex? The insight you get from pondering these questions will make you less susceptible to distractions.

313. My wife says I should enjoy her "naturally," but is it too much to ask for shaved legs and brushed teeth?

That depends on what you want: a pleasantly clean person or a sterile object? There's nothing wrong with the first and nothing right with the second.

Hygiene is a common way that people play out sexual power struggles. Couples get to argue about who is right and wrong, rather than face whatever issues of intimacy, abandonment, or control are really bothering them.

There's nothing wrong with wanting a clean partner. But will this really make the sex easy and satisfying, or will some other problem arise? Do you and your wife, in fact, accept yourselves, each other, and the messy nature of real sexuality? If not, all the shaving in the world won't bring you closer together.

By the way, are *you* that squeaky clean?

314. Am I the only one who thinks alcohol is *un*sexy? I hate when my spouse smells from it, and it doesn't help the sex, either.

The reality of alcohol is, in fact, pretty unsexy. Under its influence, people have less control of their bodies, they say inappropriate things, and they are less sensitive to others' needs. Interestingly, this is why many people drink before sex: It makes them less inhibited and less aware of whatever anxiety they have about sex. Unfortunately, this rarely makes them sexy to their partners; millions of people agree with you about this.

Drinkers also smell bad, although I don't think that's one of their reasons for drinking.

Both the alcohol industry and media perpetuate the myth of alcohol's sexiness by showing attractive people drinking before and after sex. In a sex-negative culture in which we've all learned to be anxious about sex, anything that makes people feel *less* is going to be considered sexy.

If you're unhappy with your partner's drinking, discuss it with him or her outside of the sexual situation. Talk about what your partner does, how you feel at the time, and how you'd like to feel during sex instead. Set specific limits and stick to them. While unpleasant, this is the only way to preserve your self-respect and possibly motivate change.

315. I don't like being given orders: "Touch me here; no, not that way!" Why can't people just relax and enjoy what you're doing?

The way people compare unwanted sexual communication to being ordered around, you'd think that army life is just like difficult sex. I wonder what our commander-in-chief would say about that.

People *can* relax—when they're having an experience they like. We all have an obligation to know what our mate likes and to be flexible and provide at least some of those things. If there are ways you'd prefer to be given information about your partner's preferences, by all means let your partner know so he or she can use them.

If your partner can't relax in *any* kind of sexual situation, you have the right to request some change.

316. We have a problem—my wife loves porn movies, but they just turn me off. What should we do?

Recall Klein's Second Law of Sexuality: If it doesn't feel good, don't do it.

Let's give you the benefit of the doubt and assume that you've experimented with a few different kinds, none of which work for you. Your wife can certainly watch the films by herself, perhaps as a prelude to being with you. Maybe there are creative ways you can both enjoy them; for example, with the sound off, or in small amounts rather than watching an entire film. Would you like more of the sexual attention she seems to give the films?

Be creative and suggest substitutes you can both enjoy, such as erotic magazines. What about engaging the spirit of hedonism in totally different ways, such as through lingerie, candles, or a vibrator?

How do you two solve any of the other conflicts that all couples inevitably have? Could those methods work with this issue?

317. I enjoy talking dirty during sex, but my spouse thinks it's crude. What should we do?

One option, of course, is not talking dirty. But before taking such a drastic step as giving your spouse what he or she wants, collect some information. What does "crude" mean? Is the problem that you are using all street words, or just a few? Does your partner know you're being playful when you talk that way? Is there some other way to talk about bodies and sexy feelings that you can both enjoy?

In an effort to control childhood sexuality, parents and teachers put a taboo on kids' "bad words" as early as they can. Consequently, it's very hard for people to change their attitudes about this. Getting your mouth washed out with soap is an experience no one forgets. I certainly won't . . . ugh.

"We are not taught to think decently about sex," said George Bernard Shaw. "Consequently, we have no language for it except indecent language."

Frankly, if your partner is willing to *do* "dirty" things, I'd lighten up on the need for him or her to *listen* to them.

318. I just can't stand making love with the television on—which my boyfriend likes to do. What should I do?

Tell your boyfriend that sex with him is far too intimate to share with *any* creature, living or nonliving. Also, remind him how much he enjoys your total attention during sex—and sensuously suggest that he's too good a lover for you to settle for most of his attention—you want it *all*.

If it's the flickering light he enjoys, suggest candles.

17

Etiquette

To succeed in the world it is not enough to be stupid, you must also be well-mannered.

—**Voltaire**

319. How do I tell my husband to shave or brush his teeth before lovemaking without being unromantic?

By not criticizing him for being a slob. Instead, let him know how eager you are to make love—and how a freshly washed man turns you on. You can also suggest that you go into the bathroom together, making grooming part of sex rather than an obstacle to it.

Don't let your husband criticize you for wanting him to be a little cleaner for sex. On the other hand, our partners can't always be Martinized (you know, "fresh as a flower in just one hour"). Demands about hygiene can be a disguised form of hostility or a way to sabotage sex. It's important to balance our desire for cleanliness with other aspects of sexuality.

320. Is there some way to get out of making love if you change your mind in the middle? What if you're willing to continue but you just don't want to do a certain thing?

You don't need to "get out of" making love. Lovemaking should be an activity that both parties consent to freely. Once you feel trapped or obligated, you're no longer making love. You're involved in a sorry power game that no one can win.

You can interrupt sex in the middle the same way you leave a store in the middle of trying on a dress or a restaurant before you've finished ordering. You look at your partner and say, "This just isn't working for me, and we need to stop now, okay?"

Getting into bed with someone is not a commitment to do anything but be friendly and gentle. While interrupting sex five times in a row will probably discourage a sixth invitation, you have the right to change your mind for *any* reason (and your partner, of course, has the right not to like this one bit).

If you want to interrupt a game, or choose a different position, or change the rules altogether, just tell your partner. If he or she can't be flexible enough to make room for your needs, suggest joint counseling, or consider changing partners.

321. What's wrong with me? I enjoy sex, but my husband is always done before I am, and I'm left feeling frustrated.

It sounds as if you and your husband both define sex in terms of his sexuality. This is not only unfair, it's unrealistic.

Many women, for example, find it takes them longer to be physically prepared for intercourse (as evidenced by sufficient vaginal lubrication) than it takes their male partners (as evidenced by erection). Similarly, most men climax from intercourse sooner than women—in fact, most women will not climax from intercourse without additional stimulation of the clitoris by hand or mouth.

Thus, it isn't unusual for intercourse that physically satisfies a man not to satisfy a woman. This means that if a couple wants to have intercourse (and, of course, not every sexual encounter includes it), the partners need to be sensitive to each other's ideal pace. A woman should not start intercourse before she is wet enough; a man should not assume that his climax means that sex is over.

Many couples begin intercourse after the woman climaxes, or arrange to stimulate her after intercourse ends. Regardless of how you do it, no one should feel frustrated or self-critical when sex is over. To put it another way, sex should not habitually end with one partner still desiring fulfillment.

If you wish, masturbate after intercourse. Don't feel you need to apologize or, indeed, to leave the warmth of your own bed, for this natural, self-nurturing activity.

322. I walked in on my roommate having sex last week. What should I have done? What should I do now?

Unless you were invited to stay, you should have left. If you've already apologized and worked out a way to avoid this problem in the future, you can simply leave it behind you. Put the incident in perspective—as great fantasy material.

323. Before getting into bed with a man, should I tell him if I'm having my period? Should I assume he won't want sex?

While not absolutely mandatory, it's a good idea to tell. Some men are almost phobic about menstruation and will appreciate the chance to gracefully decline the invitation to make love. But don't assume that every man will respond this way; many have learned to accept menstruation as a fact of life, just as you have. So mention it in a casual way, ask if it's okay, and then accept whatever response you get.

The AIDS virus can be transmitted during menstruation, so unless both you and your partner are monogamous, using a condom is a must.

324. Is there a polite way to suggest that a supposedly single person perhaps isn't?

There are polite ways to hint around, but no, I don't think there's a polite way to say, "There's evidence to suggest that you're far more married than you claim to be. Can you prove you're single?"

The closest to a "polite" way is the adult, nonhostile, straightforward way. Simply say what's on your mind, be open to the response, and trust your feelings.

325. I guess I'm old-fashioned, but I don't want a lover talking dirty to me. How do I get my partner to stop?

Your partner, presumably, does not want to talk in a way that turns you off. (If that's not true you have a much bigger problem.) So just put your arms around him or her and say, "I like your sweet words better than your raunchy ones. Will you please use them? Those sweet words will definitely get you better results."

326. How do you ask someone to use a condom? Whose job is it to bring this up?

Each person is 100 percent responsible for assuring condom use during sex. In an ideal world, sexual partners would be falling all over each other trying to say "Let's use a condom" first. And each partner would be clear: no condom, no sex.

I don't think we should ask our partners' permission to use a condom. That makes us apologetic and makes condom use negotiable. Neither should be true. "Let's use a condom" expresses your position in a friendly, clear way: "I want to, we're going to, and it's no big deal." From there it's just a short step to "I have one over here," or "Let me put it on you," or "Oops, can you please help me out?"

327. I have a dear friend of the other sex whom I would like to make love with. How do I approach this person without possibly ruining our friendship?

Unfortunately, there is no way to do this without running

some risk, be it large or small. The best you can do is minimize the risk by being friendly, gracious, and sensitive.

Although you don't want to mention this casually while waiting in line to renew your driver's license, you don't need to make a federal case out of it, either. Pick a time when you're feeling close and you have some privacy. Tell your friend that you are committed to your friendship; that *nothing* is more important to you; and that you're going to take a risk and share something.

In a close friendship like this one, withholding a feeling as strong as yours isn't entirely appropriate. So share the feeling: "I want to talk about my feelings for you"; "I desire you"; "I'd like you to become an even bigger part of my life"—whatever. You're sharing a feeling, so you can't be wrong.

If your friend says "Great, let's go," talk about what this means to each of you. That may be the less romantic way to go, but it's crucial if you want to maintain your friendship and avoid misunderstandings.

If he or she is not interested in acting on your feelings, you need to accept that. In this case, make it clear that things can go on as they were; ask if anything else needs to be said, and then drop it. The following week ask if there's any unfinished business left over from the conversation. If there is, deal with it; if not, let it go.

328. How do I tell someone I'm interesting in necking (and if that works out, perhaps a bit more) but not in making love?

First, *you* have to accept your right to set such limits; and the fact that this is not a terrible burden to your partner.

Our society is kind of quirky about this; it must be teenage boys who have successfully created the myth that once two people go so far, they have to go "all the way." It's as if light kissing and hugging are stops on a local train, but anything more puts you on an express train that can't stop until intercourse.

Real lovers appreciate necking and other such things for what they are, not merely as "foreplay." It's considerate to announce your limits ahead of time so a prospective partner can decide if he or she is interested. How do you do this? Warmly take the person's hand and suggest that you're not ready to think about anything serious like sex but that you would enjoy a few quiet moments to kiss and hug.

329. This friend I've known for years turns out to be gay! When he said he was interested in me, I felt sick. What right does he have coming on to me like that?

Whoa! The fact that this person is gay seems to have suddenly distorted your judgment. He's still the friend you've always admired; he's merely stated that he's interested in you in a new way.

This is the saddest part about coming out of the closet—the nongay people suddenly change but believe it's the gay one who's different. Perhaps you feel betrayed about having been misled for years. Your response illustrates why your friend did so.

The proper response to someone's interest that you do not wish to return is either to pretend you aren't aware of it or to say "no thank you." Neither should be done with a sneer. By the way, this man's interest in you is no reason to question your masculinity. Like many women, many gay men like manly guys, too.

330. This woman at work recently came out as a lesbian. What should I do—congratulate her? Tell her it's okay with me? Wait for her to bring it up?

You don't need to tell her it's okay with you. She'll know that you're okay about it by the way you treat her. If this woman is like most gay people, she'll be perfectly satisfied to have her homosexuality ignored. If you're close enough friends to say you admire her courage for coming out in a homophobic world, do so. If not, just let her be who she is, and be her friend if you like. That's all that most people want from each other.

331. Don't you think it's rude for someone to use drugs during sex?

It depends on how it's done and with what results. Perhaps your objections are pragmatic. A person using drugs may be less than totally present. While some drugs increase body awareness, others decrease it. There are those who become less responsive while high and those who become so responsive that they neglect the needs of their partners.

On the other hand, objections are frequently emotional. Sometimes partners feel left out or "square." And although people often use drugs simply to enhance a sexual experience, their partners often decide there are different reasons: "If she loved me she wouldn't get high"; or "You're using drugs just to escape from me and our lovemaking."

Discuss these conflicts *out* of bed, when it's easier to see this as a simple policy discussion and it's easier to feel like a team.

332. Ouch! How do you get a woman to use less teeth when giving you oral sex?

This is a common question for which there is no perfect answer. Part of the problem is that the easiest ways to provide "less teeth" also give you less of what makes oral sex so enjoyable.

Still, a warm smile and "That'd be even better with less teeth" is usually the first step.

If your sexual relationship is comfortable and playful, just tell your partner the problem and encourage her to try several different techniques. Use her fingers or a banana to illustrate what you like; you can even share X-rated videos for ideas and examples.

The problem is trickier in a less relaxed relationship. Many women feel defensive if they feel their oral techniques are under attack. They may also feel less inclined to experiment. Any approach requires patience, encouragement, and appreciation.

333. Oops! I called someone the wrong name during lovemaking. What should I do?

Author Philip Nobile, among others, suggests that everyone call their lovers "Darling" or "Honey" to avoid just such a moment.

For now, all you can do is apologize. (If you haven't already done that, you have an even bigger problem.) Do *not* make excuses, which will only get you in more trouble. Remember, a closed mouth gathers no feet.

Do something quietly intimate for or with this partner, and in the future, refer to it occasionally as "our special thing." Time, and your subsequent treatment of your partner, will determine the rest.

334. My partner yells out to Jesus almost every time we make love. How can I put an end to this?

Some say that atheists have trouble with sex because they have no one to call to during orgasm. Somehow, "Life energy!" or "Universal truth!" just do not have the same ring as "Oh God! Oh God!"

I'm assuming you aren't uncomfortable with displays of passion, you just dislike your partner bringing a certain religious flavor into your bed. If the passion is the problem, I urge professional counseling. Let's assume, however, that it isn't.

Whatever your problem with your partner's expressions of passion, you need to discuss it honestly—as *your* issue, not your partner's. This will eliminate defensiveness and locate responsibility for the problem where it lies—with you.

As we near orgasm, we literally lose control over our voices, along with the rest of our physical selves. This is one of the best parts of sex. At climax, our bodies want to roar, shake, bite, scratch, and claw. Since none of these is "polite," many of us settle for varying sizes of moans. Some partners even inhibit that. Be glad yours doesn't.

335. I'm embarrassed by sounds coming from my vagina when I make love. What causes this? How should I handle it?

During sex, a thrusting penis (or other object) can push air into the vagina, which expands as you become aroused. When the penis withdraws during or after lovemaking, the air escapes with a whoosh.

Since the angle and fit of the vagina change with different positions, you can experiment to see which ones reduce the sounds. If you discuss your discomfort with your partner, you may learn to laugh at the sounds. Better yet, ignore them. Why judge what your body does while experiencing pleasure?

336. I'm delighted with my new sexual relationship, but for now, I don't want anyone to know about it. How do I tell my partner about my wishes?

Past third grade, I don't think you can get away with "This is so special, let's just keep it a secret." You need to tell your new partner exactly why you desire secrecy. And if you're serious, you'd better do it soon. Stalling this conversation for fear that it will damage the relationship is short-sighted, impractical, and unfair.

On the other hand, it's reasonable to expect some discretion from people, including our lovers. Start the conversation by mentioning that "Although it's been difficult, I haven't discussed the big news with anyone in my life, nor will I. What about you?"

337. My boyfriend and I are on the verge of splitting up. How do we remain friends even though I don't want to be lovers anymore?

Call me old-fashioned, but I believe in ending relationships Montana-style. That's where the other person moves to Montana. For years, I've watched my patients swear that they will be friends with their future ex-spouses. I support them as best I can, even though this never seems like a practical idea. It rarely works out, even in California.

One of the reasons people attempt to stay friends, I believe, is to cushion the pain of separation. While the idea does provide comfort during the early, most wrenching parts of the separation, it usually only postpones the final stages. What people gain in illusory comfort they lose in the extra time it takes to get finished and move on.

How can you best attempt to remain friends? Agree on strict boundaries: hugging but no kissing, lunch but not dinner, whatever. Both people need to take 100 percent responsibility for keeping such agreements, which can be difficult.

338. Periodically I end up in bed with a really selfish lover. How should I handle this?

You can spot selfish lovers when they tell you their favorite kind of oral sex is 68: "You do me now," they say, "and I'll catch you later."

Selfish lovers are people who are far less interested in your pleasure than in their own. They come in both sexes and in many varieties.

These include the person who reaches the peak of arousal (and self-absorption) almost immediately; the person who doesn't like to move around very much; the person who enthusiastically encourages you to do "a little more, yes, just a little more, yes!" for thirty or forty minutes; the person who forgets you exist the second after his or her orgasm; and so on.

You can go along with a selfish lover and take what comes your way; you can encourage a selfish lover over and over to touch you this way or that; or you can confront a selfish lover and explain that even though you enjoy the sex, it's just too frustrating and it needs to be different. Some selfish lovers will respond. Others will ask what's wrong with *you*. That's the tip-off to head for the door.

339. How long should you wait before dating an ex-lover's best friend?

It depends on the kind of relationship you want with your ex-lover and what kind this friend wants with your ex.

In general, I think it's self-destructive to go immediately from one relationship to the next. We leave the past unprocessed, we increase our vulnerability to making mistakes, and we don't learn. Endings require various kinds of emotional processing, such as anger and grieving, before we are emotionally free to start new beginnings.

You'll be ready when:

• You don't think of a new partner as "Jane's (or John's) friend" but as your friend
• You're not afraid of your ex getting back at one or both of you
• You can stop looking at your ex, wondering what he thinks about you and about your new companion
• You've thought over the possible implications; e.g., testing for AIDS
• You're ready to discuss exactly what the new relationship means, which may be different to you than to her/him, and
• You don't see this new relationship as the solution to all your problems. After all, no relationship is.

340. How do you tell someone you have herpes and still get them to make love with you? When should you do it?

Let's modify the first question: How do you tell someone you have herpes? After all, being ethical trumps getting laid.

The way to tell is to tell. Unless the other person has herpes, you'll have to explain what that means: that you have periodic outbreaks; that your body usually signals you right before each one; that you're contagious for four to eight days before, during, and after an outbreak; and that, with a condom, sex is pretty safe the rest of the time.

You simply have no right to lie to prevent someone from being scared and running away. If you do tell and your partner doesn't run away, you can relax, knowing you've done the right thing and that you now have nothing to hide.

I believe that people are genuinely touched when someone reaches out and reveals they have herpes. Doing so in the earliest part of a would-be sexual relationship—say, before your second "necking" session—shows you are an honest, caring person, just the kind of sexual partner people like.

341. Is it rude to ask a new partner about an AIDS test?

No, assuming you're willing to discuss your own as well. Do it as a teammate, not as an adversary.

Anyone who is offended by a gently worded inquiry about AIDS is either immature or out of touch with reality. You're better off without such a partner.

342. This girl I really like is offended by something I suggested we do (we started making love about two weeks ago). I don't mind not doing it, but now she says we're through. Why couldn't she just say no instead of making such a big deal? How do I get her back?

These are two different questions.

Your suggestion may have reminded her of a painful old situation. Or she may have thought it was a steppingstone to something really offbeat, which she couldn't handle. Or she may have felt you were suggesting she is a certain kind of person, which she found insulting.

Have you told her you want to continue seeing her and that your sexual suggestion was, to you, a minor request? Have you asked her why she reacted as she did? If you have, and you're still estranged, there's probably nothing you can do to get her back. At least you discovered her way of dealing with emotions before you became more involved.

18

Communication

Love is just sex misspelled.

—Harlan Ellison

343. Why do some people have so much trouble talking about sex?

Partly because they were raised in homes in which sex was considered bad, something not to be discussed, and something no one was supposed to be interested in.

A second reason is that talking about sex requires us to admit that we're thinking about and having it. It also requires us to acknowledge that we're doing it because we enjoy it—that we're making love instead of doing something more "productive," like earning money, cleaning the house, or watching "Wheel of Fortune."

Finally, many people are afraid of what they would actually say. If I speak frankly, will my partner turn off? Think I'm weird? Leave me? For the frightened, insecure, or guilt-ridden, saying little or nothing feels safer than saying too much.

344. Aren't there ways of communicating about sex besides talking?

Definitely. Some people think buying a Porsche is one such form of nonverbal sexual communication.

There's also the power of touch: soft, seductive, shy, reassuring, or urgent. And there are so many places to touch, as varied as hair, face, nipples, navel, and toes. You can also place your hand on your mate's, or your mate's on yours, and gently demonstrate what you like first-hand.

Then there are the twice-removed, coded forms of sexual communication, like what you wear when a mate comes home, or the invitation to shower together, or your effort to clean up the bedroom for no obvious reason.

Touch and symbolic communication work fine as long as both partners understand the same code. Words can be considered a last resort—ideally, a dependable one—when other languages don't work. If this happens, don't blame each other. Afterwards, explore the breakdown and attempt to standardize your special secret codes one more time.

345. Shouldn't sex be natural and spontaneous, making all this "communication" unnecessary?

Between the influence of the Church, the government, the mass media, and capitalism, sex in America stopped being natural and spontaneous long ago—if, indeed, it ever was. It will never be natural and spontaneous again.

These days, we are all bombarded with repetitive images of how sex should be. Because we work so hard to create experiences that match those images, it's hard to stay in the present and create sex spontaneously, moment by moment.

Making babies can still be natural; it doesn't require any thought or understanding. Sex with other, specifically modern, goals such as intimacy or pleasure requires more than genitals—it requires two minds connected to each other in a meaningful way. We can either criticize the fact that this requires communication, or treat it as an opportunity and enjoy the challenge.

346. Sexually, what should we actually communicate about?

Sexual conversation typically falls into three main categories:

1. Feelings: These include anxiety, anger, and delight
2. Desires: These include what I want (slower, harder) and what I don't want (no fingernails, please)
3. Conditions: These include things about me (I need to brush my teeth first); about you (I need you to look at me); and about our environment (I need more privacy, less light, a cleaner bed)

Don't worry, you don't need to know which category you're communicating in. Just do it.

347. I try to talk to my partner about sex, but then I'm criticized for being "unromantic." What should I do?

Let's hope you're not discussing your sexual relationship during reruns of "I Love Lucy."

For some people, *any* clear communication about sex is uncomfortable and therefore unromantic. You need to ask how—if at all—your partner is willing to talk about sex with you. If the answer is "not at all," you know where you stand, and you can act accordingly. A single person might head for the door, while a coupled person might head (hopefully, with partner) to a therapist.

On the other hand, there may be ways your partner enjoys communicating about sex, and you simply need to discover them. Some people like a more clinical language than others, while some like a more silly, friendly language.

Perhaps your partner feels you're constantly critiquing your lovemaking. Or maybe your partner feels pressured to change and has learned that "communication" means instruction, not dialogue. Solution? Naturally, communicate: Ask your partner what he or she wants to do.

348. I don't like talking about sex. Shouldn't my partner just know what I like?

Of course—if your partner is a protégé of Kreskin the mind reader. If not, how should your partner "just know?" Many people assume that being in love releases a special ESP hormone; others like to think their partner is a sex expert. Both are ways of avoiding taking responsibility for our sexual experiences.

Unless you want to be treated like part of a very large group ("most men"; "most women;" "people of that age"), you need to tell your partner enough about you so that you can be touched and made love with as a unique individual.

349. Telling my partner what I like in sex takes the fun out of it. What should I do?

This reminds me of those bumper stickers that say "If you think education is expensive, try ignorance."

If you think telling your partner about your needs takes the fun out of sex, try *not* telling your partner. You'll be surprised at how much *less* fun that is.

Sex can be full of surprises even if you talk about your likes and dislikes. If straight talk just doesn't work for you, try developing a private language with pet names for sexual acts and for each other's body parts.

350. How do you get someone to talk about their feelings after sex?

Cartoonist Nicole Hollander says her Spirit Guide is quite clear about this: In June 1997 men will begin talking about their feelings; within minutes, women all over America will be sorry.

The big question here, I think, is why you want a partner to discuss his or her feelings after sex. There are plenty of good reasons, such as the desire for closeness, confusion about a partner's response, or particular delight or dismay about what has occurred.

If, on the other hand, you simply need reassurance after every lovemaking occasion, I can understand a partner becoming uncooperative. Such serious insecurity is not your partner's problem. It is best handled by a mental health professional.

Are there other ways that you could get what you want without your partner having to talk about it? More hugs, for example, or face caresses, or squeezing a fresh glass of juice might be a solution that works for both of you. What exactly do you want?

351. During sex I frequently want to say "I love you," but I've learned that this can be a big mistake with some partners. How do I deal with my frustration about not being able to say what I feel?

Your sense of inhibition and isolation is one of the unfortunate, inevitable aspects of casual sex. It's very adult of you to recognize this and want to accept it.

Many people have extremely powerful, meaningful sexual experiences with casual partners. "I love you" simply does not mean, in such situations, what it does in a committed relationship.

What we really want to exclaim, as part of these spiritual moments, is, "I love me" or "I love our moment together" or "I love my connection to the universe." It's wonderful to feel this way. But such phrases don't quite roll off the tongue, and these sentiments are foreign to our culture's consciousness.

Expressing an ecstatic state with mundane words cannot be done accurately. But some partners want to take such words literally upon returning to the mundane world, which has caused problems since the beginning of time. You are quite right to discipline yourself away from any words that are likely to be misinterpreted.

Saying "I love you" to some casual lovers during sex is like throwing gasoline on a fire. You can't predict or control how big the response will be, and you can't undo it if you don't like the results. Think about channeling some of your passion in other directions, such as writing or painting your feelings and experiences. Tell a friend. Eat a few cookies and ponder the essential unfairness of existence. Learn to say "I love *this*."

352. Should lovers keep sexual secrets? If so, what kind? When and how should we share them?

Virtually everyone keeps sexual secrets—that is, withholds relevant sexual information from his or her partner(s). The most common ones are: how I like to be touched; the fact that I masturbate; how my body really responds to sex; something important that happened in my past.

Unfortunately, withholding such information leads to isolation, resentment, and sexual dissatisfaction. It also discourages the healing of painful past experiences.

This is not to say that every single secret should be shared. Sometimes partners clearly tell us that they don't want to know certain things. Some reasons to share are destructive: to punish a partner, to test a relationship, or to get rid of guilt without intending to change.

On the other hand, there are many good reasons to share: to increase closeness, improve sexual satisfaction, end the need for additional lies, and help heal painful past experiences.

For more on this subject, see my book *Your Sexual Secrets: When to Keep Them, How to Share Them.*

19

Sex Roles

In our civilization, men are afraid that they will not be men enough; women are afraid that they might be considered only women.

—Theodor Reik

353. What is meant by the term *sex roles*?

Sex roles are the sum of behavior, feelings, and thoughts that society attributes to human beings based on their gender. Americans used to do that with race, ethnic background, and age; while people are becoming more sophisticated about these, many still think that girl humans should want to be nurses while boy humans should want to be doctors.

In the area of sexuality, sex roles dictate that men are supposed to initiate sex, desire it more frequently, and be more aggressive during it; women are supposed to be more passive, know less about it, want it less, and not be too lusty. In real life, these sexual traits are distributed about evenly between men and women.

354. Doesn't nature divide the world into male and female?

Of course. Nature programs animals and plants into several specific activities based on their gender. Most of what animals do, however, is *not* gender-based.

Humans are like animals and also different from them. We can learn, express our individuality, and acknowledge our biology without worshiping it as inevitable destiny. We can be male or female and make our own unique decisions at the same time. This is part of what makes humans special.

355. Doesn't religion divide the world into male and female? There must be a reason.

Today's major religions evolved during a time when people were scarce and reproducing was considered a sacred duty. Thus, early religious doctrine divided life's responsibilities according to whether or not someone could carry a child—that is, according to gender.

Today we have a different view. Most people believe they can honor God in ways that don't involve having children. And many want more out of their lives and relationships than children, no matter how satisfying they are.

Today's religions divide the world according to gender partly because of tradition. They also do it because the interpretation of ideoloy and doctrine belongs exclusively to one (the male) gender. Consciously or not, this powerful group frequently favors its own sex when writing canonical policy.

356. Boys and girls relate differently to sex. If this isn't just natural, how do you explain it?

Part of the difference we observe is natural. It results from real gender differences such as pregnancy, menstruation, hormones, and the earlier and shorter puberty of girls.

Biology, however, need not be reinforced by culture; all

societies take steps to soften various biological realities. We recognize the disadvantage that frailty gives the elderly in crowds, for example, and so we make special arrangements for them in buses and theaters.

Besides, there are no biological facts to support many common social ideas, including: boys need sex more than girls; boys cannot control themselves sexually as well as girls can; and girls are more emotional than boys.

The many cultural, nonbiological reasons that boys and girls relate to sex differently include:

• Different parental messages about the purpose of sex
• Different social messages about the value of the male and female body
• Different limits on the permission to enjoy sex
• The responsibility put on girls to control male sexuality, and
• The contrasting messages society gives about permanent relationships: For girls they are something to look forward to; for boys they are the inevitable penalty of growing up, and the price paid for sex.

357. Why complain about sex roles—after all, men and women do relate to sex differently, don't they?

Yes and no.

For one thing, sex roles trivialize the *similarities* between men and women, such as the desire for touching. For another, sex roles ignore the basic fact that women can be very different from one another, just as men can be very different from one another. So dividing the world according to who has a penis and who has a vagina really distorts things.

See below for more good reasons to complain about sex roles.

358. How do sex roles affect intimacy and pleasure?

Think about how you create sexual satisfaction. Unfortunately, sex roles block us from doing just these things, by preventing communication; encouraging a sense of powerlessness; creating an air of judgment and performance anxiety; isolating us from one another; and discouraging us from being ourselves. Intimacy and pleasure become low priorities when our pride and self-esteem are on the line.

For example, we're told that a "real man" initiates sex, is a sex expert, and doesn't discuss his feelings. A "real woman" is responsive but not too enthusiastic, doesn't give her partner "too much" information about her past or her desires, and makes her partner feel adequate. Such rules are the basis of "normal" sexual behavior—and sexual frustration.

Many people, I believe, feel resentful about the roles they get stuck with simply because they were born male or female. As this resentment builds, it undermines sexual desire, spontaneity, and intimacy.

359. All my life I've been told about the importance of being a "lady." How are you supposed to have sex in a ladylike way?

How you're *supposed* to do it is by staying in control of yourself; not talking about it before, during, or after; not letting your body express itself by sweating, moaning, or clutching; and, most of all, by not enjoying it "too much." This is *not* a formula for sexual pleasure or intimacy, which women have been typically discouraged from expecting.

This dreadful ideal was taken to its extreme in England a century ago. Expecting one's wife to have sex was considered unrealistic, almost brutish, and the majority of respectable London husbands visited prostitutes regularly. We are mostly beyond such bizarre ideas about sex, although women still get double messages about whether or not having and enjoying sex is okay for them.

In reality, you need to choose: being a "lady" during sex or being sexually satisfied. Note that men don't have to make a similar choice; they can get sweaty and yell during sex, then put their clothes on and retain their self-respect. I urge you to do the same; you simply need a more down-to-earth ideal of acceptable female behavior. Try "woman" instead of "lady."

360. When women complain about sex, why don't they at least appreciate that they don't have performance anxiety like men?

Unfortunately, this isn't true; women as well as men feel anxious during sex about "performing" well. This anxiety is inevitable because of our culture's rigid ideals about what sex is supposed to be like.

Typically, men are anxious about getting erect quickly enough, delaying ejaculation long enough, and giving their partner a big enough orgasm quickly and without instruction.

Women have their version of this anxiety too. They feel pressured to arouse a man, get him erect, and give him an orgasm—preferably, the biggest one he's ever had. And they feel pressure to lubricate rapidly, be very excited, and have their own orgasm as soon as possible.

361. Is it still true that when spouses disagree on sexual frequency, it's always the man who wants more?

"Still?" It wasn't necessarily that way in the past. It has always been more difficult to accurately assess women's sexual interest than men's. That's because we describe women's sex drive with words like "frigid", "slut", and "nympho." We can't expect to know the truth about something we fear and distrust in this way.

As women are increasingly given permission to express their true sexuality, their grievances about unfulfilled desire are finally being voiced and heard. That explains why their level of dissatisfaction seems to be increasing.

The range of sexual desire is far wider among men as a group, and among women as a group, than it is between men and women. In my clinical experience with couples' desire conflicts, each gender is the high-desire partner about half the time.

362. Almost every woman I sleep with seems embarrassed or self-conscious about her body during sex. Is this normal? What can I do about it?

Unfortunately, this is all too common. To hear most

women talk, you'd think that breasts only come in two sizes: too big and too small. This self-criticism is brought to you courtesy of our capitalist economy, which thrives on making people feel sexually inadequate—and therefore eager to purchase whatever new product promises to make them sexually adequate.

In this larger sense, there's very little you can do. On a personal level, you can simply let your partners know what you appreciate about their bodies, both verbally and by touch. You can also gently interrupt repetitive self-criticism; many women don't know just how much of it they do, nor how unpleasant it is to listen to. On the other hand, be sure to stay out of the amateur therapist trap. Even professionals take Saturday night off.

By the way, the preceding assumes that you're not doing anything to make women uncomfortable about their bodies, like comparing them to movie stars or ogling women on the street when you're out on a date.

363. I get uncomfortable when my partner fingers his nipples during sex. How do I get him to make love like more of a man?

The more important question is why you'd want to. Needing to "act like a man" can be confining, erotically deadening, and boring for all concerned. Once we have to behave according to certain standards, we start monitoring our sexual responses, becoming spectators instead of participants.

Besides, what does "acting like a man" mean? To various men, that could eliminate such enjoyable forms of expression as moaning with pleasure; touching one's own penis; enjoying being dominated; and to some, even cuddling or kissing.

Think about the famous matador confronted by a neighbor who saw him washing dishes in a frilly apron. "I'm surprised to see you doing something so unmanly!" said the neighbor. "Unmanly?" replied the matador with a powerful confidence. "Hah! I know I am a man," he said. "And so *everything* I do is manly."

364. Shouldn't a woman have sex whenever her husband wants it? We men go to work whether we want to or not.

Traditionally, many men have expected their wives to be uninterested in sex but obediently available nevertheless. Is this really the level you want your sexual relationship on—obligation? Such an approach guarantees resentment on both sides, whether it is expressed outwardly or not. It also makes your wife an opponent rather than a partner.

When one spouse wants sex far less frequently than the other, the issue is often not sex at all. Power, anger, money, and the division of labor are just some of the things that can be involved. I urge you and your mate to honestly discuss your sexual interest—perhaps with the help of a professional—and to really listen, rather than judge.

With all of the unpleasant chores adult life demands, I don't see the point of making sex one too. When a woman doesn't want sex, she may be interested in sharing something else— some hugs, a cup of coffee, a game of Scrabble. The answer to your question, ultimately, depends on your vision of what a relationship is about.

By the way, should a man have sex every time his wife wants it?

365. I'm confused. Do women like to be dominated in bed or do they want sexual equality?

"Women," you know, are a very diverse group with differing needs and interests. Your best bet is finding out what your particular partner wants.

Some women—like some men—like to be dominated in bed *occasionally*. But that doesn't mean they want this all the time. Besides, "dominator" and "dominated" are roles that people agree to play out together. The question of equality doesn't refer to the existence of those roles but rather to the satisfaction and respect each person is entitled to *regardless* of the sexual role chosen.

There's a big difference between wanting to enjoy being dominated in bed and being told you have no right to expect enjoyment because you like being dominated. People want equality regardless of their preference; sexual satisfaction demands it.

366. Is it true that women give sex for love and men give love for sex?

It used to be the case far more than it is now. That's because women used to bargain for love and men for sex; now, men admit their interest in love and women their interest in sex more openly.

Traditionally, love for women meant financial security. That is, sex was a commodity they could trade for a man's pledge of economic support. Now that many women are financially self-sufficient, they have less need to barter sex for the promise of money.

There's still some truth to the old cliché, however. Women are still taught to withold sex as part of their husband-selection strategy. And men are still taught that falling in love is the beginning of the end of their freedom and youth.

What's true today is that most people want both love and sex. Sadly, many settle for one or the other.

20

Monogamy and Affairs

As we all know from witnessing the consuming jealousy of husbands who are never faithful, people do not confine themselves to the emotions to which they are entitled.

—Quentin Crisp

367. What is monogamy?

"When two people are under the influence of the most violent, most insane, most delusive, and most transient of passions, they are required to swear that they will remain in that excited, abnormal, and exhausting condition until death do them part." That's how George Bernard Shaw described it.

Literally, *monogamy* means being married to one person for your entire life. People usually use it to mean an agreement of sexual exclusivity in a current relationship.

368. Is monogamy possible?

It is certainly more difficult than it has ever been (and that's saying quite a bit).

When most people had the courtesy to die at the age of thirty-five, lifelong monogamy was a far simpler commitment than it is now, when people routinely live to eighty. What's more, there is less social support for marriage now than ever before. To take just one example, less than 25 percent of the sex shown or implied on television is between married couples.

Mixed-gender work environments also make monogamy difficult, particularly since work is where most of us are at our most attractive. And after spending the bulk of their waking time working, rearing children, and keeping house, most people have very little time or energy left over to enhance their marriages.

"Even in civilized mankind," however, "faint traces of monogamous instinct can be perceived," said Bertrand Russell. As several American couples can attest, monogamy is possible. Certainly, it takes something special; too bad no one is sure what it is. Maybe Robert Mitchum had it right. He attributed his forty-two-year-long marriage to his lack of imagination.

369. What exactly is "being faithful?"

Every couple defines this differently. For some it requires exclusivity only in intercourse; for others, in all sexual activity; for still others, in emotional as well as physical involvement. Some people even define "being faithful" as meaning no sexual *fantasies* about anyone else. For them, thinking is the same as doing.

None of these definitions is right or wrong, because the concept is simply a way of defining relationship agreements. Only when people differ on the definition, or have trouble living up to their agreements, is the definition important.

In the days when relationships were mostly about property and child rearing, fidelity was defined primarily as sexual. Now that we also want intimacy from relationships, many people believe that fidelity has an emotional component as well.

Of course, some people define fidelity as being truly sorry when they are unfaithful. As Joyce Cary once wrote, "Sara could commit adultery at one end and weep for her sins at the other, and enjoy both operations at once."

370. Why is monogamy so important to some people?

For various people it is important because of their fear of abandonment; their low self-image, which makes comparing oneself to others painful; or their desire that someone "prove" his or her commitment.

In our society, however, jealousy and the need for monogamy run deeper than individual psychology. They are firmly rooted in our definitions of relationship and our concept of private property. In America we say that jealousy between lovers is "normal," and indeed it seems so.

But people in faraway places or other times would strongly disagree. While the desire to be loved and connected to others is a deep human need, the desire to possess another or to be exclusive with another is something that is learned, not something we are born with.

And that's one reason why, as writer Mignon McLaughlin put it, "No one has ever loved anyone the way everyone wants to be loved."

371. Why is monogamy so much harder for men than for women?

To be a bit more accurate, monogamy is harder for many men than it is for many women. That said, how to explain it?

The evolutionary approach says that men try to spread their sperm all over the place to maximize their immortality, while women try to keep a lid on things because they have to take care of the results of sex.

The psychoanalysts say that boys, to become men, have to unlearn their earliest attachment (to mother), while girls, to become women, simply reinforce the attachment. This makes men wanderers and rejectors, and makes women stayers and hangers-on.

I prefer the social explanation. What fantasy is a male

taught to have his whole life? Pursuing, scoring with, and then eluding as many women as possible. What is the classic female fantasy from girlhood? Finding, capturing, and settling down with Mr. Right.

Monogamy, then, is the fulfillment of the lifelong female goal and the defeat of the most powerful male fantasy. It's not surprising that men talk about marriage as "surrender" and tell newly engaged men that "we all have to go sometime." Women learn to anticipate monogamy, while men learn to fear and resent it.

372. We plan to marry sometime next year. How do I convince my sweetheart that we should be faithful to each other now?

This sure looks like a disaster in the making. If you two can't agree on how to live your lives now, what will make it any easier after you marry?

There is validity to what each of you wants. The conflict is crucial; how you settle it will be a model for how you handle other conflicts that lie ahead. Until you settle this issue, I encourage you to put the marriage on hold.

The most you can do is tell your mate how much this particular issue means to you, and exactly why. Talk about how you feel, not about your mate's intentions. You should also try to understand his or her position in as much detail as possible. Then the two of you should should discuss the meaning of this conflict, your respective willingness to insist on something the other rejects, and what this suggests about the future.

How do you convince someone to be exclusive? You can't. An ultimatum may work, but if you resort to one, you'll probably regret it—whether it works or not.

373. I told my fiancé that if he's still interested in other women, he can't really love me. Don't you agree?

Fairy tales and soap operas tell us that true love inevitably leads to monogamy. Real life suggests otherwise.

Exclusive interest may be your definition of "real" love, but this is a belief, not a fact. The important issue is whether you and your mate can agree on this or some other belief about love. If you can't, the relationship is headed for trouble.

"Interest" covers a lot of territory, from fantasizing to looking to flirting to hungering to making love. Particularly in our oversexualized culture, demanding that someone have no sexual interest in others whatsoever is unrealistic and self-destructive. Wanting sexually exclusive behavior is a more realistic demand, albeit a difficult one for many to comply with.

Author Hugh Prather once said he was more interested in how someone treated him than in whether or not someone "really" loved him. If you and your fiancé can agree on how you plan to treat each other, call that "love" and consider yourself ahead of the game. I urge you to come to an understanding about this complex subject *before* you get married.

374. Why do people have affairs?

People get involved in affairs for a variety of reasons: for sex; for understanding or companionship; to feel important; to express anger; and to seize power in their lives or relationships.

People often begin an affair for one reason and continue for quite another. For that matter, many people are never really sure why they begin or stay in an affair.

It's too simple to say that people get into affairs because they don't love their spouses enough or because they lack self-control. It's much more complicated than that. Affairs fill a need for those involved, often one they do not recognize or take seriously enough.

375. Every magazine and television show talks about affairs, but *everyone* can't be doing it. Just how common are affairs?

Well, everyone's not doing it, but a lot of people sure are. It's impossible to get an exact figure, because many citizens refuse to answer sex surveys or they lie when answering them.

While recent research by various popular magazines, Shere Hite, and the Kinsey Institute has generated a range of numbers, most surveys consistently point to more than 50 percent of all marriages experiencing at least one affair at some time.

The fact that everyone talks about affairs indicates a wide interest in the subject, suggesting that many people do, have done, or will do it. But this is by no means a modern phenomenon. Roman men, when returning home from traveling nineteen centuries ago, would send someone ahead to let their wives know, so as not to catch them with other men.

376. What should I do if I suspect my partner is having an affair? Everyone gives me different advice.

Why are you discussing this with everyone? That in itself reflects a breakdown of marital communication.

I strongly believe you should discuss your suspicions with your mate. Don't do this in a screaming, accusatory way; rather, raise the issue as a problem that the partnership needs to deal with. Do not try to test or trap your spouse. Present the facts as you see them: not as damning evidence but as information that needs to be explained.

At some point, describe exactly what marital/sexual agreements you want both of you to keep and ask if your partner has a commitment to these. "Trying" is not good enough; either someone is committed or not.

If your partner's explanation of his or her behavior is plausible, and if he or she desires the same agreements you do, drop the suspicions. If not, marital counseling is probably indicated. Either way, however, don't make a drama out of a situation.

377. I recently ended an affair that I wish I'd never started. Should I tell my spouse about it?

The answer lies in another question: why tell? Several common reasons are bad ones: to get rid of guilt, to punish a partner, and to manipulate someone into leaving you.

On the other hand, there are good reasons for telling a partner: to heal the wounds and self-doubts that a partner has suffered because of your denial; to explore the lessons learned about the relationship; to increase intimacy; and to discuss safe-sex implications.

You must examine your motives for wanting to tell your

partner. How do you think he or she will respond? How will your relationship progress from that point? Will you be glad you told? Will your mate?

378. I had a short affair and recently stopped. Do you think I've ruined my marriage?

Marriages are rarely ruined or ended by affairs, particularly brief ones. Rather, the damage is usually done by the problems that lead people to have affairs. I urge you to address those, with or without your spouse, as soon as possible.

The affair itself leaves you with three things to deal with. First, is your mate likely to find out about it? If so, you're better off telling him or her about it yourself. Second, how are you going to deal with any guilt you feel? And third, how are you going to grieve the loss of an important person or relationship in your life—without turning to your spouse for sympathy?

Handling these three issues along with your marital problems will help minimize the affair's impact on your marriage.

379. Last year my wife told me about an affair she had recently ended. I believe that it's over, but I still think about it, which kills my interest in sex. What should I do?

It sounds as if you haven't forgiven your spouse. After all, suffering is a form of nostalgia. If you feel partly responsible for "causing" the affair, you clearly haven't forgiven yourself, either.

What do you want? Your partner can promise she won't do it again, but there are no guarantees; a relationship requires trust. If you still feel wronged, tell your partner what you need. If she really wants to put this behind her, she'll respond. But don't attack her, renewing the conflict. Work together creatively to figure out what's needed to finish healing you and the relationship.

If you insist on tormenting yourself or your partner, marital and/or individual therapy is called for.

380. I'm very attracted to someone in my office. I recently found out

this person feels the same way. How do I prevent myself from having an extramarital affair?

Mostly by deciding you won't. It's like being on a diet. The single most important step is not being negotiable; i.e., "really" wanting something is not a good enough reason to have it. With this person, you must simply decide that your desire will not be a factor in your decision-making.

Just as the smart dieter stays out of bakeries, you must monitor your own vulnerabilities. Don't work together alone at night. Don't wear your sexiest clothes to work. Don't buy the perfect little thing for your friend when you see it. You get the idea.

At the same time, do mourn the loss of possibility. Do cry, rage, or otherwise express yourself—away from this person— and deal seriously with the unfairness of life. Then you'll be in a position to examine what you're not getting from your marriage, and take steps to create it.

381. How do you prevent a spouse from having an affair?

You don't. Your spouse will make that choice him- or herself. All you can do is make sure you have agreed to the same marital contract. How? Simply ask. If you like, you can remind your spouse how much this contract means to you and explain that you'd consider it a profound violation if he or she broke it.

Preventing your spouse's affair is, thankfully, not your job. If you have evidence of an affair, share it with your spouse. If not, enjoy your marriage—the only protection from affairs there is.

382. Please settle a disagreement. I see this friend occasionally. If we haven't actually made love, should it be considered an affair?

There's no right or wrong here; any satisfactory answer must come from inside the relationship, not outside. Intercourse is not so much a *definition* of an affair as a symbol of how one feels. So whatever it is *about* lovemaking that you've agreed is outside your marriage, that's the quality that determines if you have to forgo a given activity. For various marriages, that includes sexual intimacy, emotional closeness, intense pleasure, commitment, and sharing special things.

Other ways to know if this relationship is prohibited under your marriage's "affair" clause are whether or not you want to introduce your friend to your spouse and whether or not you feel comfortable hugging and kissing your spouse in front of your friend.

Virtually anything can be a form of infidelity, even holding hands. Adults know there are many ways to make love. Intercourse is only one.

383. I think my husband is having an affair—with another man! What does this mean? What should I do?

First, ask your husband what's going on. It could be a misunderstanding.

Your husband is the only person who can tell you what it means. Ask him, and listen. Although your anger, sadness, and other feelings are valid, try to deal with them separately from the process of understanding him.

Your husband may be gay or bisexual (or straight and experimenting). He may not even know what he is at this point. Only after many long conversations should you attempt to make decisions about your marriage. You may want him to choose between you and his male lover. You may decide to accept your husband's male partner as long as he sees no other women. Other couples develop other arrangements.

This sort of thing is far more common than most people think. The best book on the subject is *When Husbands Come Out of the Closet*, by Jean Gochros.

384. We've both agreed to be exclusive with each other, but how do we keep our sex life from getting dull?

Keeping an exclusive sexual relationship fresh is a lifelong process. It is an opportunity, not a problem, and it must be a project of the partnership, rather than one partner.

Various couples find it helpful to share fantasies; read sexy stories together; and make dates for sex, encouraging each other's anticipation. Some couples even enjoy going to the same nightclub separately, flirting with others, and then "meeting" each other and going home together.

Ultimately, attitude is the most important ingredient. The key is to approach sexuality as an unlimited vista, in which two people can invent, do, and enjoy anything that comes to mind or body.

385. I recently heard that even married couples should think about safe sex. Why?

Most married people think their partners are monogamous. Surveys and marriage counselors make it clear, however, that many aren't. If your spouse is having unsafe sex with someone else, sex with that spouse is not completely safe.

Some researchers speculate, in fact, that married couples are among the highest risk groups for AIDS, because they typically take no precautions with each other. It's a very difficult subject to raise, because doing so involves honestly discussing sexual behavior outside one's supposedly monogamous marriage.

21

Spirituality

> Someday, after we have mastered the winds, the rains, the tides, and gravity, we will harness the energies of love. Then, for the second time in the history of the world, man will have discovered fire.
>
> —Pierre Teilhard de Chardin

386. What is meant by the "spiritual" aspect of sexuality?

Most of us experience sex on a mundane level; that is, as part of the same world in which we drive, eat, watch television, and so forth. However, we can also experience sex on a spiritual level, transcending our normal earthly bounds in several ways.

This kind of sex does not stop at "pleasure." It goes beyond pleasure to an extraordinary experience of the self.

387. Why are the spiritual dimensions of sexuality important?

Sexuality has a miraculous potential that most of us never touch. As Indian mystic Shree Rajneesh said, "Ninety-nine percent of people know sex only as a relief; they don't know its orgasmic quality. They are not having true orgasm, just genital release. True orgasm is a state where your body is no longer felt as matter; it vibrates like energy, like electricity."

Experiencing this state of vibration:

• Is a marvelous chance for self-exploration
• Brings extraordinary richness to relationships
• Allows people to experience the perfection of their bodies, and
• Is deeply healing—especially for people whose self-image has been poisoned by shame-based teachings about sexuality

Sex can provide deep momentary pleasure; it can also nourish the soul. Spiritual sexuality is about deepening the pleasure while accepting the nourishment that sex can provide.

As Tantra master Azul states, "The split that has taken place in the West between spirit and matter, between the transcendent and the secular, between the male and the female, and between the body and the mind, is healed in spiritual sex."

388. What kind of experience does spiritual sexuality provide?

First, it is a chance to lose the ego. "I" becomes submerged into "now." The boundary between "I" and "you" becomes thinner and less important. You experience your self as energy, an energy that some people call "love."

Second, it is a chance to transcend time completely. Time does not actually cease, of course, but it ceases for you. It goes on, but you are not in it. You don't notice the loss, because every moment still has a place. That place, for each moment, is now.

Third, it is a chance to reunite with nature. Instead of observing the universe, you can reconnect with it. You experience your self as expanded, connected to the biggest entity there is—life.

We moderns have no satisfactory vocabulary for discussing spiritual sexuality because we don't learn to think of sex in this way, and we generally don't talk about "energy" but about "real things." Those who do talk about energy are usually called poets, priests, or nuts.

389. How do I achieve this spiritual sexuality?

For starters, try some of these:

Turn off the mental instructions about what you're *supposed* to do sexually. Let your body do what it wants, without wondering if it's right or even if it's sex. If you feel more like kissing than like having intercourse, do it; if you partner's arm suddenly looks good enough to lick, lick it.

Enter arousal unafraid, letting excitement build without defending yourself. Don't hold yourself aloof, and don't keep yourself "together," not even to "perform" better. Keep breathing. Let your partner get as emotionally close as possible. Trust your sexual energy, your partner's sexual energy, and the sexual moment.

Feel yourself and your sexuality to be beautiful, perfect, and flowing out of you limitlessly. See your partner's body and sexuality that way too.

390. How can sex have a spiritual dimension when it involves mostly pleasure and self-gratification?

"Sex should be playful and prayerful," said Shree Rajneesh, suggesting that the two are one. Pleasure itself is not contrary to spirituality; actually, accepting pleasure consciously can be a powerful form of meditation.

When we pursue pleasure with greed, fear, or anger, the result is not spiritual at all but pain for ourselves or others. Unfortunately, Western culture sees all pleasure as contaminated by this one side of it. In a society deeply suspicious of pleasure, we learn to pursue it burdened with guilt and to enjoy it only partially and self-consciously.

When sex is pursued "playfully and prayerfully," when it is seen as a celebration rather than a physical release or an emotional validation, it can be spiritual. Under such circumstances, the more pleasurable it is, the more spiritual it can be.

391. How can sex be spiritual when it involves the body, which is so imperfect?

You've put your finger on part of the priceless gift of sexuality—the opportunity to experience the *perfection* of the body.

Part of our modern psycho-spiritual crisis is our alienation from nature and our bodies. We see our bodies as problems to be solved rather than as divine miracles to celebrate. Any religion that sees our bodies as dirty rather than beautiful is more interested in controlling people than in honoring the sacred. No god is glorified by having its creations demeaned.

392. Is spiritual sexuality the same as loving someone?

Loving someone does not guarantee experiences of spiritual sexuality. Unfortunately, our culture's romantic myths teach us to expect that deep love always leads to deep sex, which is not at all true.

Spiritual sexuality is a special form of bonding that makes partners feel love for each other, whether they are deeply connected in other ways or not. Our culture's romantic myths suggest that this sexual ecstasy is the same kind of love that can sustain a long-term marriage. Alas, this is frequently *not* true.

Spiritual sexuality requires trust, comfort with one's body, a shared vocabulary, and a joyful attitude. Many people can best find these in a special loving relationship. Others can experience spiritual sexuality in a more casual context.

As the mystics say, sex is beautiful. There is no need to hide it behind the beautiful word *love*.

393. If sex is so spiritual, why does my church tell me to be wary of it?

Because of history.

A negative attitude toward sex was not an important part of ancient Judaism or the earliest Christian movement. But for political purposes, the church adopted the ruling Greco-Roman tradition's discomfort about sex. This required a dramatic re-interpretation of sacred texts.

Theologian Raymond J. Lawrence, Jr. says, "The Bible, correctly translated, does not contain any significant sex-negative teaching. Modern misinterpretations reflect the destructive wish to eliminate sexuality from the human experience—a wish that is neither moral nor spiritual."

394. If sex is spiritual, why is religion so specific about what kinds are allowed and what kinds are "dirty?"

Not all religions are. But in the early struggles to control Christianity, sexual dogma was a key weapon. Arguments raged about the superiority of some kinds of sex over others, with each faction being influenced by its own school of Greek philosophy. Celibacy—even *within* marriage—also had powerful supporters. Eventually, the winning sect claimed that sex was permissible only for procreation.

This made sexual behaviors focusing on pleasure sinful, a position still held by the Church hierarchy. The decision about sex being dirty originated as a political one, not a theological one.

Those who focus on such details as orifices and positions show a fundamental misunderstanding of sex and a distrust of human beings and their sexual energy. The only thing that makes sex "dirty" is the same thing that makes *anything* "dirty"—doing it with an exploitive or destructive spirit.

395. Why talk about sexual spirituality? We already have plenty of guidelines about sexual morality.

"Morality," said satirist H. L. Mencken, "is the theory that every human act must be either right or wrong, and that 99 percent of them are wrong."

Since *morality* involves judgments about the goodness and badness of behavior, it is really a set of ideas about making decisions. *Spirituality*, on the other hand, involves experiences of celebration and connection.

The two are totally different. But for many people, unfortunately, *morality* has become the opposite of sexual pleasure and creativity. Many orthodox religious believers seem to feel that the less someone is involved with sexual feelings and behavior, the purer or more enlightened he or she is.

As theologian Raymond J. Lawrence, Jr. notes, "The lust for sexual innocence continues to be a powerful force in modern religious life. It poisons the sexual development of both children and adults. It sees human sexuality as the opposite of human goodness—which is destructive to both." And, we might add, an insult to God.

396. Since today's young people don't feel any guilt about sex, how can you expect them to know that it's spiritual?

First, let's get the facts straight: Young people feel lots of guilt about sex. Too much, frequently, to discuss condoms honestly or carry a diaphragm.

But that's beside the point, because understanding the spiritual aspects of sexuality does not require guilt. When people trust themselves and their sexuality, they can relate to sexuality's beauty, power, energy, and ability to make them feel a part of the cosmic order of things.

397. If sex is so spiritual, why does it ruin so many lives?

Lives are ruined not by sex but by bad sexual decisions.

Even the purest things—art, charity, parenting—can be used in destructive ways. Sometimes, for example, people choose to have children without considering everything involved. The result is pain for everyone.

The same is true with sex. Depending on how it is considered and chosen and used, it can express beauty or ugliness. This is why we should be teaching young people about sexual decision-making and its consequences, rather than telling them to "just say no." And this is why information about sexuality and contraception should be freely available—so people can make enlightened, rather than hurtful, sexual decisions.

398. Isn't seeing sex as "spiritual" part of the problem? People today *worship* sex.

Yes, some people worship sex, the way others worship money, fame, their children, and so on. Although worshiping any of these is a poor idea, that doesn't make the objects of worship bad.

Seeking spiritual sexuality is not the same as worshiping sex. It means focusing on the parts of sex that transport us beyond ourselves to our special relationship with all of life.

In our sex-negative culture, some people are so suspicious of sex that *any* joyful relationship to it looks like "worshiping." That's why Marlene Dietrich observed that "in other parts of the world sex is a fact, in America it is an obsession."

399. Can casual sex be spiritual? If so, how?

A spiritual experience is one in which we are connected to a different, larger, perhaps divine world. This possibility is simply part of the nature of sexual energy and is available whenever people are open to it.

To be open, different people need different things. Some need a committed love relationship; others do not. Indeed, some people deliberately use sex as a vehicle for spiritual experiences, and they spend time finding partners who feel the same. We can label these people "promiscuous," or we can look past labels to the meaning this behavior has for those involved. It may or may not be spiritual.

Remember, "casual" is only one way to describe casual sex, and not everyone defines casual sex as bad. Many participants feel deeply positive about it.

400. Do other cultures see a spiritual aspect to sexuality?

Yes, many cultures, past and present, understand that sexuality has a spiritual component.

The Cherokee Indians, for example, have practiced their Quodoshka teachings for centuries. They believe the human body is sacred, and so they have a spiritual attitude about nudity. And they believe that learning about sexuality is a way of honoring Mother Earth.

Halfway across the world, priests and poets in India developed the concepts of Tantra. In contrast to the Western conception of orgasm, the tantric orgasm does not represent the peak of excitement, which can go no further. Instead, it is the valley of relaxation, which is infinite. It is a deep, soothing meditation, restoring energy rather than depleting it.

Interestingly, virtually all cultures that honor the spiritual part of sexuality see it as a gateway to intense pleasure.

401. How can I enhance the spirituality of my sex life? Can I do it without getting involved in formal religion?

The first part of this journey should be identifying whatever negative feelings you have about sex. Taking such an inventory helps you know where you're starting from and where the obstacles are.

There are many paths to spiritual sexuality. These include breathing exercises, which expand the potential for deep orgasm; physical activities, such as pelvic rocking and Kegels (see question 248); and changes in beliefs, such as de-emphasizing intercourse and the genitals.

Developing new sexual attitudes and behaviors takes time. You will learn to pay attention to subtleties of energy and your body that were previously invisible.

Take advantage of the many wonderful guidebooks available. These include the luscious *The Art of Sexual Ecstasy* by Margo Anand and *Sexual Energy Ecstasy* by David Alan Ramsdale and Ellen Jo Dorfman.

22

Homosexuality

If God dislikes gays so much, how come he picked Michelangelo, a known homosexual, to paint a Sistine Chapel ceiling while assigning Anita to go on TV and push orange juice?

—Mike Royko

402. What is a homosexual? What is a lesbian? What do *gay* and *straight* mean?

Throughout history, homosexuality has been defined in many ways. In recent Western society, the label has been applied to anyone who admitted *any* same-sex experiences or interest.

Today we know that this describes a very large proportion of the population. So it is much more descriptive, and accurate, to say that a homosexual is someone whose sexual thoughts, feelings, and behavior are *usually or exclusively* for those of the same gender.

Gay and *straight* are slang for, respectively, homosexual and heterosexual. The expression *homosexual* appeared for the first time in Europe in the late nineteenth century. *Lesbian* is the term most female homosexuals prefer. This is why you sometimes hear or read the expression *gay men and lesbians.*

403. What is the Kinsey Scale?

One of the great discoveries of researcher Alfred Kinsey's pioneering work in the 1940s and 1950s was the prevalence of same-sex experiences in the lives of "normal" heterosexual Americans. Kinsey found, for example, that about half of all males and a fifth of all females have at least some overtly erotic same-sex experience between adolescence and middle age.

Kinsey recognized, therefore, that *homosexual* and *heterosexual* are not mutually exclusive categories but affinities that all people have and deal with in one way or another. He created a seven-point scale (0 through 6) that rates *all* aspects of a person's sexuality—thoughts, feelings, fantasies, and behavior—on a continuum ranging from exclusively homoerotic to exclusively heteroerotic.

Thus, we can refer to a person as a 0 (exclusively other-sex oriented), a 2 (primarily other-sex oriented but more than incidental same-sex behavior or fantasies), a 6 (exclusively same-sex oriented), and so forth.

Traditionally, the world was assumed to be populated primarily by 0s; anyone from 1 through 6 was considered a (sick) homosexual. But it makes more sense to call 0s and 1s "essentially heterosexual," and 5s and 6s "essentially homosexual." Many people are 2s, 3s, or 4s. Some call themselves bisexual, some feel straight, some feel gay, and some don't label themselves at all.

"The world is not divided into sheep and goats," said Kinsey about sexual identity. "Nature rarely deals with discrete categories. Only the human mind invents categories and tries to force facts into separate pigeonholes."

404. How many people are homosexual?

It really depends on who you include in your definition.

Do you mean people who are exclusively homosexual their whole lives? Bisexuals who have a long-term same-sex relationship at some point? Essentially straight men and women who have one or two spontaneous same-sex experiences?

In a sense, the concept of "homosexual" is so imprecise that the question has little meaning. Although various surveys differ, the accepted figure for "mostly or exclusively homosexual" is around 6 to 10 percent of the population.

405. What causes homosexuality?

Social scientists used to know the answer to this question: growing up with a weak father and strong mother. Then someone noticed that this described the vast majority of American families. So we're not so sure anymore.

Actually, it now appears that there is a strong genetic component to homosexuality. That is, most gays are born, not made. This fits with what most gays (especially men) say, which is that they knew they were different very early in life.

Some people define themselves as gay only later in adulthood, after they have lived as heterosexuals for many years. This change may reflect a gradual self-awareness that takes years to develop, or it may take someone by surprise. For some women, homosexuality is a conscious choice for political or other reasons. This is rarely true for gay men.

The origins of sexual orientation, like those of personality, are far too complex to map completely. At this time there is no way to predict who will be gay and who will be straight.

406. How do you cure homosexuality?

Attempts to "cure" homosexuality were very popular in the 1950s and 1960s. Either voluntarily or by force, many unhappy gay people were "treated" by psychoanalysis, behavior modification, hormones, and electroshock. Virtually all were "failures," because their basic orientation could not be changed.

A small number of extremists still claim to "cure" homosexuality with aversion therapy. Gays are shown erotic same-sex pictures and are subjected to shocks or other punishment if they get excited. The idea is to make homosexual arousal so painful that it declines and eventually disappears.

Such treatment may shut off someone's sexuality altogether, but it cannot change his or her identity. There is no "treatment" to turn homosexuals into enthusiastic heterosexuals.

407. What is a bisexual? Isn't that someone who refuses to admit what he really is?

A bisexual is someone who can enjoy sex with both genders. This, says Woody Allen, doubles the person's chances for a date on Saturday night. Some bi's are open to both genders equally, while some prefer one sex and have partners of the other sex less frequently.

Are bisexuals confused or stubborn? Neither. Many sexologists believe there are two kinds of bisexuals. The first is one whose sexual identity, for whatever reason, is not yet fixed. The second is one whose sexual identity is fixed; it just happens to include both genders. Neither of these is the same as someone denying what he or she "really is."

Either way, bisexuality is a viable sexual identity shared by millions of people. It is as valid as a homosexual or heterosexual identity.

408. Do gays hate members of the opposite sex?

Some do, some don't. While some gay men have virtually no female contact, there are many wonderful friendships between gay men and straight women.

While some lesbians get along fine with men, many prefer a separate, female-centered lifestyle. Other lesbians do hate men and feel dominated, oppressed, enraged, or frightened by them. Many of these women, when children, were sexually molested or physically abused by men, and they generalize these bad experiences to all men.

Many heterosexuals are totally mystified by homosexuality, and hatred for the opposite sex seems like the only logical way to explain it. But like heterosexuality, homosexuality is about what a person is drawn *toward*, not what a person is escaping *from*.

409. Exactly how do homosexuals have sex?

The same way straight people do: by kissing, hugging, smiling, rubbing, and putting their fingers, mouths, and genitals wherever it feels good.

For both straight and gay couples, according to sociologists Philip Blumstein and Pepper Schwartz, a good sex life is central to a good overall relationship. When it comes to sex, homosexuals and heterosexuals are far more similar than different. Various straights and various gays like their sex oral, manual, anal, nongenital, and solo.

That said, we can note several differences between the sexuality of homosexuals and heterosexuals, and between lesbians and gay men. For example, according to *American Couples*, Blumstein and Schwartz's comprehensive study, "Gay men, as a group, are much less monogamous than other couples," while "lesbians have sex less frequently by far than any other type of couple."

Gay men have more anal sex than other couples. The study also showed that kissing is most consistently part of lovemaking for lesbians and least consistently for gay men, with heterosexuals in between.

410. How do homosexuals decide who plays the boy and who the girl?

Many don't, which gays often consider a prime advantage of homosexuality. Many say that sex and intimacy do not need a "boy" and "girl," that two "people" is sufficient.

On the other hand, some gays enjoy playing one or the other role, usually called "butch" and "femme" or "top" and "bottom." Heterosexual couples also do this, often without being aware of it. And as you have probably observed, it isn't always the man playing the "top."

411. Some gay men are so . . . feminine. Why must they be that way?

First of all, most gays are invisible, because they act like everyone else. Gays who get media attention tend to be effeminate men and macho women, so these stereotypes tend to stick in our minds.

It is helpful to distinguish between sexual orientation (gay versus straight) and sex-role behavior (acting in ways we interpret as "masculine" or "feminine"). Straights as well as gays experiment with expressing themselves in ways associated with the other sex. Many men who appear "effeminate," for example, are straight.

Alienated from (and abused by) popular ideas about gender, perhaps gays and lesbians are more willing to tamper with its sacred symbols. Of course, many people are uncomfortable with such behavior in others; by challenging our definitions of male and female, they shake the predictability of our world. That's why no one questions the supermacho man, even though he is much further from the average than the slightly effeminate one.

412. What is "camp?"

"Camp" is the deliberate manipulation of gender roles, either for fun or to make a statement. As a creative response to society's sexual oppression, gays entertain themselves and amuse or shock heterosexuals by playing with clothes, makeup, art, and attitude.

Straight society has historically enjoyed "camp" in certain ways, such as through female impersonator shows. It is when gays take camp out of the theater and into the "real world" that mainstream society gets nervous.

413. What is the "closet?" How exactly does a person "come out?"

"Being in the closet" is slang for hiding one's homosexuality from family, friends, and others in the straight world. Many gays do this to avoid the economic, social, and physical punishment usually directed toward openly gay people in America.

People "come out of the closet" for different reasons. Some are forced out by circumstances, some eventually can't stand hiding anymore, some do it on principle, and some are "outed"—publicly identified by radical gays to make homosexuality more normal and visible in the larger community.

Coming out is not a public announcement but a long-term process of refusing to hide or let others' judgments run one's life. This may be done by introducing a lover honestly, or not pretending to be interested in the "right" gender, or not laughing at "fag" jokes, or not hiding actual living arrangements from visitors.

414. If gays are so proud of being gay, why do they hide their homosexuality?

Imagine yourself, heterosexual, in a world run by homosexuals. Unlike most people, you may not get legally married. Adopting children is almost impossible. Your private sex life is accepted as proof that you're an unfit parent if you get divorced.

People tell vicious "hetero" jokes on television and everywhere you go. You're good at your job, but you'll probably lose it if someone finds out you're a hetero. You take good care of your apartment, but you'll get thrown out if the landlord finds out you live with someone of the other sex. You have a mate whom you love, but if you hold hands in the park or supermarket you'll get stared at, cursed, even chased by the police.

You're basically law-abiding and patriotic, but your lovemaking is against the law, and you know heteros are prohibited from joining the military and from holding public office. You love your religion, but you're told that God hates you and you may not serve Him.

Would you be out of the closet, letting everyone know you were one of those hated heteros? Or would you protect yourself, your lover, your career, and your life by hiding the most basic part of who you are?

415. How can you tell if someone is gay? How do gays spot each other?

While there are plenty of gay male florists and lesbian truck drivers, homosexuals are found in every single neighborhood and profession. In that sense, it is impossible to spot them, because they are literally everywhere.

How do they spot each other? The way that any interested people spot each other: through eye contact, slang or in-group expressions, trendy fashions, and the like.

And like other people, gays frequently miss each other. "Do you think that person is gay?" is asked at least as often by gays as it is by straight people.

416. If you're gay does that mean you're mentally sick?

In 1957 Dr. Evelyn Hooker gave psychological tests to groups of gay and straight men, none of whom were in therapy. When a number of psychologists scored the tests without knowing whom they belonged to, no differences were found between the two groups.

Ten years later Dr. Mark Freedman compared lesbian and heterosexual women. This study showed no evidence that gay women had any more emotional problems than straight women.

These studies reflect the experience of thousands of therapists across the country: that gays have the same emotional strengths and weaknesses as everyone else. In recognition of this reality, the American Psychiatric Association removed *homosexuality* from its official list of emotional disorders in 1973. Gay people's relationships, needs, and problems may now be evaluated and treated as human ones.

417. If homosexuality is normal, why is the Bible against it?

"If homosexuality were the normal way," said Anita Bryant during her vicious attack on the human rights of 20 million Americans, "God would have created Adam and Bruce." Bryant must also believe, responded educator Dr. Sol Gordon, that if being black were normal, God would have created Amos and Andy.

Two thousand years ago, the Apostle Paul was very concerned about separating Christian converts from their old cult practices, such as same-gender sex. While his writing focused more on detaching people from the non-Christian past than on condemning specific things, this context was eventually lost, and his writings were taken literally.

Paul was also personally tormented about sexuality. He believed that celibacy within marriage was ideal and that sex was at best an evil necessary for childbearing. Thus, sex that could not produce children—notably homosexuality and masturbation—had no value and was therefore wicked.

The Bible demands that we divine humans interpret it. How else can we deal with, say, the requirement to marry one's dead brother's widow or to stone adulterers to death?

How shall we interpret it? Fortunately, the Bible offers a compelling, absolutely clear vision: with love and tolerance. So in dealing with homosexuality, specific words against it must be weighed against this recurring theme. The Bible states in majestic simplicity that you must treat a homosexual with the same respect with which you wish to be treated. Many Christian and Jewish denominations have officially declared so. And many are now ordaining homosexuals.

Almost all people who take the Bible's condemnation of homosexuality literally believe, at the same time, that other parts of it must be interpreted in accordance with modern life. Such a selective reading says far more about such readers than it does about the Bible.

418. Why are gay men so sexually active?

One explanation looks at the traditional male sex role in our society: Since men are much more open to casual sex than women, the possibilities for casual sex among groups of men are enormous.

A more complex explanation looks at the issue developmentally. Because of confusion, denial, and fear, most gay men miss the sexual experimentation of adolescence. When they get the chance to explore their sexuality as adults, they have more resources—time, money, privacy, knowledge, even institutions such as bathhouses and bars.

Adult gay men, therefore, can act out the sexual experimentation that adolescents cannot and have needs that straight men may not. Also, their potential partners (other gay men) are not scripted to resist sex (as are women) but are, instead, equally eager to experiment.

In a less homophobic, less sex-role-scripted society, gay and straight men would probably be more like one another.

419. Why hasn't AIDS convinced homosexuals to stop what they do?

To a large extent it has: High-risk sexual behaviors like anal intercourse and anonymous sex with multiple partners have dramatically decreased in the gay community. In fact, gays have changed their behavior during the AIDS epidemic faster and more completely than any other group.

However, if your question is, "Why hasn't AIDS convinced many gays to go straight," the answer is because sexual orientation is not a choice, it's an inborn characteristic. Besides, AIDS is not a gay disease. Gays who do not and have not practiced unsafe sex are no more likely to get it than straights who behave similarly.

420. Why is homophobia so widespread? Why do some people think it's "natural" to find homosexuals disgusting?

Homophobia is the fear or hatred of individuals because they are gay. Homophobia takes many forms, such as "fag" jokes; job discrimination; fear that gays are prone to molest children or seduce straight people; and the fear of being seen in public with gays because of what people might think.

Understandably, many straight people reject homosexual *behavior* for themselves. Rejecting homosexual *persons*, however, is different. Fearing them is unnecessary; hating them is unfair; beating them or chasing them out of an apartment or job is evil.

Some 20 million Americans are gay, probably including one or more of your neighbors, co-workers, sports idols, or even children. They deserve the blessings promised all Americans: the right to privacy, to fairness in housing and jobs, and to be left alone.

421. Why do some people have such deep hatred for gays?

Considering that some churches teach that God hates gays; that some educators believe that gays are child molesters; that some men believe that gays are out to seduce straights; and that some politicians believe that gays are bent on destroying our country, it's amazing that *everyone* doesn't hate gays.

American advertising contributes, too. Because so many ads rely on getting people to question their sexual adequacy (so they can sell products pitched to relieve this anxiety), they plant a troubling question in people's unconscious: Am I man enough? Woman enough? This makes homosexuality frightening because it undermines people's confidence in their hetero-sexuality.

Remember James Garner's gangster character in the film *Victor/Victoria?* Deeply troubled that he was attracted to a man dressed as a woman (the "man" later turned out to be Julie Andrews), he questioned his masculinity. This was so painful that he actually went to a bar and goaded men into beating him up so he'd feel like a man.

When a straight person's sense of sexual identity is this fragile, homosexuality can trigger deep emotional turmoil. It's easy to blame and hate gay people for it. Besides, although everyone knows and sees gay individuals all the time, most people don't know it. This makes it easy to see gays as "them" rather than "us," as things rather than people. And that makes hatred easy.

422. How can I prevent my kids from becoming gay?

This is an understandable desire—not because there is anything wrong with being gay but because in a homophobic society, being gay involves a lifetime of stress and danger.

As far as we know, there is nothing a parent can do to affect a child's sexual orientation. Your best bet is maintaining a home in which affection is honestly shown, sexuality is respected, and maleness and femaleness are both valued.

Ultimately, parents should be more concerned with a

child's ability to love than with the gender of the people the child chooses to love.

423. What should I do if I think my teenager is gay?

The most important thing you can do is let your child know that you love and support him or her no matter what. If that isn't true, find an adult relative, neighbor, or friend who does, and share your concerns with this person.

Certainly, you (or this other adult) can gently raise the issue of homosexuality. But your child may be uncomfortable discussing the issue or may not even know whether he or she is gay. Another way to communicate about the subject is to leave reading material around the house. This will both provide information and indicate your willingness to discuss the issue.

If you have any guilt or anger about the subject, deal with it yourself. Your feelings aren't your child's problem, and they will only add to the difficulties. In the meantime, read Don Clark's *The New Loving Someone Gay*. And get in touch with PFLAG (Parents and Friends of Lesbians and Gays). They have an excellent national organization and supportive local chapters.

424. What should I do if I think my husband is gay?

Share your concerns with him and find out if he thinks he is or if he's been having sex with men. Keep in mind that these are not the same thing.

If he denies each of these, you can dismiss your suspicions; be skeptical and investigate further; or you can leave.

If, on the other hand, you husband admits to a sexual interest in men, sit down together and discuss your marriage. What does each of you want? One or the other of you may want to separate. Other couples solve this dilemma by opening the marriage: a lover for you, for example, or male lovers for your husband but no other women.

You can think of your husband's sexual encounters with men simply as affairs or as something more complex. Either way, a support group or counseling will probably be helpful. A particularly good book on this subject is Jean Gochros's *When Husbands Come Out of the Closet.*

If your husband has been involved in anal intercourse (particularly as the receptive partner), you should both be tested for HIV. Have only safe sex until you get the results.

425. I sometimes have erotic fantasies about my own sex. Does that make me gay?

No, although it certainly makes you typical.

The real question is, How do you relate to your sexuality? To whom are you basically attracted? Who turns your head in the supermarket? Who do you hope notices you at parties? A straight person answers these questions "Generally, the other sex, not my own."

Still, as discussed in chapter 13, there's plenty of room within a straight sexual identity for same-sex erotic fantasies.

426. I'm straight, but I think I'd like to have gay sex once. Am I sick? How do I find someone to do this with?

No, you're not sick. This is a common fantasy, which many people eventually indulge. Call it "same-gender" rather than "gay" sex to help keep it in perspective and feel more like your familiar self.

There are many ways to meet perspective partners. You may have a friend who is interested (gay or straight) or a friend who has a friend. You can go to a bar where gays or bisexuals hang out, but as in any pick-up bar, you run the risks of getting into some unsafe situations. You can also check the classified ads in a big city or alternative newspaper.

Once you locate Mr./Ms. Right-for-a-Night, relax, get to know the person a little, and communicate your desires and preferences. If you suddenly get terribly uncomfortable, don't feel obligated to go through with your original plan. You are *never* required to have sex no matter what you have implied or promised. No one should ever have unwanted sex.

427. My wife wants us to invite this gay couple she met over for dinner. Is this a good idea? How should I act?

Since your wife likes them they're probably nice people. If you're in the mood to make some new friends, invite them over. Otherwise, forget it. If you do have them over, plan on enjoying yourself, treat them like people, and don't do or say anything different than you usually do.

428. I see that gay couples are starting to adopt babies, which can't be good for the children. Isn't that selfish of these people?

First, let's separate emotion from fact: According to world-famous sex educator Dr. Michael Carrera, "There is no evidence that a parent's sexual orientation predicts what kind of a father or mother he or she will be. Gay men and women have already shown that their ability to be loving, nurturing, and fit parents is not related to their sexual orientation."

Since a couple's sexual orientation is not a parenting issue, the relevant question is, do they have the desire, and the emotional and material resources, to be parents? Since gay couples cannot fall into parenting unintentionally, or take parenting opportunities for granted, gays who choose to raise kids usually do it with special commitment and attention.

Most kids, of course, periodically feel that their parents are ruining their lives. Kids of gay parents sometimes feel this way too—because it's totally normal, not because of their sexual orientation.

We should also remember that, according to Dr. Carrera, "more than 95 percent of the children who live with a gay parent have a heterosexual orientation."

429. There's a new teacher in town, and rumor has it that he's gay. Is he dangerous to have around the kids?

Not because of his homosexuality. As discussed in Part V, the overwhelming majority of sex crimes against both boys and girls are committed by heterosexuals.

By the way, are you going to believe those rumors, meant to discredit someone who has no chance to respond? Why not arrange to meet this teacher and judge for yourself if he's a good person?

430. Is it true that many famous Americans are or were gay? Why didn't I know this before?

If you consider people like Walt Whitman, Leonard Bernstein, Martina Navratilova, and Gore Vidal famous, then yes, it's true.

Why aren't more people aware of the homosexuality of public figures? In a gay-hating society, many public figures hide their homosexuality to protect their careers. More to the point, our media and educational system systematically denies the existence of homosexuality in prominent people. Whitman is a good example.

Our society does not want prominent people associated with a characteristic considered negative. Ignoring homosexuality may be the easiest way to handle this issue, but, ironically, it totally dishonors the person we claim to admire.

Part IV

Concerns

23
....

Erection
Difficulties

**The sexual organs express the human soul more than
any other part of the body. They are not diplomats.
They tell the truth ruthlessly.**

—Isaac Bashevis Singer

431. What causes erections?

An erection is a reflex action, like a sneeze. It starts when
the brain interprets "sexual arousal," which can be physical or
mental stimulation, including memories, fantasies, and input
from the various sense organs. The brain then sends a message
through the spinal column to begin a complex chain of events.

Assuming the man is relaxed enough to allow the process
to occur, extra blood is sent to the pelvic area. This blood fills
up the spongy tissue of the penis, which is arranged in three
long cylinders. The brain's instructions also restrict the veins'

ability to drain the blood from the penis, and so it stays filled. The pressure of that extra blood against the inside walls of the penis is the firmness we call "erection."

The body can short-circuit this complex process at any point along the way if the man is too anxious, angry, frightened, tired, or sad.

432. What's supposed to give a man an erection—how turned on he is or the way a woman turns him on?

Many men think their virility demands they get hard just from thinking about sex or undressing a woman. I call this the "look ma, no hands" erection.

While this is often true in adolescence, a man's system changes as he matures—and it better, given how much sexual stimulation surrounds us every day. To get and stay erect, most adult men need to have their penises touched or otherwise stimulated. Many also need other physical contact, such as kissing or smelling.

On the other hand, each man must ultimately turn himself on. He must get and stay relaxed, give himself permission to enjoy sex, volunteer to lose control, and define a given situation as sexual. Without these, the most talented hand or mouth in the world won't give him an erection.

So the accurate answer is neither A nor B. It's yes.

433. I heard that there's a bone in the penis. If so, where does it go when you're not erect?

There is no bone in your boner. As discussed in question 431, erection is caused by increased blood flow being trapped in the spongy tissue of the penis. There's no cartilage or voluntary muscle there, either.

434. Why can't you predict the size of a man's erection from the size of his penis when soft? Don't all penises expand the same amount?

No. Some penises become erect by enlarging a small amount, while others enlarge a lot. Some men have less penile cylinder capacity than others. More importantly, some men start out with their cylinders more filled than others. And finally, some men fill up their cylinders more when erect than others. These variables combine to make erection size unpredictable.

Why do men measure differently on these three dimensions? Mostly genetics.

435. Sure, you therapists all say that size doesn't matter, but how small is too small?

It depends on what you want. To father children, size doesn't matter, sperm count does. To please a partner, size doesn't matter, attentiveness does. To enjoy yourself, size doesn't matter, relaxation does.

To feel self-confident, adequate, or manly—well, that depends on the individual. For some guys a dozen inches wouldn't do it, although they imagine it would.

Physicians say that an erection less than two inches long may reflect hormonal or other problems. Anything bigger than that is likely to be okay.

436. Don't laugh, but my penis seems to be too large; every girl I sleep with complains of pain. What should I do?

The vagina can expand to allow a baby through. So if your penis is smaller than a baby (okay, a tiny baby), you shouldn't have a problem.

Perhaps you are attempting intercourse before your partners are aroused and lubricated enough. Or perhaps you keep meeting women who don't lubricate very much, and you need to use a commercial product (K-Y, Astrolube, etc.). Maybe your partners simply aren't relaxed enough to let your penis in. What can you do to make them more comfortable?

You might also try other positions, including side-by-side or woman on top.

437. I like to have a couple of drinks to loosen up before sex, but my doctor said this could cause erection problems. What did she mean?

Because it is a central-nervous-system depressant, alcohol interferes with the brain's message to the penis of "Hey—get erect!" The result can be a soft one when you want a hard one.

After this has happened once or twice, men frequently drink *more* to relax before sex, which is exactly the wrong thing to do. Physiologically, about half a drink provides the ideal balance between decreased inhibition and intact erectile function. You're lucky to have a physician who's sensitive to this issue.

438. I'm confused. During the night I sometimes see my husband on his way to the bathroom with a big erection; when he returns from urinating, it's gone. Is there a difference between this erection and the one he gets from sex?

Yes and no.

Fully functioning men become erect about every ninety minutes during each night's sleep. The last erection typically occurs very early in the morning. Sometimes one of these erections wakes a man; he may also find he was to urinate, and so he heads for the bathroom with an erection. By the time he finishes, the sleep stimulation is gone, along with his erection.

During the night, the bladder gradually fills with urine. The resulting pressure on the prostate sometimes stimulates a sexual dream, which produces an erection. Again, the erection leaves soon after the man wakes up.

Some older men like to take advantage of the "head start" their sleep erection gives them by having sex upon awakening. As long as their partner is cooperative (not everyone prefers sex to sleep), this is fine.

439. Why do I get an erection easily with one woman but not with another?

The first thing to look at is the way these different women stimulate you. If you enjoy the way one does it far more than the other, that probably accounts for the difference.

Your question suggests this is not the case. Thus, it's probably an emotional issue. The most likely reasons for the discrepancy are: You feel more relaxed and safe with one than with the other; or you are upset with one (and probably not discussing it) but not with the other.

The mind lies, but our bodies don't. If you can get erect with one woman but not another, it means you have some business to take care of with the second one.

440. At what age do you lose your erection for good?

Most experts agree that at death we lose our erections permanently. Even this is open to controversy, however. Woody Allen says there is sex after death, we just don't feel it.

Actually, there is no reason that a man should lose his erectile ability simply because of age. Various medical problems that undermine erectile ability, however, are more common among older men. These include cardiovascular disease, diabetes, and prostatitis. With good health, a man past sixty, seventy, and even eighty can have a perfectly sound erection.

441. We hear that stress affects everything. Does it affect erection too?

Definitely. In sexual situations, stress can be experienced as anger, sadness, fear, or performance anxiety. Such stress can block the body's perception of stimulation or its response to it, inhibiting the erection reflex. In the same way, stress can also make an erection go away.

You may have had a situation like this, in which your partner wanted to arouse you but you were so worried about something else you just didn't get turned on. Or perhaps you thought you heard your lover's ex-spouse coming up the stairs. *No one* keeps an erection in such a situation.

442. Is it true that if you lose your erection in the middle of sex you can get it back? How?

Yes, many men have this experience. But you can't will an erection back. Paradoxically, it only returns if you don't need it to.

That means not feeling like a failure, not fearing your partner's judgment, not needing to separate from her in humiliation, and not thinking that sex is over. It's just a lost erection, that's all.

While you can fake such things to others, of course, your body won't buy a lie. So if you simply pretend you feel okay about losing your erection, it won't work. Try discussing this with your partner when you're *not* in bed. Think about how good it would feel to hug and kiss her if the problem appeared again, and imagine how sympathetic and low-key she could be if you stayed in touch with her through your (and her) disappointment.

How to get your erection back? Let it go, and enjoy sex without it. Feel free to notice and use it if it returns.

443. Okay, it's not the end of the world if you lose your erection. But what are you supposed to do when it happens?

Stay physically close, keep your sense of humor, and talk about how uncomfortable you feel. Then, if you're both in the mood, resume sex, with or without an erection.

Yes, it does sound simple. It *is* simple. Losing your erection doesn't have to mean losing your mind.

444. What are penile implants? How do they work? Who are they used for?

These are devices surgically implanted into the shaft of the penis to create erections. One type is semirigid all the time; it is bent toward the belly when not in use and unbent for urination or intercourse.

The other is the hydraulic type. A reservoir is implanted into the scrotum, connected to hollow cylinders implanted in the penis. To get erect the man pumps his scrotum, sending liquid from the reservoir into the penile tubes, which stiffens them.

Penile implants are expensive and somewhat risky. The hydraulic type, in particular, needs to be replaced or repaired, on average, about every five years. Implants permanently damage whatever erectile capacity the body still had. They are best used for men whose erectile ability has been lost due to accident or illness such as cancer or diabetes. A man should consider all alternatives before deciding on this radical treatment.

445. What are these new impotence treatments using injections?

Three drugs are used to treat impotence: papaverine, phentolamine, and prostaglandin-E. One or more of these drugs is injected with a very fine syringe into the shaft and spongy part of the penis. Acting directly on the blood vessels, they create an erection within ten to twenty minutes that lasts an hour or more. This is not, by the way, the same as being mentally aroused. You have to provide that yourself.

The drug is first administered by a physician, who does several in-office trials to establish the correct dosage (which differs from one man to another) and gauge the patient's reaction. The man is taught to inject himself and then gets a supply to take home and administer himself.

These drugs do not work for all men. Because they are so new, their long-term side effects are not yet known. The short-term problems include pain, irritation, priapism (erections that won't go down), and blood-pressure changes.

According to the new Kinsey book, the success rate for this treatment varies from 65 to 100 percent, the rate of side effects is 2 to 13 percent, and 50 percent of men eventually drop out of treatment. Interestingly, some men report that their own natural erections start returning after six to twelve injections.

446. I heard about someone whose erection didn't go away. Why? How do I arrange this?

A continued erection that will not go down is called *priapism* (after Priapus, the Greek god of procreation and erect phalluses), and you don't want it. It can be very painful, and it damages the penis's vascular system to the point where erectile ability can be destroyed forever. Priapism requires *immediate* medical attention.

Priapism is unrelated to sexual stimulation. It is typically due to a failure in the mechanism that frees the blood trapped in the erect penis. It is often a symptom of serious problems, such as spinal cord disease or leukemia.

Papaverine and related drugs are a new source of priapism (see preceding question). Patients are carefully instructed in the proper dosage with which to inject themselves. Occasionally, the body cannot tolerate the strength of the injection, and priapism occurs. And using the concept "If a little is good, more must be better," some men intentionally overdose themselves. Blood clots form, preventing blood drainage from the penis. Emergency rooms around the country are starting to report men who have been erect for four, six, even ten hours, in terrible pain.

447. Once in a while, my husband loses his erection during lovemaking. Am I doing something wrong? What should I do when that happens?

Most erection problems are not caused by a partner doing something wrong but by feelings that the man has before or during sex.

When this happens, the most important things are to maintain emotional contact with your husband, and not get pulled into a big drama about it. You want to respect your husband's distress, of course, but you don't have to agree that the sky is falling just because his penis does.

You and your husband need to discuss this *outside* of the bedroom when you're feeling close. "What shall we do about this?" is a good approach to leaky roofs and child-rearing issues; talk about your marriage's periodic erection problem the same way. That means talk about how it feels, what you want, what he wants, and what the options seem to be.

And tell your husband the truth: that it isn't much of a problem unless it's *made* a problem by his turning away in frustration or anger.

24

Ejaculation Difficulties

Sex is one of the nine reasons for reincarnation. The other eight are unimportant.

—Henry Miller

448. What exactly is an ejaculation?

Ejaculation (from the Latin for "throwing out") is the expulsion of semen from the penis, releasing the tension that has built up during the arousal phase. Ejaculation involves the spinal cord, pelvic muscles, and rhythmic contractions of various glands. It is a reflex activity like sneezing, although it usually feels a lot better.

449. Is there a difference between ejaculation and orgasm?

There is no ejaculation without orgasm, but there can be orgasm without ejaculation.

Many people make a big fuss about separating the two. For most men, the distinction is tedious and irrelevant.

450. What makes up ejaculate? Is this different from semen?

These are two words for the same thing: the teaspoon or so of fluid that comes out of the penis during climax.

Semen is mostly water. Ninety-eight percent of it comes from the prostate gland and seminal vesicles. Other glands contribute various products, including protein, sugars, and salts. If a man is fertile, his semen will contain between 120 and 600 million sperm, still a microscopic amount that cannot be seen with the naked eye.

Semen is slightly alkaline, which helps to neutralize the acidity of vaginal secretions. This is important for the sperm, which don't swim well in acidic environments.

451. What is semen supposed to look like?

Depending on a man's diet and internal chemistry, semen varies from white to gray to yellow. It usually comes out creamy and sticky, liquefies, and then dries in the air.

452. Can a man ejaculate from a partial erection or even none at all?

Yes. Erection and ejaculation are controlled by two different mechanisms.

453. What are "blue balls"?

This term refers to the painful testicles a man gets from prolonged sexual arousal without the release of orgasm. This is the last thing many adolescent boys feel before they go to sleep after a Saturday night date. The condition is also called "lover's nuts."

The discomfort is caused by vasocongestion, the accumulation of blood in the pelvic region that is part of sexual excitement. Fortunately it is harmless and gradually subsides after the stimulation ends.

Women sometimes experience a similar condition in their vulvas, which they are just now beginning to talk about in public. Shall we call this phenomenon "blue lips?"

454. After I ejaculate during lovemaking, my wife likes to keep moving or at least to caress my penis, but this is uncomfortable for me. Am I abnormal?

When we talk sex, we're talking friction. That's why lubrication is so important. As long as the friction is getting us excited, we welcome it. When we're aroused, our threshold of pain goes up so we can tolerate high levels of friction.

After ejaculation, the friction no longer adds to the excitement. And our threshold of pain quickly returns to normal. But our bodies have just been highly sensitive to stimulation of all kinds. So after ejaculation, any sexual stimulation at all, including a partner's touch or more intercourse, can be very uncomfortable, even like tickling.

Different men feel this to different degrees, and a few don't mind at all. So you're not at all abnormal. But you must tell your partner that although you don't want physical stimulation, you still want emotional contact. Too many women feel that their whole being is pushed away when their partner simply pushes their hand away.

455. I'm afraid I come too fast. What should I do?

Too fast for what?

The answer used to be, "Too fast to make my partner climax." But now we know that most women don't climax from intercourse. So the question is, once again, "Too fast for what?"

Men get distressed about this common problem because they think it makes them bad lovers, but that's because they think of sex primarily as intercourse. Couples who use their hands, mouths, and the rest of their bodies to make love don't use stopwatches to measure their satisfaction. If there's an erection or orgasm problem they just work around it, enjoying whatever is available.

Traditionally, people thought the problem was caused by too much stimulation. But the problem is actually the opposite—too much anxiety, which prevents a man from really experiencing stimulation and his response to it. The key, then, is reducing anxiety, not stimulation.

One way sex therapists help men relax during sex is by banning intercourse for a month. Men then learn to enjoy sex without the pressure to delay ejaculation. We also teach men to breathe deeply and regularly during sex, and we encourage slower lovemaking. Because it typically reflects anxiety and habit, rapid (*not* "premature") ejaculation is one of the easiest sex problems to fix.

Groucho Marx apparently had this problem at one time. A friend recommended a desensitizing cream for his penis, guaranteed to prolong erection. The next time they met, the friend asked how it had worked. "I came rubbing the stuff on," Groucho reported.

456. What are the structured techniques therapists use to help men last longer?

The most common exercises are the stop-start and the squeeze. Both educate men to identify sooner the point when ejaculation is inevitable, so they have plenty of time to slow down, try different stimulation, and refocus their attention.

The stop-start technique works as follows:

1. The man or his partner strokes his penis. He practices relaxing and enjoying the pleasure (which for many men is harder than it sounds).
2. As he feels himself nearing ejaculation, the man stops, or signals his partner to stop, the stimulation. The stop lasts for several seconds, so arousal can subside slightly, with no loss of erection.
3. The stimulation is resumed, and the pattern is repeated three times.

4. The stimulation then proceeds to ejaculation, which the man is told to enjoy fully.

The stimulation is progressively increased every two weeks, from dry hand to wet hand to passive intercourse to thrusting intercourse.

The squeeze technique is similar to stop-start, with the addition that the man or his partner squeezes the penis for four seconds when the stimulation is interrupted. This helps delay ejaculation. Stimulation then continues.

At first, the penis is squeezed at the head, near the ridge. With progress, the penis is squeezed at the base, a movement that can be incorporated into intercourse. The squeeze is applied at the top and bottom surfaces, not on the sides.

Sooner or later these techniques require communication and cooperation, which is one of their advantages.

457. It's extremely difficult for me to ejaculate during lovemaking. What does this mean? What should I do?

I will assume that you have already experimented with various positions to get the stimulation you like best. Your problem is often called *retarded ejaculation,* which means "takes a long time," or *ejaculatory incompetence,* which means "doesn't come." Ignore these threatening expressions.

Something is interfering with your ejaculation reflex. Your first stop should be a physician, who will check for prostate problems, cancer, diabetes, and neurovascular problems. He or she should also ask if you are taking any medications.

If nothing negative turns up, your next stop should be a sex therapist, either with or without your partner. Possible difficulties include anger, fear, and anxiety. Because they represent an earlier stage of trauma and adaptation, ejaculation problems are among the most difficult sexual problems to resolve.

Is it easy for you to ejaculate in ways other than intercourse? This is not unusual, and it suggests the problem is psychological rather than medical.

458. I ejaculate when I masturbate, but not when I'm with a woman. What does this mean?

If you ejaculate easily by yourself, it means that your plumbing is in good shape. Your difficulty, therefore, is probably psychological in origin. In my experience, cases like yours usually involve a fear of intimacy, of being overwhelmed, or of the man's own (considerable) unresolved anger.

459. The doctor said that after my prostate surgery I'll probably have a retrograde ejaculation. What's that?

All men have a valve that prevents semen from escaping into the bladder (and makes urination impossible during ejaculation). Surgery can damage this valve so that semen is ejaculated into the bladder instead of out the penis; bits of semen can sometimes be seen in the urine. Artificial insemination is necessary if such a man wants to father children.

Men with this condition still have orgasms. Many find their sexual pleasure undiminished, while others feel that something is missing. Having a broad-minded view of sexuality can help dramatically in adjusting to this change.

460. I have pain when I ejaculate. What could this be?

The most common cause is infection of the prostate or urethra. A hernia can also cause this problem. Ejaculation should never be painful; you should see a physician immediately.

461. Do women ejaculate?

Scientists still cannot agree about this, although there are women who definitely drip, and even spray, when they climax.

The composition of this fluid is not urine, but it isn't "semen," either. Its source in the female body is not clear, although many women who do "ejaculate" report that they do so only when their G spot is stimulated. For more information, see Alice Ladas, et al.'s book *The G Spot*.

25

Orgasm Difficulties

This is the meaning of the complete orgasm: that your frozen energy melts, becomes one with this universe, with the trees and the stars and the rocks.

—Shree Rajneesh

462. I'm a thirty-one-year-old woman, and I've never had a climax. What causes this? What should I do?

You are not alone. Sex educator Michael Carrera estimates that 10 percent of women have never had an orgasm.

There are medical reasons for this, such as neurological, gynecological, or hormonal disorders.

More commonly, there are many psychological dynamics that can block the orgasm reflex. These include:

• Fear of failure and of the resulting rejection

- Fear of losing control of yourself
- Fear of the possible intensity of orgasm
- Fear of intimacy, dependence, or of being engulfed
- Guilt about enjoying sex
- Being a spectator and waiting for the orgasm to happen
- Ignorance of the way your body responds to stimulation, and
- Traumatic past sexual experiences

Finally, there are often dynamics in the relationship that block orgasm. These include:

- Hostility toward or fear of the partner
- Unacknowledged power struggles
- Poor communication with the partner
- The partner's refusal to stimulate you effectively or let you stimulate yourself
- The belief that sex is primarily or completely for the man
- Contraception or STD conflicts

If you are in poor health, start with a physician. If not, see a therapist who specializes in sexuality. Or call your local women's center or family planning center. They frequently have groups for nonorgasmic women. Alternatively, read Lonnie Barbach's classic *For Yourself: The Fulfillment of Female Sexuality*.

463. I can climax, but only with great difficulty. Why is this? What should I do?

One of the simplest diagnostic questions sex therapists ask when confronted with this problem is, "Do you have this trouble when you masturbate or only with a partner?" If you climax easily when alone, your problem is more likely about your partner or the relationship, rather than a physical one or a personal issue like self-esteem.

If climaxing in general is difficult, it may be due to a prior trauma such as sexual abuse or because you are afraid of letting go.

Either way, the place to start is with an honest look at your feelings about your partner(s), relationships, sexuality, and your body. Tell your partner(s) you're not going to try to climax for the next two weeks. This will reduce the pressure you feel, making sex more enjoyable. Lonnie Barbach's book (see preceding question) should also be helpful. The next step is consulting a sex therapist.

464. Why do I climax when masturbating but not when making love with my partner?

Like you, most people climax most easily from masturbation. Masturbation is so much easier—you don't have to get dressed up or even clean the house.

Either you're not getting the exact stimulation you need during partner sex, or the emotions you have with a partner are blocking your orgasm. These emotions could include anxiety, fear, sadness, guilt, anger, and confusion.

Unless your mate is extremely rigid, the first problem is easily fixed. The second requires, at minimum, improved communication and self-knowledge. Therapy is frequently necessary and almost always helpful with this.

465. How long should it take to climax?

Time, of course, is nature's way of preventing everything from happening all at once. But time is relative—it seems to go slower when your relatives are around, while it seems to stand still during good sex.

The issue isn't how long it takes to climax, it's how much you and your partner enjoy getting to the climax. Some people are so anxious or goal-oriented that they rush through the journey like a mandatory trip through Jersey swampland. Instead, the trip should be so enjoyable that a tiny part of you is disappointed when the orgasm approaches, because it means that a big part of the fun is almost over.

Taking a "long time" to climax is not a problem. The problem is when getting there is a burden, a struggle to squeeze out an orgasm that stubbornly resists and eludes you. Under these circumstances, every moment is long. But when two people are really enjoying caresses, kisses, and smells, who cares how long it takes?

You're over the time limit if the seasons change more than once while you're straining to climax. Other than that, a few minutes more or less are irrelevant.

466. Is it true that therapists tell women who can't climax to masturbate? Why?

Using masturbation to teach nonorgasmic women how to climax was a dramatic clinical breakthrough in the early seventies. Pioneered by sexologists such as Lonnie Barbach, Joe LoPiccolo, and Betty Dodson, programs were developed to acquaint women with their bodies, legitimate whatever kinds of stimulation their orgasms required, and explore their resistance to climaxing.

After a woman can have orgasms from masturbation, the next step is showing a partner what she likes and climaxing from that person's touching. She can then move on to orgasms from oral sex or intercourse with additional stimulation.

Some nonorgasmic women have personal or relationship issues that require psychotherapy or couples therapy. Exercises that increase a woman's vaginal sensitivity and consciousness—Kegels—can also be helpful. They are discussed in question 248.

467. Why would a woman's orgasm be painful? What should I do?

Orgasm should never be painful. Your first stop should be a gynecologist to see if there is a physical reason for the pain. Such reasons can include problems with the urethra, bladder, or anus; constipation; and insufficient lubrication during this or recent sexual experiences.

Painful orgasm is frequently the result of a psychological problem that makes sex seem dirty or dangerous. Sometimes the sufferer has been sexually abused as a child.

468. I'm frustrated. All the other women I know have multiple orgasms and I just can't manage it. What should I do?

Mostly, you should stop comparing yourself with your friends. With all due respect, one or more of them may be, um, fibbing. More importantly, no one should expect to have exactly the same kind of sex as anyone else. Many, many women, for example, just seem unable to have multiple orgasms.

If you want to experiment, play with your breathing. Breathe deeply and slowly during orgasm, and focus on letting the sexual energy go through you, rather than pushing it out. After you climax, continue the stimulation, even if you can only tolerate the slightest pressure. As your postorgasm sensitivity subsides, you'll be able to get aroused again. As that happens, increase the stimulation and keep breathing. Another orgasm may follow.

If pursuing multiple orgasms makes sex too much like work, do yourself a favor and forget it.

469. What's so bad about faking an orgasm every now and then? I told my sister-in-law I sometimes do this, and she acted like it's a big crime.

The problem with faking orgasms is that it prevents you from creating whatever you need to have real orgasms. Your partner doesn't know that change is needed, and you have less chance to experiment. And each time you fake it, it becomes a little harder to stop faking and admit what you've been doing.

That's the practical side. Systematically misleading your partner is also unethical. Although no one likes knowing that his or her mate is unsatisfied, people are even more upset about being deceived.

470. When I don't climax my husband feels personally insulted. What should I do?

You could fake orgasms like the lady in the question above, but that would be a mistake. Especially if you have the same sister-in-law.

Like many men, your husband may feel that your orgasm certifies that he is a good lover. If so, then of course he's insulted when you don't climax. To him, you're announcing that he's lousy in bed.

The two of you need to discuss his attitude. Specifically, you need to explain that your orgasm is for you, not for him. In reality, a woman's climax depends on many things besides her partner's technical virtuosity, such as the environment and her state of mind. Explain that his investment in your experience makes you feel used and very *unsexy*.

That said, are you taking responsibility for your own orgasm, rather than expecting him to "give" it to you? The latter attitude will pressure your partner to do sex to you, rather than share it with you.

Remind your husband that you don't need to climax every time. Also, keep in mind that you can continue having sex after he ejaculates, with his hand or yours on your clitoris or vulva.

471. About half the time we make love I don't have an orgasm. That in itself isn't a problem, but what should I do when this happens?

If you're okay about it, do nothing. Certainly, no apology is necessary. If your partner looks at you with concern, smile reassuringly and continue enjoying the afterglow. Later you can calmly explain that you feel fine, you don't always come, and that sex was great.

If you have a steady partner who can't seem to relax about your mezzo-mezzo style, have a straightforward conversation—out of bed—in which you ask to be accepted for who you are. Assure your partner that you'll tell him or her if you want more stimulation at any given time, and demand that you be believed.

Many women tell new partners that they rarely climax the first time with someone and that that's okay. You might want to do something similar.

472. I really enjoy my orgasms, but I often feel sad or lonely afterwards. Why is this? What should I do?

Orgasm, you must admit, is a tough act to follow. If our expectations are high, it's easy to feel a bit disappointed when it's over. And even if they aren't, we have to return to real life at some point, and that's *never* as good as flying through sexual ecstasy.

Some people call orgasm "the little death"; perhaps they are referring to the sense of abandonment so common afterwards. Since sex involves relating to someone in a highly primitive way, returning to real life requires a separation that can be painful in a similarly primitive way.

Of course, postorgasmic blues in a problematic relationship are understandable. For some people sex is give and give, with no get. And for some, the period following orgasm is a rude awakening from the pleasant illusion of being with a real partner, not just a sex partner.

What to do? One or more of these suggestions may be helpful:

• Get plenty of afterplay, with cuddling and other attention
• Have realistic expectations of your sexual encounter, its meaning, and its consequences
• Discuss your feelings with your partner
• Have sex only with people you really care about (if that's your thing)
• Realize that you have different kinds of experiences with different partners, and plan accordingly
• Observe the emotional results of your various sexual activities and situations, and learn what works best for you

473. My partner seems to go into a trance when climaxing, and I feel deserted. What should I do?

Many people do go into a light trance as they climax. They let go of their everyday boundaries so much that they no longer have the orgasm, it has them. They become it. This is a profound, moving experience.

It's easy, however, to feel left behind when your partner is traveling to the moon—without you. The trick here is to find a balance between staying in touch with each other and letting go of each other enough to allow spontaneous, subjective experience. This requires experimentation and trust.

Let your partner know how much you enjoy being in contact, what he or she does that makes contact especially meaningful, and what it's like to feel abandoned. Then work together to solve the *joint* (not "your") problem.

26

Desire Conflicts

Man survives earthquakes, epidemics, the horrors of illness, and all the tortures of the soul, but the most tormenting tragedy at all times has been, is, and will be the tragedy of the bedroom.

—Leo Tolstoy

474. My partner and I have very different sex drives. Do other couples fight about this? How do we decide who's right?

Yes, other couples argue about this. A lot.

Just as with food, movies, and music, it's very common for people who care for each other to have contrasting tastes in sex. When it comes to sex, unfortunately, people spend a lot of time trying to decide who's right, instead of trying to create solutions.

Desire conflicts should not be framed in terms of who loves whom, or about who is sexy, or about who is psychologically healthy. They should never be about who is right. When people express their frustration by criticizing each other, they perpetuate their problems.

Rather than being adversaries, think of yourselves as teammates who are used to solving problems as a team. Resources such as creativity, sense of humor, compassion, and communication skills will help generate approaches that meet everyone's needs.

475. What's an average sex drive? I mean, how often do most people do it?

The range of what healthy, "normal" humans do, sexually, is enormous, far broader than most people assume. Some folks want sex three times a year, some three times a day. Variables like age, health, and living arrangements make an enormous difference.

In general, I think that most people overestimate how much sex others want.

If you are concerned about your own sex drive, or are unhappy with your partner's, don't refer to what other people do. You know what feels right and what feels uncomfortable. Let that information guide your communication and judgment.

476. What, if anything, is the difference between low desire and inhibited desire?

This is not just a question of semantics but an issue with important clinical implications.

Inhibited desire suggests that a person would have more desire if some block were removed. It also sometimes refers to the sexual component of a larger personality issue, such as depression. While *low desire* is sometimes used to mean the same thing, it more often describes a person's basic makeup: the fact that their desire level right now is about as high as it's ever going to be.

Therapists respond to these two situations differently, and so should partners. To someone on the receiving end, of course, the difference between the two seems about as relevant as changing deck chairs on the *Titanic*.

477. My spouse knows how much I enjoy sex. Why then deny me this pleasure?

In the film *Annie Hall,* Diane Keaton's character announces she's quitting therapy. Woody Allen's character (her boyfriend) responds, "This is very hostile toward me," and Keaton replies, "That's just like you, seeing everything I do in terms of how it affects *you,* not what it means in *my* life." We know the relationship is doomed.

Assuming your marriage is not simply a domestic battlefield, your mate is not refusing sex just to drive you crazy. The question then, is why he or she *is* doing it. Your partner may dislike sex (or sex with you), it may be physically painful, it may trigger memories of childhood trauma, etc.

If you ask in a genuinely open fashion, you will probably be able to discover why your mate resists sex. If you can't ask that way, or if your mate can't answer, pursue marital counseling.

478. Some people say that too much screwing makes you lose interest in sex. Can you explain this?

As wonderful as intercourse is, it has many disadvantages: Men can feel pressured to get and keep an erection; it's a difficult or impossible way for most women to climax; it generally requires contraception; and it requires a certain amount of physical energy.

When intercourse is the main or only form of lovemaking, these disadvantages can make someone shy away from sex altogether. So defining sex primarily as intercourse ("screwing") can contribute to low desire.

Also, some people get caught up in intercourse and lose interest in kissing and caressing. If their partners feel deprived of those things, their frustration can turn them off of sex. The solution in both cases is to enjoy a variety of sexual experiences and not get overly involved in just one.

479. How do I know if I'm frigid?

Unless you're an Arctic breeze or the penguin house at the zoo, you aren't.

Frigid is an old-fashioned, discredited expression, like *old maid*. It is oppressive and unacceptable because it is a moral judgment dressed up to sound like an objective description. It isn't at all scientific.

You may have inhibited or low sexual desire (see question 476), which in turn may reflect a physical or emotional difficulty. Or you may be involved in a problematic relationship that expresses its difficulties, in part, through sexual conflict.

I do not automatically assume that the lower-desire partner is the problem. In different circumstances, the roles might be reversed.

If you and your mate are unhappy with your sexual relationship, get help from a sex therapist or marriage counselor.

480. I'm interested in sex quite a bit—unless I'm upset, you know, angry, sad, or worried. Then I lose interest. How can I change that?

Our bodies are not designed to get sexually aroused when we feel upset. Your experience is very common.

You may want to learn to process your feelings more closely to the time when they occur. If a sexual situation comes up and your feelings are in the way, perhaps you could share them with your partner. A mate's sympathy and caring often kindles desire, or the intimacy that can lead to desire.

If you feel upset most of the time, see a therapist. If you mostly have these feelings right before making love, professional help is also indicated.

481. Am I the only one whose sexual desire changes with my monthly cycle? Should I try to overcome this? If others experience this too, when is their horny time?

Many women report fluctuations in their sexuality during their monthly cycle. This is probably due to a combination of hormonal changes and physical effects such as bloating, head-ache, and fatigue.

Sexually, different women favor different parts of their monthly cycle. Do you know your own preference? Whatever it is for you, share the information with your partner. Together you can look forward to and plan for your more interested times, and be sensitive to (and accepting of) your less interested times.

482. I love my wife, but over the years I've lost most of my desire for her. What should I do?

This is one of the most difficult problems faced by couples and therapists alike. And one of the oldest. As Marquis de Luc de Clapiers observed centuries ago, "The heaviest object in the world is the body of the woman you have ceased to desire."

The erosion of desire has many sources: accumulated anger, new needs, even our own hormonal changes. But there can be deeper, more troubling reasons. Some people fear intimacy or commitment, which unconsciously undermines the desire for a loved one. Others are so painfully reminded of their own mortality by watching their mates age that they psychologically flee by losing sexual desire.

Dealing with these or other emotional conflicts simply by changing partners is shortsighted and self-defeating, because unresolved personal issues will eventually erode the sexual desire for one's next partner as well. Therapy or another form of personal insight/change work is crucial for moving forward.

Honestly discussing the situation with your mate can be helpful and life-changing. She may very well be feeling just as you do. Whether she does or not, she certainly wants you to desire her. Why not work creatively together as teammates, spicing up sex with touching, teasing, and toys? The answer is probably not loving her more; you're better off creating sex you enjoy and desiring *it* more.

483. I hate when I'm interested in sex and my partner isn't. Does everybody in this situation feel rejected? Will I ever get over this feeling? What do other people do?

Everybody hates feeling this way, and "rejected" is probably the most common description.

But why don't we feel this bad when we're turned down for a tennis game or a walk in the park? Because with sex, we take the "No, thank you" quite personally. This is a logical result of the myth that "if you love me, you'll make love with me." We feel that if we are not desired sexually at a given moment, we're not desired at all.

I frequently work with people having trouble coping with sexual rejection. They condense an entire childhood's worth of rejections into any occasional sexual turn-down. What they hear is "You're worthless. Go away."

We all have the infantile wish to get everything we want when we want it. Overcoming the belief that this is possible is a big contribution to any serious relationship, as well as to one's personal growth. Therapy is an excellent resource for accomplishing this.

484. I've read that busy couples should make a date for sex, but planning like this really kills my sexual interest. Any advice?

Perhaps you're turning what should be a fun little game into a serious project with obligations. Planning a sex date with your spouse starts a period of titillation, anticipation, imagination, and, eventually, lubrication. When the appointed hour nears, if you realize it's an inconvenient time, just change the date. Be very regretful, of course—but just change it. Don't use your sex date to create the very performance pressure that makes you avoid sex in the first place.

Some people dislike sex dates because they involve admitting that you're having sex, even planning and thinking about it.

Making dates for sex is not necessary. It's only a tool, like lingerie or candlelight, to lure busy people into making love when their lives are distracted by other things. If you and your mate are having enough sex spontaneously, forget the dates, move directly to Go, and collect $200.

485. How can I increase my partner's interest in sex?

While I'm sure your partner appreciates this "do it your-self" spirit in the kitchen, basement, or garden, his or her sex drive is not a good project for you.

Besides, it's not your job. If your partner does want to be changed (which is probably not the case), I doubt that he or she wants you to do the fixing. Most people would experience your efforts as controlling or intrusive.

What you *can* do is get a clearer sense of what makes your partner open to sex, and weave more of that into your lives. You can also let your partner know that you're available to work on the real issues involved in your sexual conflict (as opposed to the single issue of "why can't we do it more?").

Changing a person's sex drive is one of the hardest things therapists are asked to do; attempting to change your spouse in this regard is asking for trouble.

486. I'm getting involved with a really great woman. But she was molested as a kid and says that sex makes her uncomfortable. Will she ever recover and have a normal interest in sex?

It depends largely on how committed she is to getting help. Resolving something like this is often very painful, but it can be done. After all these years, she will probably not heal much more without some kind of therapy.

Trauma is a common origin of low or inhibited sexual de-sire. It drenches sex with bad memories. And it makes a person want to defend him- or herself rather than letting go.

If your friend is resigned to being a lifelong victim and just making do, she may never change. Predictably, she and almost any man she married would fight about sex. Your story is a perfect example of why it's so important for people to know each other and be honest with themselves before deciding to marry.

487. My man's a sex maniac! How can I calm him down?

You could tire him out with nonstop sex, but that's prob-ably not what you have in mind.

Sex maniac can mean many things. Your mate may be in-sensitive to your needs, either sexually or nonsexually. Perhaps you feel he is emotionally absent during sex or that he is un-interested in you in any other way. Maybe he's a guy who talks about sex inappropriately, bringing it into every conversation.

He may want to make love with you far more than you want. People are born with different tastes. Maybe your tastes would be closer if some of the above issues were resolved.

Calling him names won't help. He needs to know what he's doing that upsets you, as well as what you would enjoy. He also needs to understand under what conditions you desire sex. You need to work together to create those conditions.

If there are no circumstances under which you'd desire and enjoy sex with this man, counseling is in order.

488. I think it's only fair that my wife initiate sex some of the time. But she says that since I'm the one who wants it, I should initiate. Who's right?

Neither of you.

Neither "fairness" nor "It's not *my* problem" is a good way to decide who should initiate sex. People should initiate sex as part of expressing themselves *and* of expressing their sense of closeness. Each of you is missing part of this pleasure.

The important questions here are: What is inhibiting your wife from initiating more frequently or more assertively? And what is making it difficult for you to be patient, letting your wife initiate on her schedule?

Both of these questions need to be faced. A good therapist will address them simultaneously, giving each spouse the feeling that his or her concern is being taken seriously.

On the other hand, if this is your only sexual complaint, you may be better off letting go of your need to be approached. Instead of "initiating," maybe your wife would be interested in inviting, seducing, or even suggesting that you initiate. These may help you feel somewhat better.

489. My spouse only agrees to sex if I've "been good." What should I do?

This system makes sense in only two situations: if there is no other way your partner can get you to keep your agreements; or if he or she doesn't really like sex. If one of these is true, some personal growth work is called for. Marriage is hard enough without one person being undependable or the other being uninterested in sex.

If neither of these tells the whole story, then you're describing a power struggle. The question is, what is it really about? What does your spouse want? Is he or she feeling controlled? The sexual relationship is an expression of some other conflict. What?

If your present situation is unacceptable, say so. Refuse to go along with the game anymore, and request that new conditions for sex be drawn up—mutually. At the same time, suggest that your spouse has some serious dissatisfaction also and invite him or her to describe it. Don't defend yourself; listen to the feelings and complaints as information to be used productively.

490. We used to argue a lot about whether or not to make love. Now we have another problem—we hardly hug and kiss anymore. We still love each other. What can we do?

This is very common. The lower-desire partner begins to fear that touching will be interpreted as an invitation to sex and stops touching. Frustrated, the higher-desire partner gets grabby when any touching is available, which only justifies the first partner's fear.

The lack of touching and hugging damages a relationship far more than the lack of sex. Partners quickly feel isolated, angry, unloved, and hopeless about bridging the ever-widening gap between them.

To break this impasse, the higher-desire partner must demonstrate that he or she can hug and be hugged without trying to make it erotic. When the lower-desire partner experiences and eventually trusts this, the nurturance and intimacy of touch can be restored to the relationship. This, in turn, will help create a forum for addressing problems and maybe even the positive atmosphere needed for increased lovemaking.

491. My partner just doesn't believe me when I say I'm too tired for sex. What should I do?

There are probably several different things going on here. Certainly, you should not be questioned, criticized, or punished for refusing sex. And fatigue is a perfectly valid reason to say no.

But has "I'm too tired" become a euphemism for "I don't want to deal with our unsatisfying sexual relationship?" If so, I can understand why your partner resents it.

It may be time to clear the air about the role of sex in your lives. I urge you to do so, rather than avoiding conflict by periodically being "too tired." Also, you probably need a different way of responding to each other's sexuality. When you're uninterested in intercourse, are you interested in hugging, kissing, or other things? Let your partner know this instead of simply rejecting all physical contact in one curt reply.

492. My partner feels personally rejected when I say no to sex. What should I do?

It's hard not to feel rejected, isn't it? You may simply be saying no to sex, but your mate feels as if you're rejecting sex-with-*me*.

There is an art to rejecting sex without rejecting the suitor, and it consists mostly of handling your own discomfort in a graceful way. This requires that you be emotionally present for a few moments, something to which your partner will be keenly sensitive.

27

Rape and Date Rape

The longer I live the more keenly I feel that whatever was good enough for our fathers is not good enough for us.

—Oscar Wilde

493. How common is rape? I hear such different estimates.

The disagreement comes from two facts. First, rape is one of the most underreported crimes there is. Fear and shame prevent as many as 90 percent of all victims from going to the police. Second, definitions of rape differ. For starters, we should declare that if a woman says no, or is unable to say no (for example, because she's passed out from drinking), it is rape.

Some 100,000 rapes were reported to the police last year. Thoughtful estimates put the actual number from twice to ten times that amount.

494. Why do some men rape women? Is it because they're oversexed and they see a woman who turns them on and can't control themselves?

Rape is rarely a crime of passion. Rather, it is usually a crime of violence in which sex is the weapon. Generally, men rape because of a desire to conquer, to hurt, to humiliate, to get revenge, or to feel adequate or superior. Rape is occasionally a crime of erotic passion, when the rapist's arousal depends on violence instead of more typical sources.

Rape victims are never to blame, regardless of what they wear or do. We don't say that people who leave their cars unlocked deserve to be robbed or that people who talk loudly in bars deserve to get beat up, do we?

495. Who would do such an awful thing? Surely, such people are sick.

Many rapists are mentally ill, with limited impulse control, a damaged sense of reality, and wild, unpredictable behavior or mood swings. On the other hand, many rapists seem to function fairly well at their jobs and in social situations. Frequently they are known and accepted by the victim. College students who rape other college students are often highly respected by their teachers and peers.

According to sex educator Michael Carrera, rapists often have the following profile:

- Have a history of violent, aggressive behavior
- Are frequently from lower socioeconomic background
- Are usually under age thirty
- Do *not* have unusual sex drives
- Have a history of drug or alcohol abuse, and
- Suffer from poor ego development and low self-esteem

Sex educator Sol Gordon adds that rapists typically feel a lot of guilt about sex and masturbation.

The fact that so many rapes are committed by more or less "normal" men should make us stop and think about what we teach boys about sexuality and power.

496. Doesn't looking at pornography cause rape? I believe men who

see those pictures or movies think women are just sex objects, there for the taking.

The scientific facts just don't support this popular belief. Even Ronald Reagan's Meese Commission could find no evidence that viewing pornography causes antisocial behavior.

Some 20 million Americans enjoy sexually explicit films and magazines each year. The vast majority of them never rape or assault anyone. And in European countries where pornography is completely legal, there are dramatically fewer rapes than in the United States.

Yes, many rapists look at pornography. They also drink coffee and watch "Cosby Show" reruns. We don't claim that either of those causes rape. It is far more likely that the *repression* of sexuality—including erotic materials—encourages sexually violent behavior. Guilt and shame are what drive people mad, not sexual arousal.

Besides, society doesn't need pornography to teach us that women are sex objects. For that we have *Cosmopolitan*, "Dynasty," Rambo, romance novels, and the fashion industry. These affect far more people far more deeply than *Playboy* or videos possibly could.

497. It's not fashionable to say so, but don't you think some women ask to be raped by the way they dress or act?

You're suggesting that some humans want to be humiliated, beaten up, threatened with being crippled or killed, and possibly impregnated or infected with an STD. This bizarre belief helps maintain the high level of rape in this country.

Saying that women should dress or act a certain way so that they will not be assaulted makes women responsible for men's behavior, which is completely unfair. How would you respond if someone suggested you were asking to be beaten up when you wore a Red Sox T-shirt to a Yankee game?

498. I know women don't want to be raped, but don't they enjoy it after it begins? If rape is inevitable, why not try to relax and enjoy it?

Men who rape are not gentle, considerate lovers who want to satisfy their victims. Rape is *sexual assault*—the sex is brutal, physically painful, often deliberately humiliating, and very scary. No one enjoys being treated this way.

Even if a woman wanted to enjoy being raped, voluntarily submitting would not help. Most rapists are interested in domination and control, and will mistreat victims regardless of the way they behave. Besides, suggesting that a woman surrender and "enjoy" being raped is like suggesting that a man surrender and "enjoy" being beaten. Wouldn't you be offended at the very suggestion?

499. I'm confused. If I don't want to be raped, why do I enjoy fantasies about being raped when I masturbate?

Enjoying a fantasy is not the same as desiring the activity you're fantasizing about. Surely you have noticed this about nonsexual daydreams.

Rape fantasies rarely include the physical pain, numbing fear, sense of outrage, and pure ugliness that are common features of rape in real life. Instead, they focus on masculine power, relief from responsibility, just enough uncertainty to make it exciting, and an odd sense of trust. These elements can create an enjoyable fantasy, particularly when you know you can stop it at any time. They are not what real rape is about.

500. Why is it sometimes said that girls and boys learn to accept and even to expect rape?

Consider what young people learn about sex and gender:

• You can tell if a woman wants sex by how she's dressed
• Men's sexual urges are so strong that they're uncontrollable
• Women who want and prepare for sex are "sluts" (therefore, women have to resist sex whether they want it or not)
• If a woman accepts expensive gifts or entertainment from a man she "owes" him sex (this is why young women should pay their own way on dates)

• It is manly to "seduce" women; getting a reluctant woman to have sex is a great accomplishment

• Women don't really want sex; they need to be swept away by alcohol, love, or force

If we wanted to develop a social environment that supported the existence of rape, *our society* is what we would create. No wonder that a recent survey at UCLA, one of America's best colleges, showed both male and female students agreeing that under certain circumstances, women owe men sex.

501. Being raped was the worst thing that ever happened to me. Six months later, I'm still a wreck. Will I ever recover?

I hope so. But if you're like most survivors of rape, you have some work ahead of you. You probably have a low sense of self-worth, feelings of guilt and shame, anger you have no good place to direct, and contradictory needs about closeness and intimacy. Your interest in sex is probably damaged too.

Whether you reported the assault or not, it is important that you get involved with a rape survivor program. It will help you acknowledge and understand your feelings, direct your anger productively, repair your intimate relationships, and heal your sexuality.

Being raped doesn't make you bad, wrong, stupid, or damaged. But like a survivor of any trauma, you do need help to get on with the rest of your life.

502. I was raped a few months ago. When I told my boyfriend what happened, he became terribly angry, yelling and calling me names. It devastated me. How could he?

This is a common reaction from men whose partners have been raped. While it is completely inexcusable, it is understandable.

We may be modern people, but our images of male and female are ancient. And the most deep-rooted image of all is that man protects woman. Specifically, a man protects *his* woman.

When a woman is raped, her man feels as if he has failed

in his most fundamental duty. It is his worst nightmare come true. The reality—that there was no way he could have prevented it—is, emotionally, irrelevant. He typically feels guilty, powerless, and inadequate. *He* feels violated. He feels he is not a "real man."

Why do men rage at their partners who are raped? The rage is really about themselves; but because it is too painful to feel, they direct it outward. This is tragic, a second round of victimization. Blaming the woman is, simply, a defense against feeling the anguish that, for men, feels far too frightening to acknowledge.

503. I'm the one who was raped. But my mate says *he* has feelings that are important, too. How could he even compare his feelings to mine?

He isn't. He's simply saying that he's upset, too, and that he needs attention. You are probably not the person to give him the emotional support he needs right now. But it is healthy to acknowledge the reality of his feelings along with yours. The traditional male posture—"I'm fine, I can handle it, let's just take care of you"—is ultimately destructive.

Just as you don't want him denying your feelings because they are too painful for him to watch, don't shut down his feelings because they seem inappropriate to you.

504. My partner was raped, and I feel paralyzed. Everything I do or say seems stupid. What should I do?

The most important thing is to get help. You and your partner should be involved in a rape crisis program, which may be available through the local YWCA, women's center, family planning clinic, police department, or county health department. They will assess your needs and offer information, support, and legal and medical assistance.

You and your mate probably need to sit down and have a long cry together. She has been violated; so has your relationship. You two have suffered a serious loss. You need to talk about how you can go through this loss together, rather than separately.

Ask her what she wants. Be gentle, caring, and ready to listen. Hold her affectionately if she wants; don't if she doesn't seem to want it. Do not try to fix everything yourself. And make sure you get the help you need, too.

505. My friend was raped and didn't report it because she was afraid of how the police would handle it. Was she right?

Unfortunately, our law-enforcement system is, for the most part, still a few centuries behind in dealing with rape. The questioning of rape victims is too often brusque, inappropriately personal, and leering. Part of the problem is that men make the policies and usually take the reports.

The courts then exacerbate the problem by attempting to discredit a woman's account through questions about her previous sexual encounters, as if each one reduces a woman's right to be safe from assault.

Fortunately, things are beginning to change. Rape victims should request female police officers and female physicians, who are now more available than ever before. In weighing whether or not to report a rape, victims should think not only about avoiding the possible pain of interrogation but also about the possible guilt they may feel should they avoid the process.

506. I used to enjoy sex, but since I was raped, I just can't. Will I ever recover?

Loss of sexual interest is very common for victims of rape. Don't blame yourself; you didn't invite this problem any more than you invited the assault.

Professional help is an important part of recovering your full sexuality after a rape. See a psychotherapist or rape crisis counselor as soon as possible.

507. What is statutory rape?

Statutory rape describes sexual intercourse with someone who, according to the state, does not have the right to consent to sex. The "victim" may not have this right because she/he is "underage," mentally impaired, drunk, or legally incapacitated in some other way.

In contrast to forcible rape, statutory rape may involve no force at all. The "victim" may have fully agreed to or even initiated the sex. Nevertheless, statutory rape is often punished as severely as forcible rape. According to sexologist Erwin J. Haeberle, "Most rape convictions are for the nonviolent statutory kind."

508. What exactly is date rape?

Date rape (or acquaintance rape, or acquaintance assault) is forced sex between people who already have some sort of social relationship. A common scenario is the following: Two people go out and have a nice time. He's interested in sex, she isn't, and he pushes and insists until he forces her or she acquiesces out of fear or disgust.

A variant of this scene involves alcohol. The couple is having fun and drinking. When he initiates sex she resists, but the alcohol weakens her ability to withstand his pressure, both physically and mentally.

509. How common is date rape?

Estimates vary, but most studies of the last thirty years indicate that at least 40 percent of college women experience unwanted sexual aggression. E. J. Kanin's 1969 study in the *Journal of Sex Research* is equally revealing. In a sample of four hundred college men, 22 percent said they personally attempted to have sex by force that year. Presumably, the actual figure is even higher.

Date rape is many women's first sexual experience. However, because they are sexually naive, many do not identify their experience as abusive. They simply think this is the way sex is. What an awful introduction to sexual relations.

510. Don't women have any responsibility for date rape?

Not for being raped—but for participating in the complex social choreography that almost inevitably leads to date rape.

As educator Warren Farrell, author of *Why Men Are the Way They Are*, notes:

- Many young women do flaunt their sexual desirability and interest as part of attracting men. When they later decline sexual involvement—in fact, become insulted that sex is suggested—men become confused.
- Many women choose men based on their looks or careers—then resent it when men selected on the basis of these superficial criteria are insensitive to their needs and wishes.
- When a man makes physical advances and a woman says no, and he persists, and for various reasons she eventually acquiesces, a "relationship language" develops in which *no sometimes means yes*. When he then suggests intercourse and she says no, should he believe this no to mean no, or yes?

Again, *no one is ever to blame for being assaulted*. Still, the cumulative effect on men of what Farrell calls "date fraud" is humiliation, confusion, and rage.

511. How can we reduce the amount of rape in this country?

The way we think about rape prevents us from reducing or eliminating it. To change our thinking, we must realize:

- Rape is not a "women's issue"
- Women do not want to be raped, nor do they invite it by their clothes or sexual behavior, and
- Rape is typically an act of violence, not of sexual passion

In addition, we need to teach young men that they must never pressure a woman for sex and that they must accept her "no" the first time she says it. We must teach young women that they should only have to say "no" once; negotiating after the first "no" only confuses young men. Just as importantly, we need to accept young women's interest in sex, so they can say "yes" when they mean "yes." Only this will eliminate the present ambiguity of "no."

Our culture must also decide that men in prison have a right to be safe from assault.

512. Why is it important to talk about rape? It's such an unpleasant subject.

We need to talk about it in order to educate the public that it happens; that it happens to "nice girls"; that victims should not feel guilty or ashamed; and that both men and women play a role in maintaining a rape culture.

It is important for children to know about rape, too. The earlier they learn that sex must never be used as a weapon, and that everyone has a right to control his or her own body, the easier it will be to reduce the incidence of rape.

513. How is it possible for a woman to be raped by her husband?

Traditionally, rape is defined as a man forcing sex on a woman to whom he is not married. This reflects the custom that married women are the property of their husbands, which gives men the *right* to have sex with their wives.

Today, our views of both marriage and sex are changing. We see spouses more as equals, with equal rights to protection and resources. And we are starting to see sex as something precious that should only be given, never taken; something that no one has a right to take from anyone else.

Thus, everyone deserves protection from unwanted sex, including children, spouses, prostitutes, criminals, and homeless, mentally unstable people. A marriage license is not a sexual license, guaranteeing one partner access to the other's body.

Still, some husbands use violence or the threat of violence to get sex from their wives. They may even batter their children, physically or psychologically, to control their wives' decision-making.

Any person who forces another to have unwanted sex is committing an assault. Husbands who do this to their wives should be called what they are—rapists. Laws are finally, slowly catching up to this concept.

514. I hear about all these men raped in prison by other men. Are there that many homosexuals in prison?

No. Prison rapists are interested in domination and aggression; victims are chosen according to their lack of seniority, their place in the inmate hierarchy, and who is protecting them.

Many prison rapists are virulently antigay. In fact, rape—which symbolizes power—is one way for an inmate to prove he's a "real man." This issue shows how misleading it can be to categorize people's sexuality based on what thing goes into which orifice.

While society is becoming more aware of and responsive to the problem of women being raped, there is still a conspiracy of silence about the overwhelming number of men raped every day in American jails.

515. What is this "morning-after pill" women can take if they get raped?

The shock of being raped can make a woman ovulate spontaneously. This makes pregnancy a concern whenever a rape has involved intercourse.

To prevent pregnancy after a rape, women can now take very high doses of synthetic estrogen within seventy-two hours of unprotected intercourse. This brings on menstruation, although the side effects include nausea and vomiting. Unfortunately, a few women become pregnant despite the drug. Because of the high hormone levels, their fetuses are then at risk for abnormalities.

28

Sex Therapy

Psychiatry enables us to correct our faults by confessing our parents' shortcomings.

—Laurence J. Peter

516. What exactly goes on in sex therapy?

Talk, talk, talk. No touching, no watching. Using various kinds of talk, sex therapy involves the following:

- *Giving information* about the way your body and emotions work
- *Giving permission* to express your sexuality in ways you are comfortable with
- *Developing communication* with your partner about your likes and dislikes, needs and feelings, and for use in conflict resolution
- *Clarifying the goals* of your sexual interactions and relationship(s)

• *Examining and changing belief systems* (religious, family, political, etc.) that interfere with sexual pleasure and functioning
• *Resolving old emotional wounds* you have as an individual, and
• *Resolving old emotional wounds* your relationship has

How does therapy do this? By helping people talk honestly about what sex is like for them and by spotting beliefs and patterns that interfere with sexual functioning. We help people explore the past for clues that explain present behavior. And we assess the communication system, power balance, and role of sex in a relationship.

Depending on the situation, this is done with an individual or a couple.

517. What types of problems can sex therapy help?

Sexual experience is the product of two processes: physical and psychological. Sex therapy deals with difficulties in each of these areas.

It can help resolve problems involving erection, ejaculation, orgasm, and physical pain. And it can also help people with psychodynamic issues such as desire, turn-ons, fantasies, sex roles, anger, anxiety, guilt, past traumas, and sexual identity.

But sex therapy isn't Rambo: It can't do everything, cleaning up the jungle, guns blazing, against overwhelming odds. For example, it can't help alcoholics whose drinking is out of control. It also can't help people who are psychotic or who are convinced that change is impossible.

Finally, sex therapy is not the right treatment for those who are so psychologically damaged that they have little or no sense of self.

518. How is sex therapy different from marriage counseling? How do I know which to pursue?

Both forms of therapy are designed to facilitate healing and change. They use similar tools and often have similar goals. In fact, there is no strict line separating the two. A case of, say, conflicting levels of desire may turn out to be an issue of power or intimacy that requires marital counseling. And a case of, say, chronic fighting may express the hidden sexual frustration of one or both partners.

If your marriage's sex problems were fixed, would there still be other difficulties? If so, start with a marital therapist. If not, start with a sex therapist. But don't be surprised if you switch treatment strategies or even therapists after awhile. The most important thing is to start with a competent professional regardless of specialty. If he or she doesn't have the expertise you need, you'll get a good referral to someone who does.

519. How successful is sex therapy?

Naturally, success depends on the skill and experience of the professional. It also depends on the problem. Rapid ejaculation and lack of orgasm, for example, are among the easiest problems to work with; far more than half of all such cases show dramatic improvement. Serious desire conflicts and inability to ejaculate, on the other hand, are much more difficult; one-third or fewer of such cases show substantial improvement.

Of course, improvement also depends on motivation. Therapy is hard, painful work, often expensive and time-consuming. So how many sex therapists does it take to change a lightbulb? Only one—but the lightbulb really has to want to change.

520. How do I choose a sex therapist? My doctor is no help.

Doctors are a good place to start, although many are uncomfortable talking about sex. A local gynecologist or urologist may be able to help. You can also get a referral from an attorney, accountant, marriage counselor, clergyperson, or family planning clinic.

You can also get reliable, nationwide referrals from SSSS (The Society for the Scientific Study of Sex) at (319) 895-8407, or AASECT (The American Association of Sex Educators, Counselors, and Therapists) at (312) 644-0828.

Regardless of your problem, do *not* go to a so-called sex addiction program. The staff at such programs are rarely trained in human sexuality.

521. What should I look for in a sex therapist?

Start with professionalism: self-respect, an obvious sense of purpose, and experience with your kind of situation. Training in psychology, marital counseling, and physiology is crucial; familiarity with religion and sociology is very helpful.

Comfort with sexuality is important, of course, and not to be taken for granted; education, reputation, and success do not guarantee it. This is difficult to gauge, but check out a therapist's body language, physical presence, and ability to talk easily about sex. Compassion and a sense of humor will also help make therapy less difficult.

Ultimately, the most important factor is how you feel about this person and how you like sharing an hour with him or her. Thus, shopping for a therapist requires that you get in touch with your feelings, and selecting one involves trusting those feelings. For most people, this process is itself a valuable part of the treatment.

522. How do I choose between seeing a sex therapist and going to a sex-addiction treatment program?

A sex therapist must have graduate-level training in both psychology and human sexuality. An addiction counselor doesn't need either and almost never has both. A sex therapist understands the wide range of human sexual behavior and doesn't try to make patients "normal." An addiction counselor has a rigid model of "normal sex" and tries to help patients change to fit into that mold.

A sex therapist sees sex as a positive force that can be legitimately used in many different ways. An addiction counselor believes that using sex to feel good about yourself, or fantasizing about person A while making love with person B, is demeaning and a sign of mental problems.

How do you choose between them? You go to the trained professional who sees sex as an exciting journey that requires healthy decision-making, not the nonprofessional "true believer," frequently "in recovery," who sees sex as a destructive force needing to be controlled.

523. What is a surrogate? Isn't that just a fancy name for a prostitute?

A prostitute is someone who gives sexual pleasure for money. A surrogate is a clinically supervised professional, trained in psychology, sexology, and physiology, who works with a therapist to accomplish specific therapeutic goals. You can see a surrogate only as part of working with a sex therapist. A full medical and psychological history is also necessary.

Surrogate therapy is used only occasionally, when talk therapy alone isn't enough. Surrogates educate patients (generally single) about sex through actual experiences, helping them redefine their sexuality in ways that are broader, more relaxed, and more open to a partner.

Activities with a surrogate can include hand massage, hugging, kissing, and masturbating together. For this reason, many describe themselves as "body therapists" or "sensuality educators" rather than surrogates.

For more information, contact the International Professional Surrogates Association, at (213) 469-4720.

524. I think I could benefit from sex therapy, but I'm uncomfortable getting undressed in front of a stranger. What do you suggest?

Good news: Undressing is not necessary during sex therapy. Indeed, it is totally prohibited. No professional sex society or well-respected sexologist anywhere condones such behavior. The same goes for patient-therapist kissing, fondling, or any kind of sexual intimacy.

Of course, the *verbal* undressing one does in therapy is much more revealing than actual nudity. Patients tolerate it because it is uniquely valuable. When you start therapy, discuss your concerns right from the start so you can relax and get the most from the work.

525. I know I need sex therapy, but should I go with my spouse or by myself?

Like most sexually dissatisfied people, you probably have a theory about where the problem lies: in you, your partner, or the relationship. For example, some 25 percent of my new cases each year start with one partner dragging in the other. "S/he's broken," the dragger will say about the dragee. "Fix her/him."

Whether you come alone or in a pair isn't actually so important. By the end of the first session, I usually have a sense of what will work best—for now. Sometimes I agree with a patient's initial choice of couple versus individual therapy. Other times I'll suggest the opposite. "I'd like to meet with just Joe [or Jane] for a while," I might tell a couple. "I'd like your spouse to join us next time," I might tell an individual.

I prefer to see the couple together the first time, because I can see more of what's going on. Even if I end up working with just one of the partners, I have a feel for the other one and for the tone of the relationship.

If there are things you want to discuss without revealing them to your partner, go alone. If not, and you can't decide what to do, go together.

526. My husband won't go to sex therapy even though we have a poor sex life. What can I do?

Start by explaining why you want to go: not to fix him or prove that he's wrong but because you want to please him and be sexually intimate with him. Right now, you two seem to need help to make that happen.

If your husband agrees with these goals but rejects therapy, ask what his plan is. "Trying harder" is not a plan. "Not getting so upset about things" is not a plan. If your husband doesn't have a plan, you have the right to ask how he expects things to improve. If he doesn't care about things improving even though you're upset, you have more than a sexual problem. You have a marital problem.

Some spouses refuse sex therapy but will go to marriage counseling. If he'll accept this, do it. Some spouses feel better if the therapist is their own gender, or if they can pick the therapist. No problem. The key is to get into the therapist's office. Once you're in the room, change can happen.

If all else fails, don't whine or threaten. Go to a counselor yourself, discharge your anger and grief, and start growing on your own.

527. My wife wants us to go to sex therapy, which makes me nervous. What does she want?

I don't know; you'll have to ask. The fact that she's this dissatisfied and you don't quite know why indicates precisely the lack of communication that can create or maintain a sex problem.

Various people come to sex therapy to discuss technique, variety, frequency, fantasies, something physical such as painful intercourse—or communication.

528. I'm very religious. Can sex therapy help me?

Probably. You know how many sex jokes that start "A rabbi, a minister, and a priest . . ."

Actually, there's a grain of truth in the humor; a surprising number of sex therapists are former or current seminary students or clergy. Besides, training in religion and spirituality should be part of every sex therapist's clinical background.

Sex therapists are supposed to accept patients exactly as they are. We're sensitive to such issues as age, race, and class, as well as religious background. We don't follow a cookbook, trying to get everyone to do or believe the same things. What's appropriate for Mr. Jones on Tuesday at 4:00 P.M. may not be appropriate for Mr. Smith Wednesday at 4:00 P.M.

Besides, every religion supports some kind of sexual expression. I work with patients to adapt these teachings creatively to their own lifestyles. This said, it is still true that examining one's own sexual beliefs is a fundamental part of therapy. So is examining your religion's attitudes about sex. If you believe your religion forbids you from doing so, that will be a problem.

Two wonderful books for laypersons about sex and religion, both written by theologians, are *Between Two Gardens* by James Nelson, and *The Poisoning of Eros* by Raymond J. Lawrence, Jr.

529. Our sex therapist asks for lots of detail about our sex life. Is this okay?

Probably. Like gynecologists and accountants, we have to ask many personal questions that no one else does.

Each question should have a purpose, though, and the therapist's entertainment should never be one of them. For example, if one of my patients were having sex with Manuel Noriega, I wouldn't breathlessly ask what's he like in bed (even though, like you, I'd be curious). It's irrelevant and therefore none of my business.

On the other hand, a question like "How do you feel being involved with someone who is in so much trouble?" would probably be extremely relevant and therefore legitimate. In fact, I might be negligent if I *didn't* ask it.

If you're uncomfortable about the questions you're being asked, by all means raise this issue with your therapist.

530. We need help but therapy is too expensive. What can we do on our own?

You are right: Sex therapy is expensive. Insurance companies don't like to cover it, their pretense being that sex is a luxury item. Considering how much people express sexual frustration through drinking, smoking, depression, and high blood pressure, this looks like a "penny wise, pound foolish" corporate decision.

Some county mental health clinics have a psychologist or social worker trained in sexuality. The only way to know is to ask. And of course, sexuality is the birthplace of the self-help book—some of which really work. Try *Male Sexuality* by Bernie Zilbergeld; *Sexual Solutions* by Michael Castleman; *For Yourself,* by Lonnie Barbach; and *Right-Brain Sex* by Carol Wells.

Spend three minutes each day listening to your mate, without judging or advising. And when you make love, regardless of how you do it or what doesn't work, slow down, breath more deeply, and focus all your attention on where you're being touched.

Part V

Parenting

29

At Home

I hate housework. You make the beds, you do the dishes—and six months later you have to start all over again.

—Joan Rivers

531. Is it okay for us to walk around nude in front of our kids? If so, until what age?

It is certainly fine for young children to see other family members nude. It lets them know that bodies are a normal thing—that is, that they are not only for sex—and that no one's body is perfect.

This assumes, of course, that the adults involved are emotionally healthy. Nudity, when used to shock or entertain children, or to gratify the adult, is never appropriate.

As children in our society get older, they become uncomfortable with adult nudity around the house. They will express this either directly ("Can't you guys wear clothes?") or indirectly (closing the bathroom door when a parent is showering). Parents who are nude with their children must be sensitive to picking up and responding to such cues.

532. Is it okay to bathe with my eighteen-month-old? My mother thinks it's fine, but my wife disapproves.

The answer to your specific question is yes, it's fine for an eighteen-month-old to bathe with his/her father. It's convenient, it normalizes nudity, and it provides a positive, pleasant environment in which your child can enjoy his/her body.

Your wife may be objecting because nudity was taboo in her family when she was a child or because she's jealous of the attention you're giving the baby.

It sounds, however, as if you're caught between your wife and mother. Are the three of you playing out this power struggle in other arenas, too? If this is the case, I urge the three of you—or at least you and your wife—to work together to acknowledge and eliminate it. If a relative or friend can't help you do so, please consider marital or family counseling.

533. My five-year-old walked in on us while we were making love last night. What should we do?

Mostly, don't panic. With a bit of thought, you can turn this into a nonevent for your child (making it a nonevent for you or your spouse is another matter).

Raise the issue soon, when you and your child are feeling close and have some time together. You may want to ask what the child saw or heard and if he or she has any questions. The important thing is to assure the child that no one was being hurt, that you were just expressing your affection in an enthusiastic way. You can add that most Moms and Dads do this occasionally and that they like to do it in private.

A lock on the door will prevent this occurrence in the future. Children can handle a locked door, especially if their own privacy is respected. Accidentally seeing parents making love will not hurt children who feel satisfied that whatever they saw was normal and safe.

534. Is it okay for my wife and me to kiss or caress each other in front of our children? My mother-in-law thinks it's terrible.

Children do not suffer from having parents who love each other openly and express their sexuality appropriately.

Your wife's mother may just be overprotective, or she may have deeper feelings about the propriety of sexuality in general. She may, in fact, be jealous of her daughter's affectionate marriage.

Your children will be exposed to plenty of distorted sexual information from the media as they grow up. Seeing regular people like you and your wife enjoy each other's bodies is the healthiest sex education they can get.

535. How do I explain to my little girl that although "playing doctor" is okay in our house, she shouldn't do it in her friend Jane's house because it upsets Jane's parents?

Life is like that, isn't it—lots of things are okay in some places but inappropriate in others. It's fine to touch yourself in the bedroom, for example, but not when the teacher is talking to you.

Different families have different rules. For example, we might eat chicken with our fingers at home, while in Jane's house, they may use a knife and fork. Another example of this is religion. Other people's religious beliefs may differ from our own. Everyone has that right.

It's important for children to realize that people can be different without someone having to be wrong. This concept is especially important regarding sexual behavior and beliefs. Most people desperately want to be right, which means making others—including, at times, your daughter—wrong.

536. When I change my son's diaper, he sometimes gets an erection. Am I doing something wrong?

An erection is a reflex, like sneezing or blinking, and is totally beyond one's control. Our bodies exhibit such reflexes in response to certain kinds of stimulation.

The physical contact of being changed can easily result in an erection, as can the satisfaction of urinating or defecating. There is nothing abnormal or incestuous about this. There is no reason to feel guilty or embarrassed or to pretend that it's not happening.

By all means, respond to this in the same way you show approval of your baby's other physical responses. And don't be afraid to use words like penis and erection with him. It's the best way to teach respect for this part of the body.

537. How do I get my seven-year-old to stop swearing?

Why does our child's swearing upset us? Sure, swearing can be rude, ugly, mindless, mean, even shocking and frightening. Need it be these things, however, when the author is a seven-year-old?

Kids, of course, want to get our attention, and they all learn that swearing does it. We get upset partly because we feel that one of our adult privileges is being commandeered by a child. We also feel our child's bad language reflects poorly on us. Neither of these issues, of course, matters to children one bit.

And where are the unpleasant words coming from? We'd like to think from "out there"—school, the street, magazines. The source we don't want to look at is our home. For example, television now portrays kids saying things it didn't allow grown-ups to say when I was young. Nothing is sacred now that "suck face" has replaced "kiss."

Parental language is often part of the problem, as children parrot what they hear at home. So if we want our children to clean up their language, we need to examine and perhaps clean up our own. Don't create a power struggle over this. Ignore it, and it will soon go away. And demonstrate that your attention can be had in other ways.

538. My five-year-old has a talent for asking embarrassing sex-related questions in front of visitors. How do I stop her?

Stopping her may not be the most important thing. You can shame a child out of almost anything, but at what price? Connecting sex with guilt is abusive parenting.

So what's embarrassing? These may be legitimate questions that your child gets no other chance to ask. Certainly, your child has learned how to get your attention. The issue, then, is why? If not for wholesome, educational reasons, what else is your child trying to communicate?

It may be a hostile, jealous reaction to sharing you. Or the child may be sexually overstimulated. What's going on in the family? What is the child watching on television? Are your visitors doing anything inappropriate? Is it possible someone else has had sexual contact with the child?

Find out what's on the child's mind instead of simply trying to quiet him or her down. And remember that this could certainly be just a phase. Ask your guests not to respond to the sexual comments, stay out of a power struggle with the child, and allow the problem to go away.

539. My husband's brother is great with our young son, and I love him dearly. But he's gay. Is he a safe choice as a baby-sitter?

I can't answer that without meeting him, but his homosexuality need not concern you.

Contact with homosexuals does not cause homosexuality in children. And homosexuality is rarely a factor in child molestation. The vast majority of child sexual abuse of both genders is done by heterosexuals.

All good parents are concerned for their children's safety. Your fear is just a special case of this, compounded by the general ignorance most straight people have about homosexuality. If you love your brother-in-law dearly, he surely has qualities you'd appreciate in your child. Let him share those qualities.

30

Sex Education

Prejudices are most difficult to eradicate from the heart whose soil has never been loosened or fertilized by education; they grow there, firm as weeds among the stones.

—Charlotte Bronte

540. Why do we need sex education in *school?* I'd rather teach my kids about sex myself.

Everyone—from sex educators to physicians to church leaders—is in favor of children learning about sex from their parents. You are to be commended for taking this responsibility seriously.

You are, however, somewhat unusual in this regard. While most parents say they believe sex education is a parental responsibility, they also admit that they aren't doing it very much.

Given most people's discomfort with and incomplete information about sexuality, this is understandable.

That's the main point of school sex education: to support parents' efforts to educate their children about sexuality. School programs do this by providing information, raising questions, encouraging parent-child conversation, and normalizing discussion about sexual activity and decision-making.

541. I'm confused. How do most parents feel about sex education?

According to research like the *Cleveland Study* of 1,400 families, most parents wish they were doing a better job of educating their children about sexuality. Thus, it is understandable that every national poll between 1980 and 1989 found more than 80 percent of adults favoring sex education in school.

These polls show no major differences between Catholics and Protestants, or between Democrats and Republicans, in support for sex education.

542. Of course I want my kids to be knowledgeable, but doesn't sex education just stimulate their curiosity and encourage them to have sex?

No. Kids don't need any outside influences to be sexually curious. All healthy children are curious about their and others' bodies, about the kissing and touching they see around them, about their own sexual feelings and fantasies, and about the puzzle of reproduction. Sex education satisfies, rather than stimulates, curiosity.

Studies by the federal government and others show that young people's sexual risk-taking is promoted by ignorance, not knowledge. The information and dialogue of sex education reduce the taboo and mystery surrounding sexuality, making premature sex less urgent and less alluring for kids. Sex education helps young people understand the consequences of sexual behavior and teaches mature sexual decision-making.

543. I'm in favor of sex education in general, but how do I know if I agree with what's being taught?

Not to worry. Every public school is required to give parents a chance to review sex education materials and course outlines before classes begin. Feel free to go to school on the announced evening, and ask the teacher as many questions as you wish.

Children must also have a parent's written permission to attend sex education classes, so permission is actually harder to give than to withhold. Still, according to a large national study done by Mathtech Corporation, only 1 percent of parents exclude their children from sex education. In fact, many parents in the study said that they were grateful that their children had such a learning opportunity.

544. Why aren't boys and girls separated in sex education classes?

Actually schools have various policies about separating boys and girls during sex education. Since there is nothing that one gender should know that the other shouldn't, separating kids makes no sense. Besides, experience shows that teaching them together has tremendous advantages.

Learning together teaches boys what girls think and feel, and vice versa. It makes the other gender people, not just sex objects, increasing responsible, respectful behavior. Separating students perpetuates the idea that we shouldn't discuss sex in "mixed company"; but it's precisely in male-female interactions that young people must be able to discuss their sexual thoughts, feelings, and decisions. Mixed classes make this crucial activity normal and comfortable.

Mixed sex education classes are an important solution to Dorothy Dix's classic statement: "The reason husbands and wives do not understand each other is because they belong to different sexes."

545. Why do boys need to know about periods? Doesn't it just embarrass them?

Boys need to know about periods because the majority of them will eventually love and live with women who have periods. Menstruation is part of life for half the world's population, and teaching boys about it shows that it is normal. It also encourages boys and girls to discuss it rather than hide or fear it.

Does teaching boys about menstruation embarrass them? If so, that's the best reason to do it. Making them comfortable with the subject will enable them to talk to *their* kids about it. That's called progress.

546. I think sex education is a good idea, but lately my son has been coming home and asking embarrassing questions. Now what?

Great! This is sex education at its finest—increasing a child's knowledge while enhancing parent-child communication. Here is a chance to share your values, teach solid information, get closer to your child, and voice any concerns you might have.

According to a 1987 study in the prestigious *Journal of Sex Research,* the likelihood that adolescents will have intercourse decreases as the number of sexual topics they discuss with their parents increases. This study was repeated by entirely different researchers the following year, with the same results.

Your most important resources are a few dependable books, honesty, and a sense of humor. By listening patiently and creatively, you can also find out what concerns or misconceptions lie *behind* your son's questions.

Remember, it's always admissible to tell your child, "My dad never discussed these things with me, so I'm a little embarrassed, but okay, let's give it a try." You can even ask someone else in the family (uncle, neighbor) to answer your son's questions.

547. Why all this stuff about clarifying values and presenting different points of view? Isn't the goal of sex ed to teach kids chastity?

No, the goals of sex education are:

• Imparting accurate information about sexuality
• Normalizing the child's sexual thoughts, feelings, and curiosity

• Examining sexual decision-making and the consequences of various sexual decisions
• Instilling a respect for sexuality, one's body, and others' sexual decisions, and
• Encouraging and facilitating parent-child communication about sexuality

When sex education achieves these goals, students examine their sexual decisions far more carefully and wisely. Studies show that many choose to postpone intercourse and to use contraception when they do begin having intercourse.

Sex education that simply teaches "just say no" to sex is unrealistic and ineffective. This approach is not enough for kids in situations complicated by alcohol, peer pressure, or the belief that they are in love. Learning communication skills enhances students' self-respect. Learning about different points of view and examining various values builds maturity and the ability to arrive at and stay with meaningful decisions.

548. What is an askable parent? A teachable moment?

These are terms popularized by respected educator Dr. Sol Gordon. An *askable parent* is one who is more interested in educating, asking, sharing, and understanding than in criticizing, lecturing, and proving him- or herself right. It's a parent who *models* openness rather than simply saying, "You can talk to me any time." Askable parents can most effectively teach their children sexual values and decision-making.

A *teachable moment* is an opportunity for informal sexual education presented by real life. Such lessons are often more comfortable and powerful than sitting down for "a talk." The astute parent can spot these moments—for example, while watching television with a child ("Johnny, how do you think that girl feels about being pressured for sex?") or even walking in the street ("What do you suppose it's like for such a young girl to have her own baby?").

For more about this model of parental sex education, see Dr. Gordon's wonderful book, coauthored with his wife, Judith, *Raising a Child Conservatively in a Sexually Permissive World.*

549. Why are some people so strongly against sex education? They must know something I don't.

No.

Several national organizations are actively fighting sex education in the schools. They say that sex education promotes "promiscuity," destroys the family, and undermines democracy. Although the goals—and results—of sex education are exactly the opposite, this crucial fact does not seem important to these critics.

These groups, like the Eagle Forum and Concerned Women of America, also favor censorship of libraries and the press and are against antidiscrimination laws and the teaching of evolution. Some explicitly oppose teaching children how to think for themselves. They really do.

It only takes a handful of strident, irresponsible people in any community to create problems for the majority of parents and children. One-third of California's school districts, for example, faced attempts to censor teaching materials during 1989, according to a study by the Educational Congress of California.

Why are such people so angry, fearful, and irrational about a program that emphasizes responsible decision-making and parent-child communication? Because they are afraid of sexuality in any form; afraid of people thinking for themselves; and afraid of trusting young people.

550. How can anyone be in favor of sex education—my neighbor says the course in our junior high school encourages homosexuality!

People who are uncomfortable with homosexuality generally interpret *any* discussion about it as "favoring" it. But your neighbor is 100 percent wrong. There is no sex education program in America that encourages homosexuality.

Sex educators generally present homosexuality as an identity that 5 to 10 percent of the population is born with. Homosexuals come from every kind of family, are found in all walks of life, and desire the same love and security as everyone else. Sex education teaches young people that homosexuals are not sick; rather, that they are human beings who deserve the same dignity and privacy as anyone else.

Your neighbor has obviously not read the school materials or heard the teacher speak. Is there a particular reason this person would make such a fuss about something he or she knows so little about?

551. Is it true that sex education uses pornographic films? Why is that necessary?

It isn't necessary, and it is *never* done. Sex education films typically cover two main areas: biology and social interaction.

The biology films instruct children on how their bodies work: menstruation, conception, erection, and the like. A few people, disturbed about all human sexuality, find this objectionable because they can't imagine approaching these normal physical subjects in a scientific way. Such people, sadly, find sexual titillation wherever they look.

The other films help students discuss various kinds of social and sexual interactions. They examine male-female dynamics, sexual decision-making, clear communication, peer pressure, sexual desire, and, in higher grades, alternatives to intercourse.

Such films do not entertain, shock, or stimulate students. Rather, they are carefully designed to help young people examine their feelings, communicate with others, take sex seriously, and ask questions.

Why do some people thrive on spreading frightening lies about sex education?

31

Pregnancy and Nursing

Children make the most desirable opponents in Scrabble as they are both easy to beat and fun to cheat.

—Fran Lebowitz

552. How will my pregnancy affect my libido?

Each woman responds differently. Masters and Johnson documented a decreased libido in the first trimester, a rise in the second, and a gradual decline in the third. Other researchers report different patterns.

Experimenting with different positions and paying particular attention to lubrication can increase sexual pleasure, which can maintain or increase sexual interest.

553. How late into my pregnancy can we still have sex?

You can have sex as late into your pregnancy as you like, depending on how you define "sex." It's more than intercourse, you know. Sex is anything from making out (without going "further") to oral sex to masturbating together. The important thing is to meet each other's needs for holding, touching, arousal, and release in whatever proportion you desire.

Though a distended belly eventually makes positions such as man-on-top uncomfortable, creative couples can find many different ways to enjoy intercourse. Any sexual activity that is painful should, of course, be stopped immediately. In general, any position that is comfortable will probably be safe.

Physicians often advise women with a history of cervical problems or premature labor to restrict intercourse or orgasm during the third trimester. On the other hand, some doctors encourage intercourse and orgasm near term's end because they help induce contractions.

554. Can I swallow my husband's semen while I'm pregnant? We both enjoy this part of oral sex.

Many couples particularly enjoy oral sex during the last months of pregnancy, when intercourse becomes difficult. Assuming your husband does not have a sexually transmitted disease, swallowing his semen, or ejaculate, poses no danger.

555. Why does my husband constantly talk to everyone about my pregnant body, especially my "jumbo boobs"?

Perhaps he is genuinely excited about the entire pregnancy experience, including your body changes. Maybe his remarks are a way of participating more in the pregnancy or of getting a bit of the enormous amount of attention heading your way. Or he may be sexually frustrated and be talking about your body as a sexual outlet.

A different question is why he is doing something that you have clearly asked him not to do (you *have* been clear about this, right?). This may be a helpful way to present the issue to him.

556. The more pregnant I get, the more my husband seems to flirt with other women. What's going on?

This situation is not uncommon. Some husbands find their wife's larger body less attractive; some resent all the new attention their spouse gets; and some have trouble thinking of their wife as both a mother and lover.

Before you accuse, attack, or panic, find out what lies behind your husband's changed behavior. Approach him as a partner who wants to address and solve a marital problem, not as an adversary who wants to blame him for doing something wrong.

Your husband may not be aware of his increased flirting. He may not know how others perceive it, and may be greatly surprised that it bothers you. On the other hand, flirting may be a frantic, frustrated attempt to get your attention.

There's only one way to find out: ask. If he doesn't want to discuss it, ask him how else he suggests you handle your increasing resentment. By the way, if you would like more of your husband's sexual attention for yourself, let him know that as well.

557. Now that we have a child on the way, how can I get my husband to stop buying *Playboy*?

I'm assuming you have already come to terms with *Playboy* sometime in the past, since you're asking your husband to stop.

So why is this change necessary? There is no evidence that children are harmed by seeing pictures of nudity or explicit sexuality, particularly if there is no violence attached. That doesn't mean you have to like such pictures, of course. But disliking them is different from calling them dangerous.

I encourage you to examine and acknowledge your real agenda here. Do you feel inadequate because your husband reads *Playboy*? Resentful because he's not satisfying you sexually? Angry because he's using *Playboy* as a way to hurt you?

Don't deny your anger or other feelings by citing your child's welfare; own up to and discuss them with your husband. This will invite him to be equally honest with you. Whatever your reasons for wanting to ban *Playboy* from the house, make it a joint decision, not yours alone. Otherwise, the issue will create resentment and assume exactly the large importance you are trying to avoid.

558. My three-year-old hasn't stopped asking questions since my wife's pregnancy began to show. What should we tell her?

Tell her the truth.

The pregnancy is a big event in your child's life; you can't ignore the questions it raises for her. Where did she come from? How does her body compare with Mom's and Dad's? What is her relationship to that big stomach Mom has? Such curiosity is healthy.

Don't be afraid that you'll tell her too much. Kids absorb only what makes sense to them, ignoring the rest. If you try to teach her too much, she'll just get restless and lose interest. One of the best books for parents about home sexuality education is Mary Calderone and Eric Johnson's *The Family Book About Sexuality*.

559. Our baby isn't even born yet, and well-meaning friends and family are already treating it as if it's a boy or girl. How can we discourage this?

Studies show that people actually treat fetuses (as well as babies) differently depending on the gender they believe them to be. This behavior includes how and how often people touch and talk to the fetus, as well as the qualities they attribute to it ("Feel that kick—he's a real tiger!" or "Feel that rocking—she's so sweet!").

Most people, unfortunately, don't understand how their gender stereotyping limits the children they love. You can gently educate the people in your baby's life, although your attempts may be met with confusion or sarcasm. It is essential that you explain your position without preaching or lecturing. So talk about giving your child unlimited horizons, rather than criticizing other people's style of communication.

560. I am concerned that after childbirth my vagina will be too loose for my husband to enjoy sex. What can I do?

For starters, you can stop thinking of this as your problem to deal with alone and start discussing it with your husband.

Is he concerned? What does he especially enjoy about making love with you? For most men, vaginal tightness is only one of many contributors to sexual pleasure.

Still, it is a good idea to help your pelvic muscles regain their tone after childbirth. The best exercise is the Kegel, discussed in question 248. You're best off starting now, *before* you give birth.

561. Is it really dangerous to drink or smoke if you nurse your baby? I can't believe all those scare stories.

Anything you put in your mouth can appear in your milk and affect the baby. This even includes vegetables such as asparagus, which can cause gas in both mother and child.

Tobacco, alcohol, and cocaine are particularly dangerous for children. The rule is, if you wouldn't put a substance directly into your baby's mouth, don't put it into yours.

562. I sometimes need to nurse my baby in public, but I want to be sensitive to other people's discomfort, too. What should I do?

That depends on your personality and your politics. Nursing itself is really not the issue.

In America, breasts are primarily seen as sex objects, not as something connected with mothering. Thus, breasts seen in public are supposed to entertain adults (as in a nightclub or magazine) rather than nurture babies.

If you want to avoid confrontations or other people's discomfort by colluding with this bizarre appropriation of your breasts, that's understandable. Do so, and don't nurse in public. But if you feel that nursing is a normal activity, and you do it in an inconspicuous way, and you are willing to confront people with their prejudices and sexual distortions, go right ahead. It is, after all, your body. Others' discomfort is not your responsibility.

Some people try to persuade mothers that nursing in public bathrooms is a reasonable compromise. Reasonable? We should ask these people: "Do *you* like to eat in the bathroom?"

563. My husband supported my decision to nurse our son, but he always has a reason to leave the room when I do it. Why does he do this? Am I being too sensitive?

Many men have difficulty seeing their wives as both lovers and mothers. The intimacy between mother and child, particularly during nursing, is so powerful that it can feel almost embarrassing to watch. It's easy for a husband/father to feel excluded and displaced.

Many husbands are very attached to their wife's breasts and see them in strictly sexual terms. It's easy to understand how a man could look at a nursing baby and feel, "Hey, cut it out—those are *my* boobs you're playing with!"

Talk to your husband about your observation, let him know that feelings such as these are normal and acceptable, and remind him how special he is to you—not just as your baby's father but as your lover.

564. Is it okay to let my four-year-old see me nurse his sister?

Definitely. Breast-feeding is a natural activity that should be part of the family's ordinary routine. It also normalizes a woman's body, which is wonderful for a young male. When your son loses interest or finds it embarrassing, he'll manage to avoid it.

565. I get a wonderful sexy tingling while I nurse. If I let myself, in fact, I get really turned on. Is this weird?

Becoming aroused is a perfectly healthy reaction to the skin contact, intimate bonding, and erotic stimulation of nursing. Because it is rarely discussed, few women know how common this response is. Did you know that some lucky women actually climax from nursing?

While overt sexual activity between parent and child is wrong, *enjoying* your sexual feelings, even looking forward to them, is natural and positive. Perhaps this is difficult because you fear your arousal means you are a potential child molestor, or if your child is a girl, that you are a "latent homosexual." There is no factual basis for either concern.

Our bodies are wonderfully responsive to stimuli of all kinds. Ways of handling your arousal might include writing or painting about it, or being sexual later, with a partner or by yourself. Accepting your feelings will enable you to fully enjoy them, and to encourage a sexually healthy environment for your child.

32

The Single Parent

The real menace in dealing with a five-year-old is that in no time at all you begin to sound like a five-year-old.

—Jean Kerr

566. When is it okay to have my lover sleep over while my child is home?

Your child should know you have a caring relationship with someone before he or she spends the night. If you establish that, and if your child knows that sex is part of adult caring and intimacy, you won't have to be secretive about it, which teaches that sex is shameful.

The three of you should have a relationship in several different contexts before your friend stays over. This will have its own complications depending on the child's age. For example, most three year-olds go through an "owning Mommy" stage. Most fourteen-year-olds go through a "disowning Mommy stage."

This is a situation in which it's better to err on the side of caution. Like many other single parents, you may have most or all of your sex away from home. A lot of trouble? Yes. But as you already know, part of the cost of having children is not getting to use your own house exactly as you'd like.

567. How much should my boyfriend and I touch each other in front of his six-year-old?

Certainly, no *more* than you feel comfortable. But that's probably not your question.

Affection is different from sexuality, even if that difference is hard to describe. Feel free to express affection in front of the child; that is, the delight in being connected with and valued by someone.

Most people can watch others hug, lightly kiss, and playfully pat each other without feeling uncomfortable. Most children can handle a bit of this, too, especially if they don't feel excluded. Passionate kissing, groping under clothes, and sexually stimulating each other, however, generally makes others feel uncomfortable. Such behavior associates sexuality with exclusion or guilt in a child's mind. Don't do it.

In general, don't do anything physical in front of a child that you wouldn't do in a crowded supermarket.

568. I've been dating the same two men for six months. What should I tell my daughter?

Tell her the truth: that you're fond of each, enjoy your time with each, and that you like having more than one special friend. Mention that this doesn't mean you want to be friends with just anyone; these friends are special to you, and that's why you spend special time with them.

569. How can I teach my teenager sexual self-discipline when I'm having unmarried sex myself?

First, you need to ask yourself whether you feel *you're* exercising sexual self-discipline. Abstinence is not its only form, you know. If you feel good about your own sexual decisions, it's easier to see them as consistent with the values you want to teach your child.

As sex educator Sol Gordon says, there have to be some advantages to being a grownup, and sexual intercourse is one of them. Just as your child doesn't get to make the same financial or recreational decisions that you do, his or her sexual horizons should be more limited as well.

You can certainly discuss the considerations you go through in your own sexual decision-making process and encourage your child to learn and use these as well.

570. How can I keep my ten-year-old from telling his dad about my social life without suggesting there's anything wrong with it?

By explaining the difference between secrecy and privacy. Privacy means we don't share things even though we don't feel they're bad or wrong. Use examples from your son's life to make your point; surely, there are things about him he doesn't want you telling the world.

Also, remind him of your family's new structure. Dad is no longer privy to some things he used to be, nor are you. Your son can be sad about that—in fact, he may be sharing information as a way of trying to keep the family "together"—but you can help him deal with his feelings in other ways.

Let your son know it is not in his best interests to be in the middle of things, nor can he bring you and your ex closer together. And make sure you aren't unconsciously encouraging your son to play this role.

571. Whenever I bring a new friend home for the first time, my ten-year-old manages to talk about sex or my previous lovers. What should I do?

This behavior could represent many different things. For example, it might be about jealousy, or the fear of losing you. It's even possible that your child hasn't quite learned that this is inappropriate conversation, although you've probably said so many times. You must make it clear that this behavior is not cute and that it is uncomfortable for *everybody*.

On the other hand, your child may be sexually overstimulated. This could happen, for example, if you are confiding too much in your child, or if he or she is seeing too much sexual activity in your house, or your ex's. It's even possible that your child has been sexually approached by someone somewhere else. You might want to check this out.

Or are you simply bringing too many people home too frequently?

572. Lately, my thirteen-year-old daughter dresses and acts suggestively whenever my boyfriend comes to visit. Should we just ignore this, or talk to her about it?

She may be dressing this way with everyone, and you haven't noticed. Or she may be trying to compete with you, or expressing her anger at you sharing your time with someone else. Or she may desire the validation of her budding sexuality from a male.

How does she feel about your boyfriend and his visits? Titillated? Crowded? Excluded? Is your ex dating, or is he alone? Your daughter may be expressing sadness about his emptiness by undermining your richness.

Without criticizing her, discuss the way she looks and acts. How does she think people see her? What messages is she sending out? She is too old to simply say "I don't know"; she needs to start thinking about how things look to others. Emphasize that she doesn't have to spend all her time thinking about people's expectations, but part of being an adult in the world is acknowledging others' perceptions.

573. Last week my fourteen-year-old said he was ashamed of my ''immoral'' sex life, which hurt a lot. What should I do?

First of all, fourteen-year-olds are famous for their self-righteous judgments about everything. This is the time when they are developing their moral sense. As they start to realize that the world isn't as black and white as they would like, they make a last desperate attempt to simplify the world with their rules.

More to the point, however, you need to separate emotionally from your child. Needing the approval of a fourteen-year-old can cripple your parenting ability. He is free to dislike the people you spend time with or the amount of time you spend with them. But your child is in no position to understand the subtleties of adult sexual decision-making.

Make it clear that you appreciate his concern for your well-being, that you care about his discomfort, and that you're willing to explain your decisions to a certain point. But also make it clear that when he confronts anyone with such strong judgments, he closes the door to dialogue and makes closeness difficult.

574. How do I get my ex to stop quizzing me on my sex life? She says she's just being friendly and concerned.

You do this in the way you get anyone to stop talking to you about subjects you don't want to discuss. You say, "I appreciate your interest, but that's something I'd rather not discuss. By the way, that's pretty exciting news about Stevie's science-fair project, isn't it?"

Ex-spouses sometimes discuss each other's personal lives as a way of staying connected. They may say they dislike it, but it can be a soothing form of nostalgia.

575. What do I say when my adolescent son asks me if I'm "boffing" my woman friend?

You can, if you wish, say, "I don't feel comfortable discussing that." Talk about the concept of discretion and how people typically appreciate this quality in their friends.

If you like, you can ask why your son wants to know such a thing. He may have sexual fantasies about your friend (which is fine), he may be afraid you'll abandon him for her (which you can reassure him about), or he may even be testing your discretion regarding *his* life. Suggest that all these feelings are legitimate and that you'd like him to handle them in a different way.

Is there a reason that he might be hostile about your relationships?

576. I've been dating this great woman for about eight months. The problem is, our thirteen-year-olds seem to have a crush on each other. What should we do?

If you want to make the crush stronger, forbid the kids to see each other.

What exactly is your concern? If you're afraid they're going to have sex, it might be time for you and your friend to discuss sexuality with your kids.

If you're afraid that the kids' relationship may interfere with your own, discuss this with the kids in a straightforward way. Find out if your child's crush is a displacement of feelings about your new relationship, or your girlfriend. How would your child feel if your relationship ended tomorrow?

Eventually, you can discuss the possibility that the two kids could become half-siblings and ways in which this would affect their future relationship. But your initial reaction should be mild; give things some time. As you know, crushes at this age often go away on their own.

It might reduce some of the erotic charge in the kids' relationship if you do a few things together as a "family."

33

Child Abuse and Incest

The obscurest epoch is today.

—Robert Louis Stevenson

577. What exactly is child sexual abuse?

This is an important question, because there are now so many different definitions that the term has little precision. Some people insist, for example, that "sexual abuse" includes such varied events as a fifteen-year-old girl seducing her thirteen-year-old brother; a mother undressing each night in front of her twelve-year-old son; and a father vaginally penetrating his four-year-old daughter.

Including such a broad range of behavior in the term "sexual abuse" makes it possible for sincere people to claim that one out of three girls is molested or that half of all Americans have been sexually abused.

The defining dynamics of child sexual abuse, I believe, are power and secrecy. Sex abuse involves coercion—one person feeling required to submit to the other's will. The domination can be overt and physical, or more subtle and psychological. The forced secrecy can also be overt or implied, and often leads to the victim feeling ashamed or crazy.

Defining actual acts of sex abuse is difficult, because defining sex is so difficult. Clearly, adult-child sexual touching, as well as oral, anal, or genital penetration, are sex abuse. Coercively using a child to sexually arouse an adult, such as by forcing him or her to view an explicit film, is also abusive.

Although we'd prefer that sex abuse be a black-and-white issue, we should keep in mind that even the most loving families have unhealthy psychological patterns and power dynamics. It confuses things terribly to define sex abuse so broadly that it is seen as part of every child's life. All adults have moments of poor judgment, inexperience, selfishness, and lack of rational attention. The fact that these sometimes involve sexual energy or the body does not necessarily make them instances of sex abuse.

578. How common is child sexual abuse? I hear so much about it—is it increasing?

Although it seems that everyone has an opinion about this, there is no way to know the truth about either question.

I estimate the incidence to be about one in ten people. Is the problem increasing? Certainly, reporting has become more sophisticated and inclusive. We've given the horror a name, making it easier to speak about. Because of publicity, more children are speaking up than ever before, and more adults abused as kids are coming forward to acknowledge their pasts.

At the same time, the eighties and early nineties have seen an increase in the stresses that create family problems like sexual abuse: isolation, teen births, economic insecurity, community breakdown, alcoholism, drug addiction, and domestic violence.

Perhaps both things are true: Sexual abuse is increasing as families and communities continue to deteriorate, and reporting of it is increasing as it becomes more legitimate to see and discuss.

579. I heard a therapist on television say the whole family "colludes" in sexual abuse. What does this mean?

When child molestation takes place within a family, that family is generally not healthy. Typically, it requires some awful thing like a child being molested for part of its stability. Elements of such unhealthy families include an unhappy, even violent, marriage; dramatic power imbalance between spouses; distorted communication; a lack of intimacy; and the abuse of alcohol.

Thus, all adult members of such a family contribute to the context in which molestation takes place. Some collude by not seeing the obvious; some by ignoring or denying the child's complaints; some by submitting to the perpetrator's other unreasonable demands; and some by indirectly encouraging the child to accept the situation so as not to make things "worse."

Note that this is not the same as blaming family members or excusing the perpetrator in any way.

580. Does every incest experience seriously damage the child?

At present, there is no way to know. That's because virtually all research in this area starts with the assumption that incest is always destructive.

It is far easier to study people with symptoms or complaints than those who are not distressed. The legal, medical, and psychological fields are set up to investigate not the *effects* of incest, but the *negative effects*.

Research published by psychologists David Finkelhor, Paul Okami, and others substantiates the anecdotal evidence that some incest has nonnegative effects. It seems to depend on the degree of coercion and the age difference between those involved. Incest between those close in age (such as siblings) that involves no force can apparently be experienced as neutral or even positive.

Some people condemn incest in any form as morally unacceptable. This, of course, is totally different from proving that it always damages those involved.

581. How could someone actually molest a child—surely, such people are mentally ill?

The term *mentally ill* may not be a helpful one when dealing with sex abuse, because so many millions of people commit these acts and because conventional treatments of mental illness are often ineffective with this behavior.

A few perpetrators are psychotic, sociopathic, or similarly impaired. They have no idea of the damage they create. Most molesters, however, seem normal much of the time. They function at a reasonable level in their professional and personal lives. It is only when they give in to their need to assault a child that they show how dangerous they are.

Certainly, child molesters are disturbed, but there are too many to simply dismiss them all as "mentally ill." After all, what would that say about a society that produces so many year after year? In fact, here are some common cultural beliefs that encourage perpetrators to see their behavior as acceptable:

- Children are the property of their parents
- The father is the unchallenged ruler of the house
- Alcohol dependence is not a serious problem
- Sex is something that males want and females withhold, so it's okay to grab it any way you can
- It is wrong to talk openly about sex
- Kids should not control their own sexuality

582. In this day and age of sexual abuse, how can anyone send a child to a day-care center?

Statistically, day-care centers appear to be the safest place for children in terms of sex abuse. The truth is that the vast majority of sex abuse takes place in the home.

There are, of course, some day-care operations that are unsafe, but this it not common. I think many people want to believe that day care is dangerous so they don't have to face the reality that the problem is "us"—family—not "them"—strangers.

This is similar to the public's perception that kidnappers of children are usually strangers. According to the FBI, more than 95 percent of child kidnappings are done by a relative, often a parent in a custody dispute. It's far more comforting to think of the problem as being "maniacs" than as being Dad or Mom.

583. How can a person recover from having been molested?

I believe the key steps are acknowledging that the abuse took place, breaking the pattern of silence; nurturing the inner child, which, betrayed back then, prevents the adult from trusting; and recognizing that having been molested does not need to be the center of a person's identity or personality.

Ironically, there are many sex-abuse recovery programs that succeed with the first two and fail on the third. They teach people that they are primarily victims and/or survivors and help them reorganize their personalities around this damaged identity.

Each person is different, of course. Some need to confront the perpetrator, others get symbolic revenge, while many just want to forget. Helpful resources include group and individual therapy, reading, and meditating.

Some signs of overcoming the experience include not feeling responsible for or ashamed of having been molested; not being afraid of the perpetrator now; and no longer seeing molestation as the central, defining experience of one's life.

584. My partner is currently in therapy, working on having been molested. What can I do to help?

The one with the best answer to that is your partner. Ask him or her. Ask periodically, even when the answer is "nothing."

Typical feelings of people working on this issue in therapy include anger (at perpetrator, self, and others), powerlessness, self-criticism, fear, and sensitivity to things that used to seem harmless—say, the smell of pipe tobacco, the view from a theater balcony, or the sound of violin music.

The most important thing you can do is continue to love and accept your partner. This may require patience regarding sudden mood swings and changes in sexual or other routines. If you want help with this, suggest a joint session with your partner and her therapist.

Edie Savage-Weeks, veteran California psychotherapist in this field, suggests the following ways that people can support partners currently in treatment for having been molested:

- Believe the abuse really happened, even if it seems impossible
- Gently remind your partner that you're not the perpetrator, and help maintain your relationship during this tough time
- Know that the frequency, content, and continuity of your sexual relationship is going to change several times; be patient, and don't take the difficulties personally
- Give your partner extra time and space, with fewer daily responsibilities if possible
- Acknowledge your partner's fear that he or she is a potential molester, and make temporary changes in child-care arrangements if necessary
- Have fun together, even if you need to coax your partner a bit

585. I've recently realized that my stepfather molested me for several years when I was young. He's old now, and pretty harmless. Should I confront him about what he did?

There is no right answer to this question. Ultimately, you have to explore the benefits and disadvantages of doing so, and choose accordingly.

When, many years later, a former perpetrator is molesting

a new generation of children, that person must be stopped. The situation you describe, however, is more ambiguous. How will you feel during and after the confrontation? How will he? How will this affect the rest of the family?

When you think about the confrontation, what are your goals? There are crucial differences between wanting an apology, wanting to express anger, and wanting to punish someone.

The desire to put the experience of being molested behind you is understandable and healthy. The question is, what is the best strategy for doing this? Talking with a professional counselor (or at least someone you are close with) will help you clarify your objectives and feelings.

586. If an adult molests a child of the same gender, does that mean the adult is homosexual? Will the child grow up gay?

Probably not.

The vast majority of same-gender molestation is committed by heterosexual adults. One reason is that for many offenders, the relationship is as much about power as it is about sex. Another is that molestation can be a way for an adult to act out repressed same-sex fantasies without tarnishing his or her heterosexual self-image. This is one more way in which homophobia is dangerous for everyone.

Sexual abuse, of course, typically affects a child's future sexuality. But there is no evidence that same-gender abuse leads to homosexuality in the victim. Sexual orientation results from a number of factors, almost certainly including biology. The same-gender nature of abuse is usually not experienced as its most prominent feature. And molestation often begins after the child's sexual orientation is already set.

Certainly, some heterosexual victims of same-gender abuse eventually wonder if they have somehow invited this "homosexual relationship." This can undermine a person's sexuality, but it cannot "make them" gay.

People who grow up to be homosexual can have an extra difficulty with same-gender abuse because their adult sexuality echoes their painful childhood experiences. This, of course, does not make their homosexuality wrong.

The belief that homosexuals must be kept out of teaching and other child-related professions is clearly refuted by everything we know about child molestation: The vast majority of children molested by adults of the same gender are victims of heterosexuals, not homosexuals.

587. Please settle a disagreement in our house: Do children ever lie about being molested? I say they do, my wife says they don't.

This is another one of those issues that we *used* to understand 100 percent—that children never lie about abuse. However, "developments in recent years make this notion an anachronism," according to Dr. Richard Gardner, Columbia University Medical School psychiatrist.

First, there are increasing cases of one parent coaching a child to accuse the other falsely during a custody battle. Second, very young children literally cannot tell the difference between fact and fantasy. And third, children are being led by misguided social workers and other interrogators to "remember" abuse through promises of rewards if they "tell like the other children told."

The University of Minnesota's Dr. Sharon Satterfield, who is highly experienced and respected in the courtroom and in the counseling field, says, "Society would rather not admit that children lie. It makes life more complicated and shows the dark side of families and of honored professions."

588. It seems that those accused of being child molesters have their lives ruined even if they're proven innocent. I teach third grade, and I'm getting nervous—don't I have any protection?

Perhaps not. Local prosecutors and social workers are now building reputations on busting alleged molesters. Scared and feeling powerless in the face of child abuse's curse, communities are shunning anyone so accused.

Many people in the child abuse field have a "guilty until proven innocent" attitude. If children cannot remember any abuse, they are said to have abuse-induced amnesia. If the accused are model citizens, this is considered proof of their cunning and deceit. Thus far, there seems to be no way to clear one's name.

Anyone working with children these days should be extremely conscious about appearances. Unions should be encouraged to have policies on how allegations will be handled *before* any are made. Individuals should interview and select a lawyer knowledgeable in this area so that if allegations are made, an aggressive defense can be started without delay. Legal insurance to pay the costs is as important an investment as car insurance.

589. What are the warning signs of sexual abuse?

Common symptoms include:

- Inappropriately sophisticated knowledge about sexual behavior
- Inappropriately intense sexual interest or behavior
- Unexplained pain or bruises, especially on or near the thighs or genitals
- Several children telling similar stories
- Sudden unexplained fear about certain persons or places, and
- Sudden changes in a child's personality

Unfortunately, these can all be features of normal development as well. If you suspect that your child is being abused, speak calmly with him or her and with others in the child's world.

590. What should I do if I suspect my child is being sexually abused?

Don't panic.

It is important to deal with any anger, fear, or guilt *separately* from your investigation of possible abuse. Mishandled, your emotions could both jeopardize the inquiry and result in unwanted consequences.

I would advise *against* calling the police or government at first. In many communities, well-meaning new laws have removed the discretion to handle cases individually. Your child may be taken out of your home against your will simply because of an allegation. Once that happens, you have no control over the way interrogations are handled.

If you are concerned, investigate local resources and laws anonymously. Find an experienced therapist who does not reflexively report every suspicion of abuse. He or she will help you sort out your feelings and any evidence, and can interview the child in a calm, neutral environment.

Your community's yellow pages, crisis hotline, family planning clinic, or marriage counselor's association should be helpful.

591. Why do so many professionals in the sex abuse field sound like religious crusaders?

This is the most important and least asked question about the entire sex-abuse issue.

First of all, there are many decent, courageous, extraordinary people working in the difficult field of sex abuse today. They save lives, families, and communities.

The sex abuse counseling profession is loaded with people who identify themselves as victims or survivors of sex abuse. Unfortunately, many are using their jobs to work out their own rage and fear about having been abused. While a handful admit that they are activists, others will not.

Some sex abuse prosecutors are also angry and vengeful. On a witch hunt for perpetrators, they seem less interested in truth or family health than in prosecution. A disturbing number seem quite willing to bend the law they are sworn to uphold when they deem it necessary.

As Dr. Richard Gardner of Columbia University Medical School recently said, "These individuals harbor significant resentment, which they vent . . . in the work setting . . . concluding that an alleged perpetrator is indeed innocent deprives them of their vengeful gratification."

One reason this field attracts so many angry people is the widespread social agreement on how awful the crimes are. It is a perfect place for people to vent their negativity without having to take responsibility for it. Also, the current social consensus about sexual abuse makes it dangerous to challenge these people and their methods. So those with the rage and hidden psychological agendas are left to define and run the field. They are the main source of the public's (mis)information and energy about this issue.

Bibliography

Anand, Margo. *The Art of Sexual Ecstasy*. Los Angeles: Tarcher, 1989.

Barbach, Lonnie. *For Yourself: The Fulfillment of Female Sexuality*. New York: Doubleday, 1975.

——. *Pleasures*. New York: Harper & Row, 1984.

Blumstein, Philip, and Schwartz, Pepper. *American Couples*. New York: Morrow, 1983.

Calderone, Mary, and Johnson, Eric. *The Family Book About Sexuality*. New York: Harper & Row, 1989.

Castleman, Michael. *Sexual Solutions*. New York: Touchstone, 1989.

Clark, Don. *The New Loving Someone Gay*. Berkeley, CA: Celestial Arts, 1987.

Comfort, Alex. *The Joy of Sex*. New York: Crown, 1972.

Dodson, Betty. *Liberating Masturbation*. New York: Body-sex, 1974.

———. *Sex for One*. New York: Crown, 1987.

Farrell, Warren. *Why Men Are the Way They Are*. New York: Berkley, 1988.

Friday, Nancy. *My Mother, My Self*. New York: Dell, 1987.

———. *My Secret Garden*. New York: Pocket Books, 1983.

Gochros, Jean. *When Husbands Come Out of the Closet*. Binghamton, NY: Haworth, 1989.

Gordon, Sol, and Gordon, Judith. *Raising a Child Conservatively in a Sexually Permissive World*. New York: Simon & Schuster, 1989.

Hartman, William, and Fithian, Marilyn. *Any Man Can*. New York: St. Martin's, 1984.

Hite, Shere. *The Hite Report on Female Sexuality*. New York: Dell, 1976.

———. *The Hite Report on Male Sexuality*. New York: Knopf, 1981.

Kahane, Deborah. *No Less a Woman*. New York: Prentice Hall, 1990.

Kensington Ladies' Erotica Society. *Ladies' Own Erotica*. Berkeley, CA: Ten Speed Press, 1984.

Klein, Marty. *Your Sexual Secrets: When to Keep Them, How to Share Them*. New York: Berkley, 1990.

Ladas, Alice, et al. *The G Spot*. New York: Dell, 1983.

Larue, Gerald. *Sex and the Bible*. Buffalo, NY: Prometheus, 1983.

Lawrence, Jr., Raymond J. *The Poisoning of Eros*. Roanoke, VA: Augustine Moore, 1990.

McIlvenna, Ted, et al. *The Complete Guide to Safe Sex*. Beverly Hills, CA: Specific Press, 1987.

Metzger, Deena. *Tree*. Berkeley, CA: Wingbow Press, 1990.

Nelson, James. *Between Two Gardens*. New York: Pilgrim Press, 1983.

Nin, Anaïs. *Little Birds*. New York: Harcourt Brace Jovanovich, 1979.

Ramsdale, David Alan, and Dorfman, Jo Ellen. *Sexual Energy Ecstasy*. Playa del Rey, CA: Peak Skill, 1985.

Reinisch, June. *The Kinsey Institute New Report on Sex.* New York: St. Martin's, 1990.

Satir, Virginia. *The New Peoplemaking.* Palo Alto, CA: Science and Behavior Books, 1988.

Starr, B. D., and Weiner, M. B. *The Starr-Weiner Report on Sex and Sexuality in the Mature Years.* New York: McGraw Hill, 1982.

Steinberg, David. *Erotic by Nature.* North San Juan, CA: Shakti Press, 1988.

Wells, Carol. *Right-Brain Sex.* New York: Prentice Hall, 1989.

Whipple, Beverly, and Ogden, Gina. *Safe Encounters.* New York: Pocket Books, 1989.

Zilbergeld, Bernie. *Male Sexuality.* Boston: Little, Brown, 1978.

———— and Lazarus, Arnold. *Mindpower.* Boston: Little, Brown, 1987.

Additional Reading

Adams, Jane. *Sex and the Single Parent.* New York: Coward, McCann, & Geoghegan, 1978.

Boston Women's Health Collective. *The New Our Bodies Ourselves.* New York: Simon & Schuster, 1984.

Carrera, Michael. *Sex: The Facts, the Acts, and Your Feelings.* New York: Crown, 1981.

Cassell, Carol. *Swept Away.* New York: Bantam, 1985.

Gordon, Sol, and Snyder, Craig. *Personal Issues in Human Sexuality.* Boston: Allyn & Bacon, 1986.

Haeberle, Erwin. *The Sex Atlas.* New York: Continuum, 1983.

Leight, Lynn. *Raising Sexually Healthy Children.* New York: Avon, 1990.

McBride, Will. *Show Me!* New York: St. Martin's, 1975.

Morin, Jack. *Anal Pleasure and Health.* Burlingame, CA: Yes Press, 1981.

Yates, Alayne. *Sex Without Shame.* New York: Morrow, 1978.

Index